SUSTAINABLE CITIES IN DEVELOPING COUNTRIES

DEDICATION

This book is for Roma Singh. She once played in rice paddies, then, rarely among girls in Patna, graduated to medical studies. Hers is a life of welfare for women and for one funny man.

Sustainable Cities in Developing Countries
Theory and Practice at the Millennium

Edited by Cedric Pugh

Earthscan Publications Ltd, London and Sterling, VA

M006130

First published in the UK and USA in 2000 by
Earthscan Publications Ltd

A catalogue record for this book is available from the British Library

ISBN: 1 85383 619 2 paperback
       1 85383 624 9 hardback

Typesetting by JS Typesetting, Wellingborough, Northamptonshire
Printed and bound by Creative Print and Design, Ebbw Vale
Cover design by Declan Buckley

For a full list of publications please contact:

Earthscan Publications Ltd
120 Pentonville Road, London, N1 9JN, UK
Tel: +44 (0)20 7278 0433
Fax: +44 (0)20 7278 1142
Email: earthinfo@earthscan.co.uk
http://www.earthscan.co.uk

22883 Quicksilver Drive, Sterling, VA 20166–2012, USA

Earthscan is an editorially independent subsidiary of Kogan Page Ltd and publishes
in association with WWF-UK and the International Institute for Environment and
Development

This book is printed on elemental chlorine-free paper

CONTENTS

LIST OF FIGURES AND TABLES

FIGURES

TABLES

BIOGRAPHICAL INFORMATION ON THE AUTHORS

PETER ABELSON

Dr Peter Abelson has a PhD from London University, is an associate professor in the Department of Economics at Macquarie University in Sydney, Australia and is Honorary Secretary of the Economics Society of Australia. Peter has written several books including, *Project Appraisal and Valuation of the Environment* (1996) and *Economic Forecasting* (ed, 2000), and has published many journal articles on urban environmental issues. Peter has frequently lectured on environmental management in China, acted as consultant on environmental management to the Shanghai Environmental Protection Bureau, and is the principal author of the *Urban Environmental Management Manual* prepared for the People's Republic of China with support from the Asian Development Bank.

MARIA ALLISON

Maria Allison is currently Senior Research Fellow at the Local Government Centre of the Warwick Business School, University of Warwick. She took up this position following her PhD, obtained from South Bank University in London, entitled 'Health and Housing in Cape Town: Sanitation Provision Explored Through a Framework of Governance'. Maria is currently employed on two programmes of research around organizational and cultural change in United Kingdom (UK) local government, one relating to inter-organization learning networks and change management, the other relating to leadership and the management of influence. Her research interests are in environmental health, local governance and organizational change.

BHARAT DAHIYA

Bharat Dahiya is an urban and regional planner. He holds an MA in geography from Jawaharal Nehru University, and a Master of Planning degree from the School of Planning and Architecture in New Delhi, India. He has worked at the World Bank and contributed to the implementation of the United Nations Centre for Human Settlements (UNCHS) Sustainable Cities Programme in Chennai, India. He has co-authored (with Carl Bartone) *World Bank Lending for the Urban Environment: A Portfolio Analysis* (2000). Currently, he is engaged in his doctoral research at Cambridge University in England into urban governance, civil society associations, urban environmental planning and management and the localizing of Agenda 21 in relation to basic environmental services in India. Bharat Dahiya can be contacted at the Department of Geography, University of Cambridge, Downing Place, Cambridge, CB2 3EN, UK; email: bd206@cus.cam.ac.uk.

TRUDY HARPHAM

Trudy Harpham, PhD, is Professor of Urban Development and Policy at South Bank University. Her specialism is urban health in developing countries, including mental health. She regularly provides technical assistance to municipal and central governments regarding the decentralization of health services. She directs a related PhD programme from which Maria Allison graduated.

GORDON MCGRANAHAN

Dr Gordon McGranahan is a senior researcher with the International Institute for Environment and Development (IIED), working with both its Human Settlements and its Environmental Economics programmes. Prior to joining IIED, he worked for ten years with the Stockholm Environment Institute, directing its research programme on urban environmental problems, including case studies in Accra, Jakarta, Port Elizabeth and São Paulo. He has written widely on urban environmental problems, including *Citizens at Risk: From Sanitation to Sustainable Cities* (Earthscan, forthcoming in 2000).

AMANDA PERRY

Amanda Perry is Lecturer in Law at the Department of Law at Queen Mary and Westfield College in London. She has previously held lectureships at the University of Dundee and the University of Sussex and was a research associate in India for the Law Department of the School of Oriental and African Studies in London, investigating access to environmental justice. Her current research focuses on law and development and law as a determinant of foreign investment flows to developing countries.

CEDRIC PUGH

Cedric Pugh is a professor in urban economic development at Sheffield Hallam University. He is a development economist who has lived and researched in Europe, Australasia, Latin America and Asia. Cedric Pugh has undertaken United Nations research contracts and he has written extensively for international journals since the early 1970s: his major book on developing countries is *Housing and Urbanization: a study of India* (Sage, New Delhi, 1990). Cedric Pugh can be contacted at Sheffield Hallam University, School of Environment and Development, City Campus, Howard Street, Sheffield, S1 1WB, UK.

DAVID SATTERTHWAITE

Dr David Satterthwaite is Director of IIED's Human Settlements Programme and editor of the International journal *Environment and Urbanization*. He has co-authored several Earthscan books on environment and health, including *Environmental Problems in Third World Cities* (with Jorge E Hardoy and Diana Mitlin) in 1992, of which a new updated and expanded version is being published in 2000 entitled, *Environmental Problems in an Urbanizing World: Finding Solutions in Africa, Asia and Latin America*.

CAROLYN STEPHENS

Carolyn Stephens is a senior lecturer in environment and health policy at the London School of Hygiene & Tropical Medicine, and is currently a visiting Profesora Titular in the Universidad Nacional de Tucumán in north-west Argentina. She trained in literature at Cambridge University and has an MSc and PhD in public health medicine from LSHTM and the University of London. Since 1985, she has worked on the impacts of environment and health policy on the poor in India, Ghana, Liberia, Tanzania, Brazil and Argentina principally.

FOREWORD

For the first time in history one-half of the world's population is living in cities. By the year 2025, it is estimated that more than two-thirds will be urban dwellers. While urbanization is a global phenomenon, the fastest growth of cities is taking place in the developing world where more than 90 per cent of new urbanites will locate. More people are also concentrated in large developing country cities – one in four people live in cities with a population of over 500,000, and one in ten live in cities of over 10 million. Cities are the engine of economic growth and provide jobs, services and the promise of a better quality of life. This same rapid growth of cities, however, with the associated concentration of industries, motor vehicles and impoverished slums, can be a threat to health, the environment and the ecological resource base, and to the urban economy itself, thus negating the opportunities urbanization can offer.

Achieving sustainable urban environments in developing countries, the topic of this book, requires that cities solve the formidable problems of poverty reduction, social and institutional change, infrastructure development and service provision, pollution control and ecosystem management. The successful resolution of these problems requires, in turn, a much broader vision of sustainable cities. Such a vision is suggested by the World Bank in its new urban strategy *Cities in Transition: A Strategic View of Urban and Local Government Issues* (World Bank, 2000):

> *If cities and towns are to promote the welfare of their residents and of the nation's citizens, they must be sustainable and functional in four respects. First and foremost, they must be* livable – *ensuring a decent quality of life and equitable opportunity for all residents, including the poorest. To achieve that goal, they must also be* competitive, well governed and managed, *and financially sustainable, or* bankable.

This book explores many facets of these four dimensions of sustainable cities, although not always expressed in the same terms, and it traces the evolution of theory and thinking in environmental, social, economic and political studies, all related to urban growth and development. Following an insightful and wide-ranging review of these issues by Pugh, key facets are examined in greater depth by the contributing authors. Perry focuses on the law and its role in protecting the urban environment, emphasizing the need for clarity and consistent enforcement to achieve an effective rule of law and a cleaner environment. Drawing on experiences from Bangalore in India, Perry points to the important role of the public in supporting the rule of law through environmental activism, which in turn depends on the public's access to justice. In another chapter, Stephens reflects on inequalities in environment, health and power, and what can be done to achieve greater equity. Among the recommended solutions are a move toward more transparency and the sharing of health and environmental information, higher levels of ethical behaviour by the policy élite and the enhanced participation of the poor in decision-making processes both for agenda setting and for implementing policies and interventions. The practical linkages between environmental health and governance are developed in the chapter by Allison and Harpharn. Their research on urban health in South Africa identifies the quality of urban governance as a key facilitator of improved policy and practice. They point out the gaps between the vision of how new relationships can be forged between local governments and civil society – in particular through partnerships with community-based organizations (CBOs), non-governmental organizations (NGOs), and the private sector – and the reality among low-income populations. Closing the gaps requires more efforts to identify and analyse best practice and new forms of governance, that will in turn inform future policy.

Throughout the book, attention is focused on the phenomenon of growing poverty in developing-country cities, its characteristics, and its significance in any discussion of a sustainable urban environment. In his introductory chapter, Pugh describes poverty in an urban context to include 'housing poverty' and 'urban poverty' as well as monetary poverty. Poor urban dwellers live in overcrowded and unsanitary housing, often deprived of essential environmental services such as water supply, sanitation, drainage or garbage collection, exposed to pollution and contagious diseases, with poor access to health education and services – all of which lead to further impoverishment by virtue of sickness and inability to work. For the urban poor, addressing these environmental health issues – often called the brown agenda – is the clear priority for sustainable urban development.

There are, of course, many other environmental issues related to ecological sustainability around cities – often called the green agenda – which are seen as having high global priority. A chapter by McGranahan and Satterthwaite describes the conflicts that can occur between those who prioritize environmental health issues (the brown agenda) and those who prioritize ecological sustainability (the green agenda) when considering sustainable cities in developing countries. In spite of the potential conflicts, the authors conclude that there are many areas of agreement between the two agendas and warn against creating a false dichotomy. They go on to identify measures that can help the simultaneous achievement of both agendas: more attention to demand management rather than supply-side service provision, open and participatory processes for priority-setting and investment decisions, supportive national policies for urban environmental management and sustainable development and developing a good knowledge base on environmental issues within and around each urban centre to provide for better mutual understanding of brown and green issues.

This book seeks to provide practical guidance for moving toward sustainable urban environments along with the description of the efforts made by several cities in this respect. A chapter by Pugh on the sustainability and improvement of housing and the environment in squatter settlements traces the evolution of housing policy in theory and practice. Drawing on that experience, Pugh then lays out seven operational guidelines for the upgrading of squatter settlements which, when adapted to local circumstances, have been shown to be successful. They are commended to the reader. Dahiya and Pugh then go on to describe current thinking on urban environmental planning and management, including consultative processes for cities to achieve consensus on a Local Agenda 21 for their communities. The authors discuss the particular experience of the UNCHS Sustainable Cities Programme (SCP) as an example of formulating Local Agenda 21, and examine case studies from around the world. They conclude with a detailed examination of the Sustainable Chennai Project and assess the successes, difficulties and shortcomings of applying the SCP approach in Chennai. The final example is provided by Abelson in a chapter describing the dilemma of economic and environmental sustainability in Shanghai. As its leaders seek to make Shanghai an international economic, financial and trade centre, the city has had to confront the problem of how to manage economic growth with environmental sustainability in the face of an ever increasing population that now approaches 20 million. The environmental report is mixed. Shanghai has a poor environment, but housing conditions, air and water quality and waste management have all improved in the last ten years. On the other hand, the continuing demographic pressure fueled by economic success threatens the sustainability of these environmental improvements.

For the serious practitioner and thinker, this book presents a wealth of ideas and experiences about building sustainable cities from a uniquely qualified set of individual contributors. In the concluding chapter, Pugh draws upon the previous contributions to provide millennial reflections on the sustainability and livability of cities. He leaves the reader with an appreciation of the state of knowledge on sustainable urban development together with an historical perspective, identifies the significant gaps in that knowledge base and discusses needed research. The book admirably communicates Pugh's continued call for disciplinary diversity and more interaction of pragmatism and vision – or theory and practice.

Carl R Bartone, PhD
Principal Environmental Engineer
Urban Development Division, Infrastructure Group
The World Bank
Washington, DC

PREFACE

This book is about sustainable urban environments in developing countries. That means that its scope and content cover the substantive understanding of the social, the economic, the environmental and the developmental. These are discussed and elaborated on in relation to their interdependence, their conceptual characteristics, their urban dynamics and some examples of case study expression. Also, they extend the ambitions and fill in some gaps that were recognized at the time of writing the forerunner book in 1996, *Sustainability, the Environment and Urbanization*. This means that chapters and sections are included that deal with the environmental and developmental aspects of law, and the international policies and politics of climate change. Some of the features that received attention and favourable comment among reviewers of the 1996 book have been further elaborated on and extended in this new book. These include poverty, inequality and the broader context of political economy and development studies. Also, the 1996 book attracted attention from the health professions, both in reviews and in receiving a commendation from the British Medical Association. This new book has two full chapters on health and other chapters introduce discussions on the theory and practice of environmental health.

The 'new' and 'updated' is represented in various ways in this volume. It has original ideas, some innovation in the ways of perceiving the environmental, and some recognition of the cautions and uncertainties in environmental reform. Readers will find topics that address the relationships between brown and green agendas, and others that bring to relevance community development, housing policy, self-help housing and progress with localized environmental planning in squatter settlements. This book has a subtitle that gives emphasis to theory, practice and reflections. It contains theory and conceptual development in housing, health, governance, urban change and the creative contributions of post-1995 developments in various social sciences. Practice is exhibited in the environmental reform agendas in cities such as Shanghai and squatter settlements in South Africa. Theory and practice are brought together in the elaboration of 'good practice' in the improvement of housing and local neighbourhood environments. Significant updating is given exposition and evaluation in the development of Local Agenda 21s, derived from the 1992 United Nations (UN) Conference on the Environment and Development in Rio de Janeiro, for the implementation of sustainability in human settlements.

Overall, the book has been influenced by useful comments from critics and reviewers of the 1996 book. However, not everything has been conceded. The approach to political economy has its roots in the social, economic and political realities of the developing countries. In this context, the authors have eschewed outright ideological advocacies such as neo-Marxism, neoliberalism, dependency theory or fundamentalist environmentalism. What readers will mostly find here are principles and ideas that emanate from the dialectic between the economic, the social, the environmental and the political. The theoretical compass, with relevance to political economy, also draws upon the writings of some Nobel prize-winners in the 1990s, including Robert Coase, Douglass North, Robert Fogel and Amartya Sen. These authors have variously argued that mixtures of the good, the bad and the indifferent are present in all markets, states, the voluntary sector and households. What needs to be identified are those patterns of interaction among these that lead to environmentally friendly patterns of urban sustainability. This perspective has the merit of versatility and seeking improvements rather than some unfeasible optimum in a grand theory.

The contributions of the authors were written in a period between late-1998 and mid-1999. This has some significance for the content of, and approaches to, their writing, particularly upon political economy and development policy. At the same time as we were writing, James Stiglitz and James Woltensohn, respectively vice-president and president of the World Bank, were delivering lectures and speeches for creating a new paradigm for development policy. This provided the basis for the bank's world development report for 1999–2000 and for their complementary strategic revisions of urban development. In essence, some significant international advocacies and policies broadened from sectoral and narrow-based interpretations toward priorities for the socio-political as well as the economic in development. Development was conceived as the social transformation of society over medium-term periods of 10 to 20 years. More than this, the general development of society and the economy was understood to include the urban as a centrally significant element. Additionally, the urban was reinterpreted, from within its previous sectoral boundaries to the very heart of holistic development. The contributing authors do not refer to these new World Bank initiatives, but they are all known for their approach during the 1990s when they wrote advocating the linking of general development and urbanization; it is gratifying to be able to include Carl Bartone's Foreword, recognizing that the new approach to development and sustainability is attracting increasing intellectual and policy attention.

One intellectual implication of the foregoing is that urban research agendas are likely to adopt the longer-term ethos of 'social transformation'. Again, the contributors have adopted medium-term developmental perspectives in their writing on sustainable urban development. However, it should be recognized that the next phases of research on sustainability will include greater sophistication on various transitions, including those in the urban and the environmental, in poverty, in health and epidemiology, in education and in the socio-political. Policies and processes will be evaluated for their impacts upon various transitions and their relationships to sustainable development. The prospect is exciting and the subject of sustainable urban development is set to grow in theory, in evaluation studies, in cross-disciplinary ways, and in new micro-studies.

Finally, it is the editor's pleasure to acknowledge the cooperation and contributions by authors, secretaries and professional staff at Earthscan Publications. I have become increasingly aware of the pressures of work on academic and research staff in universities and research institutes. Authors have variously had to adjust to competitive demands, to travel plans, to sickness over periods of three months and more, and to disabilities. It has needed large cooperation to bring this book to publication. Gratitude is expressed to Lynn Fox, my secretary in the School of the Environment and Development at Sheffield Hallam University, and to Akan Leander at Earthscan Publications. The subject matter in the book is important enough, but the field is growing rapidly and in diverse ways. In this, my own humoured feeling about this book is: 'Mountains will go into labour, and a silly little mouse will be born' (Horace 65–8 BC, *Ars Poetica*).

Cedric Pugh
Baslow, Derbyshire
March 2000

Acronyms and Abbreviations

BMRDA	Bangalore Metropolitan Region Development Authority
BOD	biological oxygen demand
CBP	community-based partner
CBO	community-based organization
CEO	chief executive officer
CG	consultative group
CMA	Chennai Metropolitan Area
CMC	Chennai Municipal Corporation
CMDA	Chennai Metropolitan Development Authority
CMWSSB	Chennai Metro Water Supply and Sewerage Board
CPF	Central Provident Fund
EPM	environmental planning and management
EU	European Union
GDP	gross domestic product
GNU	Government of National Unity
GO	government order
GSS	Global Strategy for Shelter
GTN	Government of Tamil Nadu
HDB	Housing and Development Board
HDFC	Housing Development Finance Corporation
HIID	Harvard Institute of International Development
HSS	Housing Subsidy Scheme
HWM	hospital waste management
HzWM	hazardous waste management
IMF	International Monetary Fund
IO	international organization
IPCC	Intergovernmental Panel on Climate Change
KIP	Kampung Improvement Programme
MEIP	Metropolitan Environmental Improvement Programme
NGO	non-governmental organization
NPE	new political economy
OWM	organic waste management
PHP	People's Housing Process
PIL	public interest litigations
PWB	Public Works Department
SAHPF	South African Homeless People's Federation

SChP	Sustainable Chennai Project
SchSP	Sustainable Chennai Support Project
SCP	Sustainable Cities Programme
SEMF	Strategic Environmental Management Framework
SEPB	Shanghai Environmental Protection Bureau
SIP	Strategy Implementation Profile
SMG	Shanghai Municipal Government
SOAS	School of African and Oriental Studies
SOE	state-owned enterprise
SWM	solid waste management
TEV	total economic valuation
TSP	total suspended particulates
UDF	Urban Development Framework
ULB	urban local body
UN	United Nations
UNCED	United Nations Conference on Economic Development
UNCHS	United Nations Centre for Human Settlements
UNCTAD	United Nations Conference on Trade and Development
UNDP	United Nations Development Programme
UNEP	United Nations Environment Programme
URBAIR	urban air quality management
WHO	World Health Organization

1 INTRODUCTION

Cedric Pugh

INTRODUCTION

The idea of sustainable urban development has been seminal and highly significant among intellectuals and policy makers in the 1990s. It is seminal in the sense that it is capable of development in its historical context, and it has become international, national and local in its policy significance. The impacts upon the urban social science literature have been profound and inventive. Before sustainability took a hold, urban social science tended to be separated into the confines of subject boundaries. Urban sociologists were interested in social structure, class, segregation, and various aspects of inequality and poverty. These interests could be applied to housing, the allocation of land, relativities in incomes and access to various urban services. Economists had similar interests, but studied them in terms of theoretical explanation, technical appraisal, measurement, and the costs and benefits of policy reform. Architect-planners had regard to macrospatial form, building technologies, and with relevance to developing countries, some pioneers such as John F C Turner brought self-help housing into relevance for low-income housing policies. Urban geographers, as guided by the conventions and scope of their subject, had eclectic interests, often undertaking household questionnaire surveys and adding commentaries on housing, social conditions and urban development. Political scientists concentrated on issues of urban government, with those in public administration specialization providing evaluations of infrastructural services and urban management. Other subjects – for example, law in development studies – were in only their first phases of influence in the urban social sciences.

By the late 1990s, much was changing, and changing rapidly, in the character and orientation of new books. The examples are many and varied, but the general thrust of change can be established from a few selected books. Fernandes and Varley (1998) brought together a collection of contributed chapters under the title of *Illegal Cities*. This book has great relevance for developmental and environmental issues in cities and towns in developing countries. The scope and aims include transitions in property rights from the 'illegal' to the 'regularized', customary law, tenure and the impact of law on the quality of life of the masses in poverty. In his concluding chapter, which gives commentary on the future of law and urban management, de Azevedo (1998, p269) writes:

> *The fact is that in developing countries law serves to distance the 'legal' from the 'illegal' city, increasing the value of the former. The areas in which the law is implemented effectively are those that house the machinery of the government, modern economic activities, and the homes of the middle and upper classes. By contrast the unregulated parts of the city suffer from low levels of infrastructural investment and poor access to the means of collective consumption, and they house the poor and marginalized sectors of society.*

In context, 'collective consumption' includes the social costs and benefits of environmental conditions, including air and water quality, along with price-access to essential services. But the words from de Azevedo say more than this. The issues surrounding 'sustainable cities' have elevated socio-legal studies and transitions in property rights in the changing urban literature. Studies of sustainable urban development become more than tabulating conditions of household living: they beckon towards the role of institutions in development, towards social inclusion and the exclusion of environmental benefits on a citywide basis, and the necessity to make the understanding of the 'urban' something more than geographical space. The 'urban' is clearly economic, social, political and environmental space, dependent upon wider national and international processes.

The forerunner to this book, *Sustainability, the Environment and Urbanization* (Pugh, 1996), has a scope that includes macro-economics, governance, urban health reforms, the political economy of development, reforms in international aid organizations, and micro-studies of households in some insanitary local environments. Although its primary purpose was to establish a collection of ideas and to survey the environmental research initiatives of the mid-1990s, by virtue of the nature of subjects it commenced by placing meaning and definition upon a young and growing literature on sustainable cities. Most of the authors who contributed to the character of the book were overtly cross-disciplinary in their approach. In some cases the cross-disciplinary approach was quite seamless, drawing upon theories, techniques and empirical work as blended mixtures from economics, health science, sociology, public policy, property rights, the valuation of environmental assets and degradation, and social opportunities in development. The conceptual and pragmatic issues of sustainability in urban contexts led authors to necessarily write in cross-disciplinary ways. One example will convey how authors dealt with sustainable urban development. Writing on the poverty and environmental health problems in local, low-income living areas, McGranahan and his co-authors (1996, p126) wrote:

The prevalence of local externalities and public goods, the importance of local institutions and the high level of diversity all underline the importance of local participation in designing and implementing improvements once the possibility of providing standard household-level services is ruled out. At the same time, how such institutions operate locally depends very much on how the state functions at higher levels, and the services centralized utilities do provide for the more disadvantaged neighbourhoods. The problems of these neighbourhoods are often compounded by the fact that standard utility services are oriented to well-defined households, rather than negotiating with and serving ill-defined groups of households and communities.

In three evaluative sentences McGranahan and his co-authors were saying that the problems and solutions to environmental poverty required complex, interdependent knowledge from across the social sciences. Transforming the language, the evaluations can be rewritten. First, the theory of economics in public goods (and social costs and benefits) argues that market or household individualism cannot itself resolve disease, squalor and premature death in such environments. Instead, some collective decision-making and resourcing is necessary, drawn from government provision, organized voluntary action and labour, and partnerships that set out responsibilities in resourcing, managing and implementing social/public policy solutions. In order to proceed, a new community-based and participatory approach to environmental planning and management is required. This will mean that work practices and policies will change because the priorities from among the poor and their affordability will almost certainly differ from standardized infrastructural provisions by government agencies. Also, affordability will have to be analysed technically to determine the appropriate cost, pricing, subsidization and choice of technology. Overall, it is an exercise in substantive reform, bringing together elements from economics, community development, new environmental planning and management, and socially adapted economic and technical appraisal. In practice, it is difficult to administer and in socio-political terms it has some uncertainties and risks of only partial success. This new book is both more elaborate and cautious on cross-disciplinary ways and on the implementation of public policy in environmentalism.

THE IDEA OF SUSTAINABLE DEVELOPMENT

The idea of sustainable development has itself been developed since the mid-1990s when it was very often associated with economic growth and social development that would not undermine environmental and developmental assets for future generations. By the late 1990s it is recognized that the scope of this is simultaneously in the economic, the social, the political and the environmental. From a perspective of historical and developmental change, this frequently means that 'sustainable development' is in a continuing state of flux that expresses outcomes of the dialectic between the economic, the social, the political and the environmental. The historical and the evolutionary does not necessarily and in all instances draw socio-political flux away from the intellectual tasks of building the blocks of theory and establishing concepts and principles. This is because the intellectual, although having abstractions and models, is also largely an exercise in persuasion and acceptance by public opinion and policy making. Of course, in formulating and implementing developmental policies it is often the case that trade-offs are made between the economic, the social, the political and the environmental. But, again this has significance for the way 'sustainable development' can be influenced and revised. Interrogative questions can be raised about the conditions which tend towards success or failure in comparative research and case studies. When failure is large and fundamental, questions arise as to whether it is appropriate to create new theory or to undertake institutionally loaded reform in order that good principles might be better utilized in practice.

In essence, the idea of sustainable development is largely about a range of different patterns of growth and social change that are environmentally and socially better than alternative patterns. Thus, the quest is not simply one of promoting environmentalism but at the same time severely inhibiting growth, or alternatively about permitting economic growth processes to do what they may and then attending in ad hoc ways to the partial destruction of some environmental assets. Put in these terms, further questions and issues become relevant. First, in an historical sweep of economic liberalism and the deregulation of markets on international scales since the early 1980s, what are the added probabilities of damage to environmental assets and some socio-economic opportunities? This is implicitly a question of distributional impact where there are winners and losers in developmental change. It is also a question about power and the way the interacting roles of states, markets, the voluntary sector and households are reconfigured in a period of greater liberalism and the internationalization of finance capital and the structural–spatial reorganization of production. As will be argued by various authors in this book, these are largely questions requiring an extensive search of ideas and evidence rather than following any preconception that ideological political economies such as neo-Marxism, dependency theory (with its assumptions of contrasting economic centrality and exploited peripherality), neo-liberalism, or even radical environmentalism provide ready-made solutions. In effect, the real world does not exhibit direct and simple teleological linkages from ideology to policy prescription, then to perfect implementation and to unambiguously good welfare. If the contrary were to be the case, the cause for environmentalism would be mostly straightforward, and evaluative social science might become redundant, or useful only outside environmental policy.

A second matter emanating from the realities of winners, losers and trade-offs in developmental change does concern intellectuals and their concepts. Along with Winch (1958) and Ayer (1993), it is reasonable to argue that the central task of social science is to bring conceptualization to complex and changing social reality, and to do this from theory, method, technique and evaluation. With relevance to agendas for sustainable development, the following can be said: sustainable development is basically about maintaining and enhancing environmental assets. Or, put in another way, consumption in the present should not reduce significant opportunities for consumption and the pursuit of lives of value in the future. However, environmental assets do not stand alone in socio-economic processes: they are interactive and sometimes dependent upon other assets. Economic assets provide the means of production, maintenance and the expansion of social opportunities, including attention to conserving and maintaining environmental assets. Of course, they can also be used in ways that degrade environmental and social qualities. Human capital is another asset that interacts with environmental assets: it provides knowledge, information and management services for environmentalism. Also, because sustainable development is partly socio-political, two further types of assets become significant. Social capital influences civic association, the quality of political processes and the character of the voluntary sector. In its positive vein it can be directed towards the public good in sustainability. But it can be negative if it is fragmented in ways that serve sectional interests that more or less reduce wider socio-economic opportunities and the economic and social value of environmental assets. Institutional capital is about the norms, rules, conventions and behaviours that influence ways of doing things. These can be formulated for assignments of responsibilities and for the resourcing of environmental common-pool resources: or, as in the case of other sorts of capital, they sometimes inhibit environmentalism. Overall, we see several interacting capital assets, having relationships of both cooperating interaction and potential conflict and substitution. The intellectual endeavour is to improve aggregate welfare in its broadest socio-economic sense – that is, not just as social policy – but sometimes with the constraint of specified absolute levels of pro-poor resourcing and environmental maintenance. The authors in this book have much to say on all the foregoing matters on sustainable development.

THE URBAN

The best starting point in discussions of the urban in the context of sustainable development is to understand it as a part of the wider developmental at the national and international scale – that is to say, it is reactive to national policy making and performance in macro-economic development, in shaping economic and social policy sectors, and in reforming institutions, including private and social property rights. And, of equal or greater significance, the urban is reactive to globalized finance capital, new communications technologies, the flows from 'real' capital investment by transnational corporations and other firms, and to various international policy organizations with environmental or economic relevance. Seen in this reactive perspective, the urban is limited in its scope and impact. But, the urban is not simply and narrowly reactive. It is also contributory and it characterizes the national and the international. For example, agglomerated industrial activity, along with city-regional and international trade, produces the products, the savings, the investments, the technologies and many of the ideas that are national and international. In this perspective, the urban is greatly significant and, although localized, is largely national and international in character. It is the agglomerated urban activity that provides the motor force for the strength and direction of the globalized dynamic, the more so in a post-1980 world of economic and spatial restructuring. More is said about the theory and social impacts of this in the concluding chapter, and it is featured in the writing of most of the contributing authors.

The previous paragraph has various social and economic inferences and implications that have fundamental significance when attention is given to the urban. The urban becomes more dynamic and expansionary when international and regional trade grows, along with large increases in population. This is true in theoretical terms (see Chapter 10) and historically. Cities and towns were founded and developed from these causes in the 11th and 12th centuries in Italy, in later centuries in medieval Europe, in the industrial revolution, and from the 1930s in developing countries. In all cases, urbanization had important characteristics in socio-economic change. These include social and occupational stratification, wide ranges of rural–urban links in agriculture and building, and urban economies of scale and specialization. More than this, these same precipitating causes of socio-economic change – that is, trade and demographic growth – also led to a hastening of institutional and legal changes that are otherwise normally glacially slow. The reasons are the economic and social necessities for finding new ways of doing things and for reforming older institutions that are inhibitory. This also implies new methods of government and urban management. In terms of policy, the significance of maintaining infra-structure and alleviating environmental nuisances increases. The social stratification will make urban poverty conspicuous and relevant to urban economic policies, sometimes aggravated by the troughs in trade cycles. At the same time, new patterns of social inclusion will emerge. Contrasting examples of this can be found in child labour in developing countries in the 1990s, to some extent associated with economic liberal-ization. In Gujarat in India, child labour has increased and intensified in the diamond-cutting and ship-breaking industries. The factory conditions create unhealthy environments and require long, hard work daily for very low pay (Swaminatham, 1998). Meanwhile, in Singapore the government progressively improved the quality and performance in schools. The approach is meritocratic, with strong streaming and the encouragement of homework – that is, a form of useful child labour. Enrolment and retention rates have increased over the years, and ethnic differences in performance reduced among Malays relative to Indians and Chinese. All of this is related to the closer engagement of parents in the education of their children.[1]

Economic aspects of the urban have taken on more complicated characteristics since the mid-1990s. One good example of this is the financial crisis in some Asian countries in 1997–98, coinciding with the drought aftermath effects of the *El Niño* phenomenon. The drought-reduced food harvests and, in urban consequences, the vast forest fires caused widespread air pollution and health problems. This led to greater attention to improved environmental policies in the World Bank's framework for an Asian recovery programme (World Bank, 1998). The financial crisis was caused by a number of interacting factors (Pugh, 1999). These included fixed exchange rate regimes in countries such as Thailand at a time when the value of the US dollar was rising, balance of payments deficits, massive short-term borrowing in the private sector, a herd-like withdrawal of short-term investment funds by foreign financiers, and large inadequacies in loaning by banks and financiers. The International Monetary Fund's (IMF's) conditionalities on financial assistance added to macro-economic austerity and aggravated medium-term poverty and inequality. Subsequently, the IMF recognized that fiscal austerities should be reduced. However, in the meantime the financial crises had led to an economic crisis which, with its slowdown in economic growth, in its turn led to a social crisis in under-employment, poverty and an increase in child labour at the expense of school enrolments. The recovery programmes, with greater or lesser effectiveness, are addressing the issues in the financial, economic and social crises. More than this, the dialectics between the economic, the social and the political are expanding reform agendas in the recovery plans. These include pro-poor programmes, revisions to social policy and the heightened significance of the environmental. The decreased growth has temporarily lessened environmental degradation in air pollution and similar impacts, but increased poverty and health risks in squatter settlements. What happens in the longer term will depend on whether legal and institutional reforms will be formulated and implemented to contain and reduce degradation. However, it is worth noting that during 1999, rates of growth, volumes of exports and other economic indicators began to improve. This reflected a strong US economy, adding to demand for exports from Asia and some reflationary fiscal policies.

In various ways the contributing authors have discussed the urban. These include the power of groups that support global liberalization, the agglomeration and urban change in developing countries, and the consequences of localized and regionally systemic macro-economic fluctuations. As argued earlier, the economic is in dialectic with the social and the political. One aspect of this is the significance of governance and institutional reform in developmental sustainability. These introductory discussions proceed with an overview of governance in its association with development.

GOVERNANCE[2]

Since the mid-1990s the idea of governance has greatly influenced development studies, including such urban subjects as poverty, environmental improvement, health, education, housing and the upgrading of squatter settlements. Governance is primarily about steering policy and practice for improved social opportunity, welfare and economic efficiency. In more specific terms, it is practised in attempts to improve state–market–society relations. An underlying supposition is that the state both influences markets and society, and is itself influenced by them. Accordingly, state, market and society roles are reconfigured with a dialectic of the economic, the social, the political and the environmental. Although these relationships and roles have been previously and extensively studied before the 1990s, the 'new' does make some differences. It switches some attention from sector studies of performance in the public sector to wider scopes and orientations. One example is that conceptualizations of welfare widen from the state's tax-transfer roles to societal welfare in household self help, in the expansion of social opportunities in markets and in institutionally loaded reform. Institutionally loaded reform includes changes to rules, norms, laws, property rights and ways of doing things. In the context of developing countries, property rights include practices in any of private, collective, customary, and informal rights and observances. This also takes institutional reform and governance into the sphere of 'enablement'. Enablement is essentially the design and implementation of economic, financial, socio-political and legal frameworks for enhancing efficiency and social effectiveness. The socio-political includes the creation and development of civil society and participation.

More can be said about governance by extending the foregoing principles. First, governance is not simply intangible and immaterial: it can be used in policy, planning and economic production. For example, in solid waste management, community-based organizations can act as entrepreneurs in organizing and marketing their services in low-income living areas. Second, and in continuity of the previous example, community-based organizations often need to interact with local government agencies in the pursuit of their roles in solid waste management. This may lead to coproduction practices where each is influenced by the other and revises its work practices for reasons of effectiveness and the affordability of urban services. Third, governance is frequently closely associated with decentralization, capacity building and partnerships, which are a part of the vocabulary associated with governance and enablement. Fourth, the 'bottom up' aspects of the 'new' ways reflect some often unstated assumptions about government. One of these is that local government cannot fulfil its responsibilities owing to limited financial and managerial resources. Another is that, in the past, governments have attempted to do both too much and too little. Sometimes they produce in spheres where markets or voluntary organizations are more efficient. But, at the same time, governments have ignored the necessity of reforming institutions and laws for welfare and development. It is also important to recognize that although the general principles of governance emphasize developmental welfare, in practice, community and government roles are influenced by localized politics. This will sometimes express narrow sectional interests and their connection to authorities. This book has substantive and varied perspectives on governance and institutional reform.

ORGANIZATION AND CONTENT

In general terms, this book has theory, new concepts, policy evaluations and some micro studies of cities and progress while implementing the recommendations from the 1992 UN Conference on Environment and Development in Rio de Janeiro. It also expresses the nature and direction of new research on the idea of sustainable urban development. In Chapter 2 I provide a wide-ranging overview of the way theory and thinking is being developed in environmental, social, economic and political studies, all of which are related to development and growth. It evaluates both separate social science subjects and cross-disciplinary approaches. One of its main features is an extended analysis and discussion of the inter-dependence among environment capital, economic capital, social capital and human capital. In Chapter 3 Amanda Perry elaborates the principles of law in urban and environmental development. Her case study is Bangalore, India, with emphasis on the enforceability and individual access to legal remedies. All of this reveals the large significance of law in sustainable development and some cautionary themes about expectations in reform. Even in some apparently promising contexts of economic development, the rule of law in environmental spheres remains fragile and incomplete.

Gordon McGranahan and David Satterthwaite have written Chapter 4, providing reflective and new ways of thinking on the relationships between green and brown agendas. They set their arguments within the framework of social equity issues in sustainable development. This leads them to examine the potential and actual conflicts between the green and brown agendas. But, they do not leave the relevant scope at this point, instead using evidence and reason to persuade us that some highly significant factors can be reconciled. The brown and green agendas are seen to have useful potential in localized environmental agendas, in urban agriculture, in the educational elements in hygiene and in managing the levels of demand for essential urban services. The authors enliven the persuasion by drawing upon comparative experience. Carolyn Stephens is another author who has a strong motivation for introducing new ways of thinking into the debates on sustainability, health and the environment. Her writing in Chapter 5 emphasizes the impact of inequalities in economic and political power in health and the environment. Also, Dr Stephens is insistent that the relevant ideas for modern environmentalism must include those from historical roots, including Aristotle, Defoe and others. By this means it becomes clearer why wealthy interests evade health and environmental significance. For modern relevance, attention is given to the role of non-governmental organizations (NGOs) and organized people in strengthening the lobbying for making power accountable. This perspective is set within an argument for education and democratization, viewed as a matter of urgency for sustainable development.

In Chapter 6 Trudy Harpham and Maria Allison evaluate comparative performances in health and governance, relating this to case studies in post-apartheid South Africa. Their writing shows the interesting ways in which governance and social development have been influencing policy in the World Health Organization (WHO). In application to the improvement of environmental and health conditions in low-income living areas, much depends upon the socio-political understandings in communities and their capacity to engage with policy and action plans. The authors argue that institutional conditions have as much determining influence on outcomes as technical know-how. Institutions that passively tolerate fragmentation can hinder the formulation and implementation of housing and environmental policy. Chapter 7, which is related to that written by Trudy Harpham and Maria Allison, is written by me. Its scope is an analysis and evaluation of policy and practice in the improvement of housing and the environment in squatter settlements. In many city-regions in developing countries, squatter settlements comprise some 30–70 per cent of the housing stock. The chapter reveals the conditions under which spontaneous physical and aesthetic improvements take place, relating these to the security of occupancy rights. Also, the rationale for the redirection of the World Bank and other international policies is explained and assessed. The chapter ends with a theory of environmental improvement, written as operational guidelines for policy makers and professionals.

In order to understand the practice as well as the theory of progress in sustainable urban development, it is necessary to review case examples and the application of environmental planning and management. Chapter 8, written by Bharat Dahiya and myself, sets out historical detail and dilemmas in the localization of Agenda 21 and the implementation of the UN Sustainable Cities Programme in Chennai, India. The localization of Agenda 21, as initiated by the United Nations Conference on Economic Development (UNCED) meeting at Rio de Janeiro in 1992, is shown to have varied performance. Variations occur in the degree of local response, in the way local governments perceive sustainable development, and in their ways of relating old 'top-down' and new 'bottom-up' approaches to environmental reform. The Sustainable Cities Programme, studied by Bharat Dahiya, has discussions of the detail of organizing and developing it in a large city with serious inadequacies in infrastructure and services. The progress has been affected by 'administrative separatism' in urban management, by gaps in institutional frameworks, and by the time that is necessary to create socio-political learning in community-based organizations. The final section of the chapter attempts to set out some general principles on first-phase implementations of international agendas. The practical issues, along with reflections upon them, are also taken up by Peter Abelson in Chapter 9. His case study is Shanghai, a city that has experienced high ambitions for its economic future and intensive economic restructuring since the early 1990s. Peter Abelson explains the historical development of Shanghai and describes its serious environmental problems in pollution, housing, transport, solid waste management, transport and land use. Overall, Shanghai expresses the major environmental and health dilemmas that occur under intensive and concentrated economic and demographic growth. The dilemmas draw forth responses in environmental policy, but in contexts where some problems are overwhelming in this present stage of development. Shanghai is now attracting much attention in the urban literature, and one good review complementing Peter Abelson's well-researched analysis has been written by Wu (1999).

My concluding chapter has some continuities and new direction compared with the forerunner 1996 book, *Sustainability, the Environment and Urbanization*. The continuities include the creation and destruction of knowledge in sustainable development, the roles of international organiz-ations, the political economy of development and some broader perspectives of the way that environmentalism is conditioned. The main emphasis in the new directions is the recent development of urban change, related to theories and evidence from agglomeration economies and institutional reform. In fact, the chapter will set out a new theory of urban change, related to environmental agendas.

DEMOGRAPHY, POVERTY AND ECONOMICS IN DEVELOPMENT

In closing this introductory chapter it is appropriate to set the underlying factors of development in the poorer countries. This is done not so much to indicate context, although that is important, as to anchor the issues of sustainable urban development in the long-term underlying conditions. Social science becomes more explanatory and illuminating when long-term conditions are brought to significance. Of course, many long-term cond-itions could enter such a discussion, but for clarity and relevance focus can be given to a few selected conditions. These will be the demographic characteristics, the circumstances of poverty and health, and major inter-national causes of growth, recession and change. All have significance for sustainable development. Demographic growth is associated with rapid urban development, with the problems of the absorption of large flows of new labour into the economy, and with the costs of pollution, environmental squalor and social services. Poverty is at once an outcome of under-development, of the masses in the informal sector because the flows of investment into the formal sector are insufficient to absorb the labour supplies. Poverty is a growing, distinctively urban problem. It is distinct-ively urban by characteristic rather than merely by volume. This is because poverty is much more than a statistical poverty line of necessary calorific costs for subsistence. In urban contexts, 'housing poverty' and 'urban poverty' are as significant as cash poverty. Housing poverty is about overcrowding, insanitary housing, high rent-to-income ratios and so forth, being at once a response to monetary poverty and reinforcing it by virtue of sickness and absenteeism from work. Urban poverty can be understood from the concepts of price–access value to essential infrastructural services, to land occupancy rights and to the net value (sometimes negative) from amenity and social costs such as pollution and contagious disease. Total welfare is an aggregate of the monetary, housing and the urban components of welfare. Some of the major economic conditions of growth, recession and change originate in the volumes and distributions of trade, in the flows of investment capital and the macro-economic fluctuation of these. They influence the growth and limitations of incomes and social opportunities.

The demographic conditions can be set out in their essential statistical dimensions. Some 30 per cent of the world's population was urbanized in 1950 at 737 million and during the last 50 years the urban population of developing countries has increased by 600 per cent. Also, whereas in 1950 the number of cities of over 1 million was 31, by 1995 this had grown to 196, with most of the increase occurring in developing countries. In most developing countries the rates of urban growth are slowing down, but the absolute numbers in the growth are vast and the urban proportions relative to the rural population also increase. One important consequence of this, as referred to above, is the increase in labour supply: this is some 35 million each year, which is set to remain close to this figure until the second decade of the 21st century. This can readily be placed into conceptual and explanatory interpretations by referring to Figure 1.1 below. Figure 1.1 graphically represents the demographic transitions that explain the comparative rates of change of death and birth rates over long periods of time.

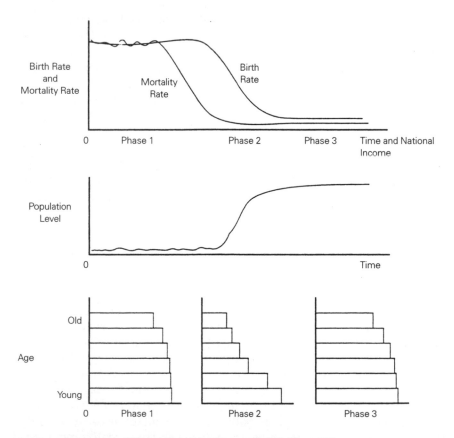

Figure 1.1 *The Demographic Transition*

Demographic transitions can be understood in a series of successive phases. In Phase 1, per capita incomes are low and the economy is dominantly agricultural. This phase is punctuated with occasional famine and killer diseases, and large sections of the population in poverty are stunted, with low body mass (see the discussions below). Both death rates and birth rates are high, and one of the major social concerns in the towns is disease and low life expectancy. Phase 2 is characterized by some initial and continuing reduction in death rates owing to the gradual improvements in nutrition and medical practices. In this phase, at first birth rates increase moderately, but then they too decrease, owing to the spread of education to women, and to improved incomes and urbanization. This leaves a growing number of women in the fertile stage of their life-cycles, with consequences for a significant and explosive medium-term growth in population. Also, the age characteristics become dominantly 'young'. In the later phases, birth rates fall further and population levels tend towards stability, but with fewer children per household, these generally reflect a greater investment in human capital. Demographic transitions are associated with rural-to-urban migration, and the developing countries have been experiencing this – since the 1930s in Latin America – with explosive growth. The urban impacts include mass poverty, squatter settlement, a large informal sector, pollution, congestion and disease. Infrastructure services and decent standard housing tend to lag behind demand and need. However, urbanization also improves average incomes and, in some circumstances, this provides the means of gradual long-term improvement in living conditions.

The health and poverty dimensions of economic growth and change lend an underlying importance to the understanding of sustainable development. The 1993 Nobel prizewinner in economics, Robert Fogel, has combined quantitative techniques and economic theory to cut new paths of understanding in the subject of growth and change. He draws upon large data sources in history, economics, sociology and health, providing new thinking in the role of innovations, the economic effects of slavery, and the relationship between health and poverty (Fogel, 1964; 1989; 1994). It is Fogel's 1994 study on the relationships between health, poverty, body mass and public policies that is especially relevant to sustainable development. Fogel found that at low stages of development large numbers of the poor were stunted (ie, they had low body mass and low energy) and were vulnerable to disease. This was associated with undernutrition and, along with low body mass, reduced potential production, productivity and income. Essentially, there was an inter-related systemic relationship between energy and health on the one hand and developmental progress on the other. Fogel concluded that in the developed countries it has been the cumulative improvements in medicine, health policies and housing that has improved the human capability to work and thereby to achieve economic growth and social development. Stunting, undernutrition and mass poverty are, of course, major problems underlying the limitations to sustainable development in developing countries.

Along with other authors, Ravallion and his co-authors (1991; 1993) have extended Fogel's approaches to the short- and long-term relationships between poverty, undernutrition and health. He shows that head counts of poverty in the range of US$24 to $31 monthly can reduce significantly with evenly distributed income growth. This contingently supports the role of growth in reducing poverty, but it also means that when a severe recession occurs, as in the Asian financial crisis of 1997–98, the head counts of poverty rose rapidly. The poor have severe trade-offs between nutrition, the capacity to do physical work and seeking improved housing and sanitary environments in urban areas. In complementary work on poverty, Anand and Ravallion (1993) argue that it is not economic growth per se that improves people's health and quality of life. Rather, it depends on the patterns of distributed growth and whether public policies expand effective health services to all social groups. The improvement in basic human indicators in health and other factors depend on the price-access to health services and increasing absolute and relative incomes in the bottom 40 per cent of the distribution of household income. Again, this places emphasis on long-term developmental change and its relevance to sustainable livelihoods and environments.

The livelihoods of households depend on various sources of income, expenditure and access to entitlements in environmental assets, in human capital and welfare. Welfare entitlements can be derived variously from self-help, from markets, from state assistance, and from mutual aid in the family and in other social networks. Viewed in this way, housing and household economics have central roles. Households combine various inputs, their work efforts and domestic capital (ie, housing and equipment) to produce meals, other goods and services, and sometimes for childrearing. This operates in a division of labour, with social cooperation, among women, men and children. Of course, this is influenced by culture, religion and bargaining within the households. Housing has importance in terms of its functional capacity to provide value in these allocations of time and resources (Pugh, 1997). Added benefits and/or costs are relevant from environmental health conditions and price-access to education in their urban settings. Another way of understanding this is to view it as 'household livelihood strategies' that achieve the necessary flows of benefits from stocks of environmental, physical, financial, human and social capitals (see Moser, 1998; Rakodi, 1999). All of this can then be used to evaluate poverty at greater depth and more generally to assess the roles of households in sustainable development. Some of these matters are elaborated on, in a number of chapters in this book. However, the economic and social opportunities of households are also significantly influenced by broader factors in the international economy.

The international economy can be described and explained in a large variety of ways. What follows is necessarily a summary and has been selected for its relevance to sustainable development. The selection includes recent changes in the direction of macro-economic policies, some important trends in public expenditure for the formation of human capital, trends in world trade and the volatility in flows of investment to the developing countries. Each of these items has a large impact on welfare and sustainable urban developments. As a set, they influence household incomes, access to education and health services, and the fluctuating conditions in economic growth and the distribution of social opportunities. The selected items also provide significant updating, in a context that many modern debates about sustainable development are anchored in the outdated economic contexts of the 1980s and the early 1990s.

In the 1980s and the early 1990s many developing countries in Latin America, subSaharan Africa and South Asia were experiencing first-phase macro-economic austerity from the IMF and World Bank structural adjustment programmes. Although the longer-term aims were to increase growth and opportunity, they reduced attention to poverty during their early phases. Concerns for poverty and environmentalism became more prominent in the early 1990s. For example, in 1990 the World Bank devoted its World Development Report to an extensive discussion of reducing poverty and the UNCED meeting was held in Rio de Janeiro in 1992. Economic policy was going through a period of evolution and review, taking it beyond simple advocacies for liberalist deregulation, privatization, the stricter control of subsidies, and so forth. The increased attention to social equity was conspicuous in the meeting called by the IMF in June 1998. This meeting included international policy makers, academics, religious leaders and trade unionists. Broad agreement occurred in several areas, but there was disagreement in others.

New directions were occurring in international economic policy. First, some lessons from the 1970s and 1980s had been learned. Sustainable macro-economic policies required monetary and fiscal discipline, largely in order to achieve growth and a framework for increasing social expenditure. Second, whereas in the past various macro-economists were arguing that egalitarianism reduces saving and investment, by the late 1990s growing numbers were saying that the broad spreading of human capital holds prospects for heightened growth and social development. Third, as led by the 1999 Nobel prizewinner in economics, Amartya Sen, it was increasingly accepted that priority should be placed upon reducing poverty and increasing social inclusion. This meant that favour was growing for empowering the poor. Fourth, caution was expressed on the view that the globalizing economy in itself was inhibiting social equity. Rather the major problem was political, especially in a declining support for tax-transfer policies. The foregoing does not represent, of course, full operational change, but rather emerging new directions. But it is clear that what has been going on since the late 1980s is much broader than neo-liberalism in its pure and simple versions of the 1983–87 period.

The second selected item – public expenditure on human capital – also offers some illumination on the updated realities of the late 1990s. For context, it is appropriate to establish some general circumstances of public expenditure in developing countries. The ratio of public expenditure-to-gross domestic product (GDP) is some 18–30 per cent, this being 15 per cent below the range in the majority of developed countries. During the austerity phases of the aforementioned structural adjustment programmes in the 1980s and early 1990s, public expenditures on infrastructure and on some subsidies were curbed. However, the restructuring of taxation and public expenditure was frequently the aim of the longer-term elements in structural adjustment. This would normally include increased tax collection and improved effectiveness in social expenditures. What, then, has actually been occurring in the modern trends in public expenditure on health and education (ie, human capital expenditure)? Gupta and his co-authors (1998) drew a sample from 188 countries, using data from the mid-1980s to 1996. They report that:

> *There were large increases in real per capita social outlays in Asia and the Caribbean, while subSaharan Africa experienced either moderate increases or decreases* (Gupta et al 1998, p11).

Some of the decrease in subSaharan countries reflects devaluation in the franc-zone countries and decreases in teachers' salaries. Health spending in GDP rose in all regions except Asia. None of this suggests any room for complacency, but it does show that recent trends do not support overall claims that the state has been rolled back in its major social expenditure programmes. The supporting data on human indicators show that on average, improvements have continued in primary school enrolments, in life expectancy, in infant mortality, in access to safe water and in access to sanitation. It should also be borne in mind that public expenditure does not provide a comprehensive view of human capital formation. Human capital formation also has resource inputs from subsistence work, self-help, markets and education which can improve childrearing, nutrition and hygiene. It can be strongly argued, of course, that public finance in the poorest countries should be expanded under international cooperation. Sachs (1999) does this for the redistribution of research and development in medicines and vaccines. He suggests that rich countries should pledge payments for the treatment and prevention of malaria and other diseases in poor countries.

Finally, it is highly relevant to look at the general characteristics and trends in international trade and finance. Trade is closely associated with urban development, agglomeration economies and in activating growth or recession. Finance is also closely associated with urban development, including business activity, housing and urban investment, and the ways its volatility interacts with the real economy and changes in head counts in poverty. Another way of looking at this is to perceive that the IMF bail-outs to Mexico in 1994 and to some Asian countries in 1997–98 have large urban impacts. The conditionalities for the loans reduce incomes and investment for the short term, and effective recovery in the longer term has further implications for the restructuring of finance and urban living conditions.

In general principle, trade can be an engine of economic growth, thereby changing the sets of social opportunities. It is trade that has fundamental causal impact on the pattern of agglomeration economies and competitive urban development. This influences the extent of environmental costs and their patterning in urbanization, along with the structuring of inequalities and poverties. Theoretical explanations are provided of these conditions in the concluding chapter. For present purposes the discussions will proceed in general outline form. Since the 1950s there has been a long-run policy to reduce protection and advance the cause of freer trade, including the Uruguay Round of 1994. For many developing countries, the IMF, the World Bank and national government structural adjustment programmes of the 1980s and early 1990s favoured freer trade. (It should be borne in mind that export-led growth and restructuring occurred in stages in the high-performing countries of Asia since the 1950s.) The economic liberalization in trade is not unambiguously good, although it beneficially speeds up the transfers of technological and managerial skills in some cases. On the other hand, many developing countries are exposed to fluctuations in prices and earnings; they face some protectionism in the developed countries such as bilateral quotas, for example, in the Multi Fibre Agreement, and some 25–40 per cent of exports in the smaller countries are often in primary commodities. Primary commodities have fluctuations in prices and incomes, and in the long term their relative prices decrease compared with manufactured goods and services which are internationally traded. Manufactured exports in developing countries have increased by 250 per cent in the 1965–90 period, but these gains are unevenly distributed. In more general characteristics, the share of world exports provided by developing countries has been in the range of 17–25 per cent since 1970, with recessions in 1990 and 1997. The 1997 recession is particularly revealing as it was caused by the contagion effect of the financial crisis in some Asian countries.

The interdependence between trade, production and flows of finance capital has large consequences for sustainable development in both the short- and the long-term timescales. Following the financial crisis in Mexico in 1995 and in some Asian countries in 1997–98, some general perspective can be placed upon global finance in the late 1990s (see, for example, *The Economist* survey, 1999). Capital flows are hypermobile and the sudden withdrawal from investment in some countries, as in the Asian countries in 1997, can lead to contagion in other developing and developed countries. The contagion is influenced by panic herd instincts among investors, by devaluations that have impacts on the relative competitiveness of nations in trade and by the recessionary impacts of first-phase economic policies. Financial crises have been much evident historically, of course – for example, in European towns in the medieval period from the 11th to the 15th centuries. This includes fluctuations in trade, building cycles and insolvency in banking systems. Since the early 1990s the IMF has evolved and changed some of its primary roles. Whereas before the early 1970s, when nations were changing from fixed to flexible exchange rate regimes, the IMF's role was to stabilize countries with balance of payments deficits, the new roles emphasize assistance to developing countries when crises occur or for the requirements of structural adjustment. Structural adjustment is intended to move a country from an outmoded economic position to an improved position promoting international economic integration. Crises require economic funding for recovery and bail-out finance: in 1994 the IMF provided Mexico with a US$40 billion rescue package.

The hypermobility of finance capital is readily apparent in the statistical trends of private capital flows to developing countries. In 1988 the total flows were some US$15 billion, which increased rapidly to US$350 billion in 1996, and decreased rapidly (largely by withdrawal) to some US$150 billion in 1998. As explained in an earlier discussion, the large influx, followed by massive withdrawal, was a major cause of the financial crisis in Thailand, South Korea, Malaysia, Indonesia and the Philippines. The financial crisis then led to contagion, not only in other Asian countries by reason of the interdependent effects on exports, but also in other developing countries in Africa and Latin America. More than this, the financial crises ran through the capillaries of economic processes to cause curbs in the growth of GDP, increased poverties and to stressed adjustments in the livelihoods of households. All of this undermined a broad confidence in the spread of market ideology and the use of only market economics (as distinct from social and market failure economics) to achieve economic recovery. Although the crises did not lead to international economic meltdown, it was a near thing. In more elemental terminology, some aspects of market freedoms became apparent as endorsing a course tantamount to a result of 'disposable people'. Market failure is inherent in financial systems, especially in the fragile systems in developing countries where they are usually small and not well regulated. The hypermobility of finance capital posed large dilemmas for the IMF and national policy makers. On the one hand, raising interest rates would curb the withdrawal of short-term investments, but deepen economic austerity. On the other hand, the alternative, large devaluations, would cause disruptive contagion and require an extensive period of economic adjustment. Also, the IMF in any event did not have sufficient resources to act as a comprehensive 'lender of last resort'. It relied on persuasion and pressure on private investors to reschedule and roll over their loans to those developing countries in crisis.

As for the longer-term policy to reduce the risks of a similar crisis in the future, it is becoming clearer that ad hoc reform is more likely than a total redesign of the international architecture of finance. The private sector has a large volume and power in relation to the IMF and individual nations. Although capital flows and investments are geographically and historically uneven, they provide benefits for development, particularly in technological and managerial spillovers. Some necessary reforms are being accomplished, including the regulation of the financial sectors and corporate business in Asian countries. The IMF did recognize that its initial approach was too conventional in terms of conditionality for austerity and subsequently it eased its view of tight fiscal restraint. For developing countries the lessons are apparent. Caution should be attached to the financial sector capability in a world of hypermobile finance capital. This means that some future crises are likely to recur, perhaps with reduced intensities, but the caution includes some preparation for withdrawal and panic. More generally, as stated above, far more circumspection is necessary in the political economy of balancing market economics, social economics and the state's roles in market-failure economics. As elaborated on in the concluding chapter, advocacy and criticism in ideology has its dangers. Much of the ideological heat either in defence or in attack of market liberalism is to some extent outdated. The major policy impact of market liberalism occurred in the development policies in the years 1983–89. In the 1990s development policies have included social sector development, greater significance being given to poverty and the rising significance of environmental agendas. More significantly, the tasks for improving markets and the social and environmental agendas are both far short of completion.

In an overall perspective, such underlying factors as demographic change, the health of the poor, social sector development, and trade and hypermobile global finance have large impacts upon sustainable development. All of this can be described in human terms. Malawi is a very poor country. Its housing policies have been rudimentary, emphasizing the provision of sites without services and supplying government housing for some public servants. Industrialization has been slow, and urban low-income settlements have the risks of disease and aggravated poverty. By contrast, Singapore was a largely fetid slum in the 1950s. Its polluted river basins have been cleansed; the extensive (and subsidized) social housing programmes have improved standards of living and the accumulation of assets among all social groups; and per capita income is ranked at fourth in the world. Continual environmental improvements add to the growth of private and social assets. Health standards are good and broadly accessible, along with family planning. Squatter settlements have been either redeveloped or upgraded with regularized tenure rights. The contrasts can be largely attributed to various economic and social policies, along with access to markets and finance capital in developed countries. In the case of Singapore, the finance sector has been well regulated and as a consequence the effects of contagion from the Asian region have been moderate and limited. Long-term underlying conditions clearly determine the prospects for sustainable urban development.

NOTES

1   Information provided in personal correspondence with Professor Phang Sock Yong.
2   This section has been much influenced by discussion with Bharat Dahiya who studied aspects of the UNCHS and UNEP initiatives in their Sustainable Cities Programme in Chennai, India.

REFERENCES

Anand, S and Ravallion, M (1993) 'Human Development in Poor Countries: On the Role of Private Incomes and Public Services', *Journal of Economic Perspectives*, vol 7, no 1, pp133–50
Ayer, A (1993) *Central Questions of Philosophy*, Penguin, Harmondsworth
de Azevedo, S (1998) 'Law and the Future of Urban Management in the Third World Metropolis', in E Fernandes and A Varley (eds), *Illegal Cities: Law and Urban Change in Developing Countries*, Zed Books, London, pp258–73

Economist, The (1999) *A Survey of Global Finance, The Economist*, London, pp3–22

Fernandes, E and Varley, A (eds) (1998) *Illegal Cities: Law and Urban Change in Developing Countries*, Zed Books, London

Fogel, R (1964) *Railroads and American Economic Growth: Essays in Econometric History*, John Hopkins University Press, Baltimore

Fogel, R (1989) *Without Consent or Contract: The Rise and Fall of American Slavery*, Norton, New York

Fogel, R (1994) 'Economic Growth, Population Theory and Physiology: The Bearing of Long-term Processes on the Making of Public Policy', *American Economic Review*, June 1994, pp369–95

McGranahan, G, Songsore, J, and Kjellén, M (1996) 'Sustainability, Poverty and Urban Environmental Transitions', in C Pugh (ed), *Sustainability, the Environment and Urbanization*, Earthscan, London, pp103–34

Moser, C (1998) 'The Asset Vulnerability Framework: Re-assessing Urban Poverty Strategies', *World Development*, no 26, pp1–19

Pugh, C (ed) (1996) *Sustainability, the Environment and Urbanization*, Earthscan, London

Pugh, C (1997) 'The Household, Household Economics and Housing', *Housing Studies*, no 12, pp383–92

Pugh, C (1999) 'The Asian Financial Crisis and its Urban Impacts', *Habitat International*, vol 23, no 2, pp157–65

Rakodi, C (1999) *Tackling Urban Poverty: Principles and Practice in Project and Programme Design*, paper to seminar 'From Welfare to Market Economy: The State, Aid and Policy Shifts in Urban Development and Shelter Programmes', Oxford Brookes University, 6 July 1999

Ravallion, M (1990) 'Income Effects on Undernutrition', *Economic Development and Cultural Change*, no 38, pp489–515

Ravallion, M, Datt, G and Van de Walle, D (1991) 'Quantifying Absolute Poverty in the Developing World', *Review of Income and Wealth*, vol 37, no 4, pp345–61

Sachs, J (1999) 'Helping the World's Poorest', *The Economist*, 14–20 August 1999, pp16–22

Swaminatham, M (1998) 'Economic Growth and the Persistence of Child Labour: Evidence from an Indian City', *World Development*, vol 26, no 8, pp1513–28

Winch, P (1958) *The Idea of a Social Science*, Routledge & Kegan Paul, London

World Bank (1998) *East Asia: The Road to Recovery*, World Bank, Washington DC

Wu W (1999) 'City Profile: Shanghai', *Cities*, vol 16, no 3, pp207–16

2 SUSTAINABLE URBAN DEVELOPMENT: SOME MILLENNIAL REFLECTIONS ON THEORY AND APPLICATION

Cedric Pugh

This chapter has a different purpose from the others in this volume. It offers a wide-ranging review of the issues and subjects within the thematic content of the idea of sustainable urban development. This general purpose accordingly provides theories, principles and new ways of thinking with regard to urban environmental issues, with relevance to the following chapters by contributing authors. The range covers the idea of sustainable urban development and the relationships between environmental, economic, social and human capital. It also explores the changing principles in the development of sustainability in economics, political economy, political science and environmental health. What follows is based on evaluation research from literature reviews and some on-location research in Asia, subSaharan Africa and Latin America. The approach is cross-disciplinary, although with some concentrated attention to each of several social science subjects.

INTRODUCTION

The idea of sustainable urban development is an aspect of wider development studies. It does not readily admit a simple summary definition, but meaning can be attributed from some appropriate blend of concepts, principles, histories and applied studies. Sometimes distinctions are made between 'green', 'brown', 'radical' and 'conservative' agendas. These distinctions do not so much draw well-defined boundaries as indicate orientations. It is quite easy to find significant examples where the distinctions raise both intellectual and policy difficulties. In 1997, forest fires set many regions of Southeast Asia ablaze. The smoke added to poor quality air in the cities and, along with the financial crisis in some Asian countries at the time, raised questions about inadequacies in both green and brown agendas. Distinctions can also break down in political attempts to divide radical fundamentalism from conservative approaches to policy. Generally, a radical approach is to adopt a strong position and to advocate the defence of nature and environmental capital as an absolute. By contrast, a conservative position would accept incremental, but significant adjustments to ongoing development. In an historical context, the radical agenda emanated from reactions to the natural resource exhaustion thesis of Meadows (1972) and similar crisis-type writing of the 1960s and early 1970s. The radical advocacy was for zero growth and the political dominance of economics. However, in a quieter and more radical way as far as practical welfare was concerned, the Singapore government installed legislation to enforce strict controls on water and air pollution in the years 1971–76. The vision was both economic and political, ensuring rapid growth, reductions in poverty and the creation of a garden city with mammoth social housing programmes and new town developments. In perspective, the routinely effective management of programmes is more radical than misplaced messages for the 'limits to growth' where that is assumed to imply zero growth.

As elaborated by Barry (1998), green ecologists have often opted for radical and even anarchic solutions for a political economy of the environment. By contrast, the urbanist with intellectual projects for sustainability has to take account of the actual prevailing economic, social and governmental conditions. Attention is thereby turned to designing and adjusting the institutional, governmental and economic conditions to facilitate sustainable development. Institutional, economic and governmental reforms have to be mediated through social and political processes. Accordingly, sustainable urban development is usually deliberated and implemented through a dialectic of the social, the economic, the political and the environmental. In these contexts, the agendas for sustainable urban development are not only for framing prescriptive conceptual foundations, but also include evaluations of comparative urban performance. Comparative studies are interrogative: they can be used to discern the appropriate institutional, economic and political conditions that enhance prospects for better outcomes. Additionally, they accumulate knowledge that is derived from collective social learning experiences, providing information and anchors for creating concepts and theories.

In another perspective, the idea of sustainable urban development has to be interpreted within its historical context. This has several relevant points. First, since the late 1980s, and more so since the UN Conference on the Environment and Development (UNCED) in Rio de Janeiro in 1992, the significance of sustainable development has risen rapidly up international and national agendas. This marks out some unique aspects of the recent historical period, with widespread articulation of various environmental issues, including the effects of greenhouse gases, the added health risks of air pollution, and the bad living conditions in squatter settlements which comprise some 30–70 per cent of the housing stock in some cities in developing countries. Second, concerns for the environment have led to rapid international policy development, some of which has been extended to the localization of environmental reform. One example of this is the localization of Agenda 21 from the guideline initiatives of the UNCED 'Earth Summit' in 1992, and its further consolidation and elaboration at the Habitat II conference in Istanbul in 1996 (this is expanded on in Chapter 8). Although the implementation of Local Agenda 21s has been fragmentary and only more or less guided by the idea of sustainability, it has activated environmental planning and management in a growing number of cities and towns. It is not only the existence of the extension of urban environmental policy that has historical significance. Substantial significance is further added because new community-based approaches are being introduced into urban environmental planning and management. This is influencing policy and practice in various spheres, such as solid waste collection and disposal, the upgrading of squatter settlements, the reform of housing policies and the reappraisal of the roles of environmental health. Reform is being enhanced and promoted by strategic policy reviews and programme development in the World Bank, the UN Development Programme (UNDP), the UN Environment Programme (UNEP) and the World Health Organization (WHO).

Historical factors interweave with intellectual developments in giving justification, reason and concept to sustainable development. The aforementioned international organizations have shaped their policies partly in relation to historical conditions. These have included the assumptions and precepts underlying late 20th-century liberalism. Examples include the globalization of finance capital, market liberalization, the evolutionary reconfiguration of state roles and the incorporation of ideas of governance into development agendas during the mid-1990s. All of this has dilemmas and contradictions, as well as some relevance and opportunities. Globalized finance is hypermobile and, in combination with other factors, the national inflows and outflows can cause a sequence of inflation and subsequent recession. This disturbs and retards economic, social and environmental development in some cities in developing countries, including those in Mexico, 1994–96, and those in Indonesia, South Korea, Thailand and Malaysia, 1997–2000. The financial crisis in some Asian countries in 1997 also coincided with the aforementioned *El Niño* effects on drought and forest fires which caused air pollution and health risks in urban areas. As noted earlier, this heightened the significance of improving environmental policies in the recovery plans for the afflicted countries in the financial crisis. Ironically, the slowed down economic development in these countries has reduced some environmental degradation in the meantime (World Bank, 1998).

Other dilemmas are associated with the new emphasis on governance which broadly refers to state–market–community relations and to the qualities of accountability, transparency and capability in government. Sometimes it is mistakenly assumed that in some unified way governance is improved by starting with civic association and democratization, then expecting that accountability and improved capability will follow. However, in practice civic association, capability in states and accountability are often independent, and each has highly variable qualities. In general terms, the theory and practice of sustainable urban development is influenced by contradictions and dilemmas, as well as by useful innovations in its historical settings. In the period 1976–96, good urban, housing and land policies were variously associated with regimes having militarist, democratic, authoritarian and leftist or rightist orientations (Pugh, 1997a). This is likely to continue for some time in environmental abatement policies.

The idea of sustainable urban development evolves not only in relation to historical change, but also in response to intellectual developments in the sciences and the social sciences. Historical significance has increased the volume and quality of knowledge in urban environmental topics. This includes the science of atmospheric pollution, greenhouse gases, international climate change and suchlike. The social sciences have been following a variety of research agendas in sustainable development. Some have revised or extended subject boundaries and topics in economics, political science, law and sociology to accommodate specialisms in the environment. The range of topics includes the valuation of environmental capital, revisions to political economy, project appraisal, governance, the theory and practice of institutions, and social development agendas. Modern discussions on the creation and development of new knowledge suggest some important aspects of process and outcome. The new will sometimes be contested by older, established sections of the knowledge industry. Also, sometimes the old will adapt and assimilate some of the new. The new is not without its own problems. Some of it develops incrementally with the risks of misconception and irrelevance being higher in first phase developments. In some cases authors will make fundamental changes in their ideological and theoretical positions. For example, in 1982 Burgess was working from a neo-Marxist basis in assessing self-help squatter settlements, whereas by 1997, with his co-authors he was writing from less ideological advocacy in reviewing policies on sustainability (see and compare Burgess 1982 and Burgess et al, 1997). Others (for example, Jones and Ward 1995) argue that major reformers in environmental policy such as the World Bank have scarcely changed at all because they are committed to neoclassical market orthodoxy. This disregards the fact that various elements in economic orthodoxy, along with new theory in institutional economics, include theories of the state and society in their environmental work. Such theories are having major impacts in social science generally, including political science, sociology and law.

The foregoing indicates that the idea of sustainable urban development is influenced by various context issues. It is a contended ground in political economy and sometimes in theoretical or empirical knowledge. Always it is shaped (and sometimes redirected) by historical change. The discussions that follow are pursued with these characteristics in mind. They commence with an analytical and conceptual view of environmental transitions and the relations between environmental, economic, social and human capital.

ENVIRONMENTAL TRANSITIONS AND
LONG-TERM ABATEMENT

One way of bringing together theory, concept, fact and meaning is to set demographic, economic, social and environmental change into a broad framework of time-based transitions. Although this approach is broadly relevant to society as a whole rather than to micro-studies, it provides information and underlying explanations of some significant factors in development. It also sets out contingent interpretations and some clarification on the relationships among economic growth, Socio-environmental development and the significance of introducing abatement polices. More generally, such an approach may concede that some sorts of patterns of economic growth can lead to some added environmental degradation, and with far greater significance there is the real possibility that alternative patterns of development and growth can add both economic and social welfare, along with improved urban environmental performance. Furthermore, even making allowance for some intellectual controversy, econometric analyses and measurements indicate that the costs of improving key urban environmental factors are affordable and modest, with some opportunities for yielding benefits in excess of costs (see Goldin and Winters, 1995; Pugh, 1996a, 1996b). Figure 2.1 comprises a set of time series diagrams, illustrating the main characteristics of demographic, economic, environmental and health transitions, including forecasts.

Section A reveals the essential broad results of the demographic transitions in developing and developed countries. The major feature is that most (but not all) developing countries are in the explosive expansion phase of demographic growth. Rising life expectancy, associated with modern medicine, improved sanitation and other positive factors, is adding some 85 million annually to the world population. This can be viewed in several perspectives. First, it adds to the problems and costs of education, health, housing and some environmental degradation. Second, with appropriate policies, economic growth adds to the generated income and technologies which, along with other factors, may improve prospects for the abatement of bad environments. Third, as argued in principles and statistics for the demographic–economic transitions in developed countries, as undernutrition is substantially reduced over long periods of time, the human energy and work capacity is expanded for productive economic life and for a better quality of life (Fogel, 1994). Fourth, economic and social advantage can be taken from policies that accelerate economic growth, extend education to women and consequently reduce fertility. Fertility rates tend to fall when women have increasing value in gainful employment, and incentives tilt in favour of having fewer, but better reared and educated children, as well as adding freedom to women's lives (Baldwin, 1995; Boone, 1996). The liberation of women adds to production and productivity, and it may improve environmental and health conditions over long periods of time. Added economic and social improvement occurs from making the work of children positive in school studies, in domestic work and in

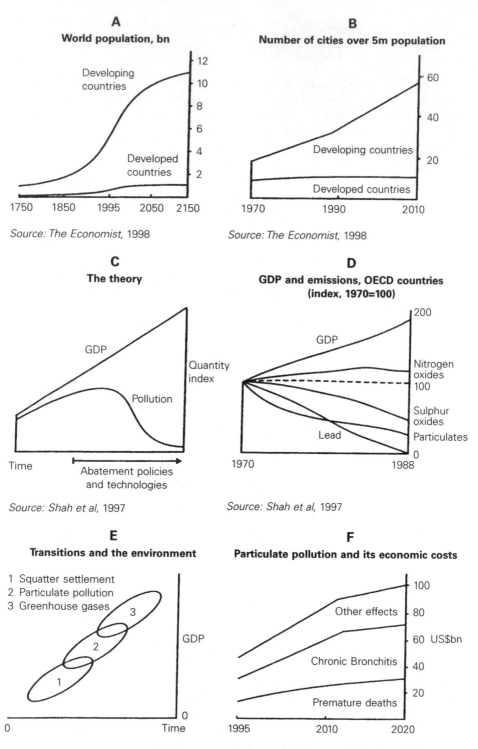

A
World population, bn

Developing countries

Developed countries

12
10
8
6
4
2

1750   1850   1995   2050   2150

Source: The Economist, 1998

B
Number of cities over 5m population

Developing countries

Developed countries

60
40
20

1970   1990   2010

Source: The Economist, 1998

C
The theory

GDP

Quantity index

Pollution

Time

Abatement policies and technologies

Source: Shah et al, 1997

D
GDP and emissions, OECD countries (index, 1970=100)

GDP

Nitrogen oxides

Sulphur oxides

Lead

Particulates

200

100

0

1970   1988

Source: Shah et al, 1997

E
Transitions and the environment

1 Squatter settlement
2 Particulate pollution
3 Greenhouse gases

3

2

1

GDP

0

0   Time

F
Particulate pollution and its economic costs

Other effects

Chronic Bronchitis

Premature deaths

100
80
60   US$bn
40
20
0

1995   2010   2020

Source: The Economist, 1998

Figure 2.1 *Developmental and Environmental Transitions*

pro-environmental attitudes and activities. Obviously development policies can be formulated and implemented within a range of positive and/or negative attributes in relation to socio-environmental improvement.

The Section B diagram in Figure 2.1 places some urban characteristics on the demographic–economic transition. Attention is given to large cities because these have special significance for pollution and sometimes for depleting aquifers, as in Mexico City, Jakarta and Bangkok. All of this adds to problems of the formulation of city-wide and localized assessment, policy, monitoring and governance. More will be said about these aspects in subsequent discussions. The diagram, of course, indicates the continuous expansion of the numbers of large cities in developing countries, although it is appropriate to recognize that most urban residents live in cities of less than 1 million people. Urban transitions have additional significant features. Cities spread and decentralize laterally, but with economic intensification in their business centres; they improve their infrastructural services, although with prolonged backlogs; and they often exhibit social and income segregations that lead to social and environmental inequalities at neighbourhood and suburban scales (see Mohan, 1994; Pugh, 1996a; Pugh, 1997a). In the very broadest sense, urbanization has environmental relevance in terms of the production of waste, mass consumption and production, the living conditions in low-income living areas, the increasing use of water, and the locales of ideas, technological change and political solutions for some abatement. Clearly, both the economic growth of societies and the environment have causal-consequential relations with each other, in two-way flows and feedback loops. This position statement is rather different from those offered by Drakakis-Smith (1996a, 1996b, 1997) who argues that the sustainable city is not about the contribution of the city to sustainable growth, but about its processes. The processes of economic, social and political change are extensively about growth and its related public policies, including environmental impact.

The foregoing position statement is illustrated in Sections C and D of Figure 2.1. Section C is a theoretical perspective. It says that as GDP rises for a medium-term industrializing phase, much environmental degradation will increase, but this is followed by medium-term reduction. The reduction is contingent on installing policy and institutional frameworks that provide the sorts of property rights, economic incentives for reducing environmental social costs and promoting socio-political development that enhances environmentalism. The foregoing is, of course, a general theoretical proposition, but says nothing about particular localized and national cases. For this it is necessary to add in historical expositions, some of which would show socio-economic reactions and political leadership for environmentalism, including in ancient and medieval societies as well as in modern developing countries. The theoretical and technical bases for this potential are elaborated on in the next section which discusses the relationships among physical, human, environmental and social capital. Section D expresses the relevant statistical time series for the performance in OECD countries in stabilizing the emissions of nitrogen oxides and reducing sulphur oxides, particulate air pollution (from inside buildings, from industrial discharges and from motorized traffic) and also decreasing lead in the atmosphere. Among various authors, Dasgupta and his co-authors (1995) have elaborated on the econometric measurements of pollution related to variations in comparative national income, broadly confirming the theory in Section C.

Neither Section C nor D displays the effects of CO_2, this having reference to global warming and the international political economy of abatement and stabilization. In scientific terms, as first established in 1827 by the French physicist Joseph Fourier, increased volumes of CO_2 absorb infrared radiation and lead to increased surface temperatures on the Earth. The expanding use of fossil fuels over 100 years of industrialization has probably increased average global temperatures in the range of 0.3 to 0.6°C. Projections for the next 20 years would detrimentally increase global warming, causing various environmental hazards and economic threats to production. The international relevance of the science of climate change was recognized in 1988 with the founding of the Intergovernmental Panel on Climate Change (IPCC) which advises governments. Consequently, the 1992 Earth Summit at Rio de Janeiro endorsed a Framework Convention on Climate Change which commenced negotiations and operations in March 1994. A series of international meetings have been held, with the one at Kyoto, Japan, in December 1997 setting out some agreements in a context of controversies and different perspectives among the US, the European Union (EU) and developing countries. The controversies originate in doubts about the accuracy of climate forecasting (presently an inexact science), about how the costs should be distributed among nations and about the urgencies for development in the poorer countries. In the event, the rather loose Kyoto agreement provided for the EU to cut CO_2 emissions by 15 per cent by the year 2010 at a cost of 3 per cent of GDP, the US to stabilize emissions by the year 2012, and other countries to have appropriate specified targets. In urban development terms, the major consequences are upon energy and industry, which contribute over 50 per cent of CO_2 emissions.

Economists have been productive in formulating policy solutions to global warming. One well-favoured approach is to create tradable emissions permits and 'joint implementation', advocated by United Nations Conference on Trade and Development (UNCTAD) (1994; 1995a; 1995b; 1997). Tradable permits are designed to achieve efficiency and effectiveness in technological innovation and in establishing overall standards of emissions control. In principle, for example, a high-technology, low-emission power station could sell its surplus permits to a less environmentally friendly power station, setting an overall framework for long-term competitive reductions in CO_2. They were written into the US Clean Air Amendment Act, 1995, in relation to SO_2 emissions. Abatement could be extended to 'joint implementation' whereby some countries would obtain credits by transferring technologies and projects for environmental improvement in less advanced countries. Taking a wider perspective, the post-1994 aim is to establish international agreements that are broader than the scope of trading permits and joint implementation. The recent literature (Grubb et al, 1993; Patterson and Grubb, 1996; Anderson and Grubb, 1997) discusses

the various political and economic difficulties of formulating and implementing useful international agreements. Among the developed countries
that have been assigned leadership initiative, the US, the EU and others
have to reconcile their divergent interests, even in 'last minute' com-
promises, as happened at the Kyoto meeting in 1997. Also, the underlying
principles and their related technical feasibilities have to be conceptualized
and set out in operational programmes. This would include aspects of
national responsibility for emissions, socio-economic impact, the capacity
to pay and degrees of flexibility in monitoring and meeting targets.
Technical simulation models would be necessary to indicate consequences
'with' and 'without' intervention. Also, experience would have to establish
some feasibilities for CO_2 control, as it has been doing in relation to SO_2.
Politically, some assumptions would be needed for the eventual responsibilities which might be assumed among developing countries. As shown
in Figure 2.1, it is the developing countries that eventually will have the
greatest interest in reducing CO_2 and other adverse emissions.

Section E of the figure provides a simplified and schematic portrayal of
environmental problems, including revealing that greenhouse gases become
more significant at higher levels of national income (for more empirical
and conceptual detail see McGranahan et al, 1996; Pugh, 1996b). Although
it is the case that for many large cities, including Beijing, Mumbai and Cairo,
there is now a coincidence of environmental adversities in low-income
housing, in particulate pollution and in other noxious/adverse emissions,
it makes some sense to see the origins of each characteristically related to
the stage of urbanization. More significantly, the squatter settlement and
slum living conditions require distinctive policy solutions, set in complicated economic and organizational frameworks. This is discussed in
further theoretical and case study detail in Chapter 7. Section F of Figure
2.1 features a few aspects of health transitions that are, of course, related
to demographic, economic, environmental and urban transitions. This
particular selection in Section F complements information in other sections
of the figure. Particulate pollution increases with industrialization and
expanding transport, causing respiratory and other health effects. The
health indicators can be transformed into economic measurements by
calculating the human capital costs of lost production from premature death
and from the foregone value of absence from gainful employment owing
to illness. The time series add to the thematic argument that the relationships
between urban economic development and the environment are properly
to be conceived as a two-way interdependence of cause and consequence.
Or, put in more basic terms, growth has both positive and negative effects
on the environment (see Sections C, D and F) and aggravated disease from
environmental conditions reduces production and productivity. This has
distributional dimensions because in many instances the poorest live
in the dirtiest and most toxic environments (McGranahan et al, 1996).
Overall, it is clear that discussions of demographic, economic, urban,
environmental and health transitions add meaning and understanding
to the development–environment relationship. Some of the foregoing
discussions also give glimpses of environmentally and socially relevant

political transitions, as seen in the international politics of global change. Political transitions have also been occurring in relation to structural economic adjustment, squatter living conditions, catastrophes such as earthquakes (for example, Mexico City, 1985), and in gradual steps towards civic association (Grindle, 1996; Haynes, 1997). In this context, 'civic association' refers to a low-income social protest and political organization which, in process, changes the relationship between the state and, at least, some sections of society which become more democratically empowered.

THE ROLE OF DEVELOPMENTAL AND ENVIRONMENTAL CAPITAL

Some modern environmental literature lacks clarity in the relationships between developmental and environmental capital. In what follows, a summarized exposition and commentary will be presented, partly departing from conceptualizations among some modern urbanists (for example, Drakakis-Smith 1996a, 1996b, 1997). My point of departure is the theory and empiricism of Ostrom (1990, 1993, 1995, 1996) in her discussion of the 'tragedy of the commons'. Accordingly, it is taken that one of the principal aims of development is to create and conserve various forms of capital, including the physical, the human, the social and the environmental. However, in Barbier's line of thinking (1998), overall sustainability can be maintained by substitution, meaning that the returns from, say, physical capital are sufficient to compensate for less returns from environmental capital. This does not ignore severe environmental risk because it is possible to write in an analytical constraint on 'minimum acceptable damage'. But, unlike some analysts, Barbier would account for the 'total economic value' of environmental capital, including inferred as well as real prices. Setting these in various economic, social and political processes, the forms of capital are interactive and interdependent, sometimes operating with mutual enhancement and sometimes with frictions or trade-offs. In terms of environmental relevance, the possibilities for mutual enhancement or conflict often centre around the idea of the 'tragedy of the commons'. The tragedy is that the interests of the individual and society diverge. The individual wishes to appropriate from environmental capital at the least cost, whereas the current and future societies would prefer conservation, restoration and enforceable limits to appropriation. As explained subsequently, the tragedy of the commons is closely associated with the 'free rider' problem in public goods (ie, those goods where the benefits are widely diffused and where ordinary pricing is difficult). However, environmental capital can be enhanced: in examples such as fisheries, forestry and infrastructure it has sometimes been possible to develop social cooperation in the assignment of duties, responsibilities and the monitoring of appropriation and replenishment.

The foregoing can be readily conceptualized and elaborated on in an analytical-diagrammatic way, as in Figure 2.2. However, by way of preamble it is appropriate to state a few contingencies. First, from earlier discussions it is clear that matters relating to global warming and suchlike require different economic approaches from those which are localized in cities and regions. The 'tragedy of the commons' varies in relation to scale and to formulating solutions. Second, environmentalism is inherently multi-objective and often multi-institutional, with these characteristics adding complexity and risks of policy failure. Institutions are norms, rules, ways of doing things and the formal and informal creation of property rights. Environmentalism frequently requires divisions of labour and coordination among various organizational–institutional forms, including coproduction among state agencies, firms, non-governmental organizations (NGOs), community-based organizations (CBOs) and households because this will bring greater prospects for effectiveness than any single institutional form could achieve. As discussed earlier, the theoretical and organizational rationale for multi-institutional frameworks and their consequent relevance to governance as well as to free markets has been elaborated on by Coase (1960), North (1990) and Pugh (1996b). Essentially, where no significant social costs or social benefits exist (ie, economic externalities with third part consequences), markets are effective and efficient on economic grounds because they reduce transaction costs. Transaction costs are the costs of formulating, monitoring and enforcing agreements and social under-standings. Such costs are relevant to environmental goods and bads, and some of the transaction costs occur in legalities, public administration and CBOs or international climate agreements. However, even when markets 'fail', it is still important to select multi-institutional and organizational arrangements on the basis of their comparative costs and benefits. North (1990) also argues that for long-term development, societies that reward productivity and production in their institutions are to be preferred relative to those with disenabling institutions for growth and development. Finally, environmentalism has a socio-political scope that extends beyond the language of rights, equality, and social justice – as advocated by Drakakis-Smith (1996a, 1996b, 1997) – to the equally significant social attributes of social efficiency, the rule of law, adaptability and accountability.

Figure 2.2 displays various forms of capital stocks or assets and some socio-economic flows linking them. The central parts of the diagram set out the production–consumption economy with flows of purchases and goods or services between households and firms. This economy is based upon various factors of production, including economic capital in the form of machines, equipment and buildings. The essential characteristic of capital is that it is expected to produce a flow of returns that will more than cover its costs. And, as noted earlier, a major aim of development is to conserve and expand capital. Households determine, among other things, their gender and age division of labour, their self-help work, sometimes their childrearing, and their savings and investment plans (Pugh, 1997c). Household consumption and home-based production for the market or for running the household can be more or less environmentally friendly according to technologies, processes, productive volumes, waste residues and impacts upon the physical and social environment. Furthermore,

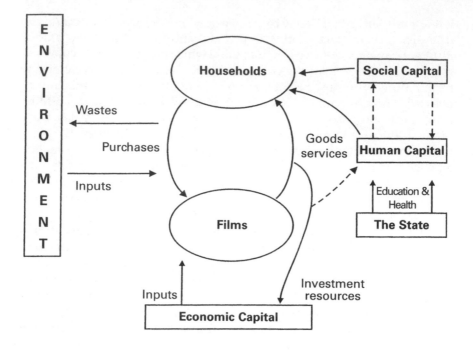

Source: Adaptation and extension from Dasgupte and Mäler, 1994

Figure 2.2 *Capital Stocks, the Environment and Socio-economic Flows*

households can be more or less productive and environmentally friendly in accordance with the social and human capital made available to them, and from reference to their employment opportunities related to their local and national stage of development. Social capital is created from networking, civic association and various social learning experiences; this can variously improve work practices in multi-institutional contexts, add to effectiveness and productivity, and in some conducive contexts make government more accountable and inclined to serve general rather than sectional interest (Evans, 1996; Ostrom, 1996; Tendler and Freedheim, 1994; Putnam et al, 1993; Putnam, 1998). Furthermore, as argued by Putnam (1998) and Long and Hornburg (1998), for relevance to housing and urban improvement social capital can take varied forms and achieve diverse purposes. Forms of politicized social capital include the formal, the informal, the independent localized and, by contrast, the networked and imported to add socio-political clout. In the context of the urban, purposes extend to linking social groups, to maintaining cohesion and to scaling up political effects. This is clearly an instrumental view of social and institutional development, and for present purposes it is related to environmental–social concepts and policies. A wider historical and anthropological evaluation would add to the example and probably extend and qualify the idea of social capital. However, using the idea of social capital in terms of adding to productivity does not make the notion tautological, but rather sets it into the broader explanatory framework, summarized in Figure 2.2. As argued in subsequent sections, social groups can sometimes have political conflicts and a lack of cohesive common purpose in environmental policies. For example, Marris and Rein (1972) found some social conflicts and confusion regarding authority among community groups and local governments in cities in the US during the 1960s.

Human capital is created from education, health and on-the-job training in firms. It can influence the leadership and operational processes in social capital and in households. For environmental significance, education and the correction of distorted or incomplete information is required where there are 'free rider' and 'public goods' dilemmas. And instituted social capital can be effective in upgrading squatter settlements, in pro-poor programmes and in housing improvement, with some examples being the Orangi project in Pakistan and the national Solidarity programme in Mexico. In a more general ethical–political perspective, Sen (1997) approves of using social capability and human capital for development, but argues that these attributes and endowments are also justified in their own right. All of this means that the form and application of social and human capital needs selection and justification because not all is instrumentally useful and justifications are wider than for enhancing production.

Finally Figure 2.2 gives a schematic view of the way that environmental capital has interdependent relationships with the production–consumption economy, with economic capital, and with social and human capital. Problems arise in valuing environmental capital because some of its value does not appear in market or social relationships. Cost-benefit and other analytical techniques can be used to a greater or lesser extent (and with important limitations) to provide implicit or simulated values (see Jowsey and Kellett, 1996). Beyond this, other considerations include priorities within environmental agendas and trade offs with other social objectives such as the reduction of poverty. At pragmatic levels, questions arise as to how environmental policies and professional practices should be formulated and operated in large cities in developing countries.

INTELLECTUAL IDEAS AND DEVELOPMENT

The first phases of post-1987 environmentalism have been deeply influenced by the development of ideas and intellectual reconceptualizations. Examples include strong roles for community-based initiatives in developing localized environmental planning and management for improving urban environments, and the development of tradable permits to curb the growth of SO_2 emissions in the US. In the earlier book, *Sustainability, the Environment and Urbanization* (Pugh, 1996a), the contributing authors were more inclined to discuss the meanings underlying sustainability and sustainable urban development rather than to establish holistic, universal definitions.

Although the discussion of meanings can lead to controversies and ambiguities, none the less they may achieve conceptual development and socio-political relevance. This can be ascertained from some summary statements and explanations from the 1996 book, but they are also influenced by subsequent thinking and a useful overall review by Satterthwaite (1997). Accordingly, sustainable urban development is understood to be part of broader development studies in economics, political science and sociology. In both its theoretical and practical political economies, sustainable development is interdependently at once economic, social and environmental with the necessities to achieve balance and the reconciliation of conflicts among these.

Within its context of post-1987 history and a political economy of enablement liberalism, environmental policies are frequently shaped by frameworks that express legal, economic and institutional conditions that are supposed to achieve various sustainabilities. In effect, the enabling frameworks will often express the currency of ideas in state–market–society relations. Among other socio-political objectives such as the reduction of poverty and the enhancement of economic growth, enablement liberalism has been influenced by the requirements of environmental reform. This means that whereas in the early 1980s state–market relations were often couched in terms of advocacy for the deregulation of markets (ie, neo-liberalism), by the mid-1990s it became more reasonable to view the evolutionary liberalism as expressing a reconfiguration of state, market, society and household roles. Accordingly, some urban environmental policies (for example, the regeneration of squatter settlements) came within partnerships of state agencies, firms, voluntary sector activities and organized households. In some urban situations this meant that the roles of each partner were expanded and diversified, sometimes within complex multi-institutional relationships. This is illustrated in subsequent sections in this chapter. Enablement liberalism and the cause for environmentalism do not mean that the path of sustainable urban development is smooth. As was mentioned previously, it can have disturbance and turbulence from global, regional crises in finance, in political conflicts in the priorities for environmental improvements in low-income living areas, and from broadspread political instabilities, sometimes including ethnic tensions and wars.

The statements on sustainable urban development can move from the general principles of political economy to some more concrete aspects. Following Satterthwaite (1997), it can be observed that sustainable development has a wide and diverse agenda of application. The coverage includes environmental hazards, improved sanitation and the capacity of localized government which is usually involved in all levels of government–national, state/provincial and local. In terms of comparative city-regional assessment and the measurement of progress and the environmental deficits of degradation, cross-border transfers would have to be accounted for in physical, social and economic terms. All of this adds to the complexity of the situation, and operational approaches to sustainability are often reduced to comparisons on specific topics such as health or to formulating general performance indicators on such factors as air quality, access to infra-structural services, and so forth. Owing to rapid changes in urban dynamics, comparisons over time have to be contextualized. As noted by Oxley and Yeung (1998), structural–spatial change is influenced by much more than rapid demographic growth. City-regions express multiple agglomeration economies of production and innovation, shaping the macro-spatial form of urbanization and the diffusion of technology. The agglomeration econ-omies of relatively reduced transport costs, access to domestic and overseas markets, and interfirm influences on developing labour skills and tech-nological innovation all attract investment, some from multinational enterprises. Thus, the changing compositional structures of production and consumption alter the levels and characteristics of urban environmental (dis)amenity. In developing countries some of the structural–spatial change simply adds similar factors of production, but in others the scaling up of technology and added economic value alters the nature of energy use, pollution and other environmental effects. High rates of economic and demographic growth also raise land values in some areas (including squatter settlements) and sometimes heighten the prospects for redevel-opment. Redevelopment not only changes environments: it can disturb social networks, place pressures on localized infrastructure and disguise the fact that if cities were developed in different forms, rehabilitation would be more economically and environmentally justified than redevelopment (Stone, 1963). The linear form of development in Curitiba, Brazil, and the ring of new towns in Singapore reduce the need for continual central-area redevelopment.

Economics

The economics of sustainability and the environment is often misconceived by the non-economists. It includes, but is not limited to, market economics whether seen from a neo-classical or Austrian School paradigm. Neo-classical economists are concerned with efficiency in markets, market failure, theoretical reasoning on equilibrium conditions, income distrib-ution, and with the roles and performance of the state. The Austrian School, by contrast, emphasizes the dynamics of markets, entrepreneurship, and the educational and freedom-promoting influences of markets. Both of these paradigms have been broadened by influences from environmental and other studies, especially in terms of the theories of institutions, property rights and the distortion of information (for a more detailed discussion see Pugh, 1996a). As noted earlier, the modern economics of the environment has had a large influence on political science, sociology, law, town planning and geography. Examples of this include Ronald Coase's theory of social costs and benefits, and his argument that institutional–organizational choice in public policy depends on comparative efficiencies and social effectiveness in associated transaction costs. Transaction costs are the costs of designing, maintaining and enforcing formal and informal agreements. These are relevant to such applications as the assignment of rights, obligations, and the allocations of costs in resource appropriation from 'the commons' and from urban environmental improvement. More broadly, Douglass North (1990) uses the idea of transaction costs, with their related (dis)incentive structures, to demonstrate how institutions influence the relative growth rates and social development of nations. His theories have relevance to governance in general development and to the design of institutions to achieve sustainable patterns of conserving economic, social and environmental capital (see the earlier discussions).

Modern environmental economics has extended the boundaries of economics largely because the 'environmental' involves an intellectual and a policy dialectic between the social, the political and the economic. This can be ascertained readily in the underlying directions of studies by Bohm (1997), Barbier (1998) and Faucheux and O'Connor (1998), but for present purposes is turned to urban relevance. For these authors the idea of sustainable development implies the integration of the economic, the scientific (for example, in health and atmospheric physics), the social, and the context for applying the theories and principles. For urban relevance, cities in developing countries add enormous volumes of physical capital which in themselves and in their productive processes lead to mixed positive and negative effects on environmental, human and social capital (see the earlier discussions). Proper environmental appraisal requires adequate accounting of the positive and negative effects, with policy implications towards enhancing the positive and reducing the negative. In fact, in modern, international and local contexts, cities increasingly require enhanced physical, human, social and environmental capital for quality of life, economic growth and the potential to redistribute resources for pro-poor and for some egalitarian purposes. The studies by Bohm (1997), Barbier (1998), and Faucheux and O'Connor (1998) indicate the way that environmental economics can add not only to intellectual understanding and welfare, but also to the abatement of environmental depletion.

Environmental economics is also beginning to place increased emphasis on the 'bottom-up' as well as on the 'top-down'. For example, and in extending earlier work by Myrdal (1968), the theory of (circular) cumulative causation links poverty and bad urban environments in mutually reinforcing ways. Again, the studies by Barbier (1998) and Faucheux and O'Connor (1998) can be adapted for application to urban conditions in some low-income living areas. Some combination of housing poverty, impediments to collective social organization and inadequacies in state-provided infrastructure result in higher than average incidences of death, disease and absenteeism from work. This acts as a secondary cause in consolidating poverty and weakening social organization for environmental improvements, thereby reinforcing the primary causes of interacting poverty, squalor and loss of income from disease. As discussed more elaborately in Chapter 7, the solutions lie in improved general development policies and in housing sector policies which join top-down administration with the bottom-up mobilization of residents. This can break the poverty–environmental nexus in the policy perspective. In the intellectual perspective, modern environmental economics is synthesized with the Coase theorem of selecting the institutional–organizational form that achieves the lowest transaction costs where otherwise the market or the state would fail to act in themselves (Coase, 1960).

The principles of institutional–organizational selection and cumulative causation can also be applied to other urban environmental examples. In policy terms, the greater the number of effective examples that are actually implemented, the greater the likelihood of expanding interactive benefits from primary to secondary levels, which of course then reinforce the primary levels in a spiral of positive development change. Air quality can be improved in policies that have related appraisal, institutional and monitoring provisions; filthy river basins can be cleansed of particulate and toxic wastes; and green taxes can be introduced to curb the growth in motor vehicle use. These sorts of policies are currently being introduced, respectively in selected Asian cities, in the São Paulo region and in Mexico City. As a set in any one city, if the policies are implemented successfully, a basic restructuring of the long-term processes of income generation, reduction of the social costs of pollution and congestion, and the achievement of healthier, more productive citizens and workers would occur. In short, the structural change becomes embedded in policies, in institutional reform and in the patterning of a more environmentally friendly urban development. Not all the economic policy interventions would necessarily conserve or enhance environmental capital in an absolute sense, but they may sometimes add to the aggregate of physical, social, environmental and human capital. This, of course, raises the question of basic objectives and procedures. As discussed earlier, a 'weaker' approach allows substitution among the various types of capital according to comparative costs and effects, whereas a 'stronger' approach would conserve/enhance environmental capital as an absolute. Trade-offs would always be relevant in principle – for example, improved human capital in the form of environmental knowledge in the present may improve environmental capital in the future. Also, in principle, a 'safety limit' could be designed into the environmental objective.

Economic research has also consolidated and extended the environmental significance in macro-economic policies (see Munasinghe, 1996; Barbier, 1998). Pre-1996 research mainly analysed the impacts of economic liberalization and structural adjustment policies on environmental conditions. Several of the pre-1996 studies suggested that market liberalism in economics achieved non-distortionary prices and this ran in favour of environmental objectives, except where environmental social costs would be significant. However, the more recent studies account for total economic valuation (TEV). TEV would include the costs of land degradation in deforestation, the social costs of disease in squatter settlement, the trade impact of enhanced exports upon the depletion of natural resources, and so on. Appraisals of TEV would add, in fact, in comparative costs and benefits, to the different uses of land, consequently adding to the accounting categories normally used in project or programme appraisal. This steers appraisal into increased, although limited environmental friendliness. Also, the general macro-economic and sectoral environmental analyses have expanded under post-1996 research. These new analytical agendas might variously include inserting environmental simulations into structural adjustment policies, relating energy sector demands to macro-economic forecasting and undertaking environmental audits of tax, subsidy, institutional conditions and pricing in water, agricultural and other sectors where distortions have been inherited from failing, past policies. For example, extensive subsidies in converting natural land to agriculture can increase environmental degradation and, as in the case of the *El Niño* drought and fires in Southeast Asia in 1997, increase health risks from air pollution in cities.

Economics has other attributes in environmentalism and sustainable development, namely in its versatile capacities for linking theory, technical analysis and the improvement of human welfare. Significant examples can be provided, relating to the economic, social and environmental regeneration of insanitary squatter settlements. The essential problem in both policy and technical appraisal is that in general terms individuals and households will work in housekeeping to maintain basic cleanliness, but not usually join together spontaneously to deal with groundwater pollution, piles of solid waste and other adverse problems in the neighbourhood. A clean household is by nature a 'local public good' in the sense that all household members share the economic benefits of readily organized housekeeping. By contrast, any hypothetical individual effort in the local environment would be ineffective because the adversities are interdependent and not confined to individual plots of land. What is required is some form of government activity or organized community leadership, sometimes in partnerships, to overcome the 'free rider' or 'prisoner's dilemma' problem. In theory, a 'free rider' will understate preferences for a cleaner, safer environment, hoping to push the costs on to others while securing the collective or social benefits of effective improvement. The 'prisoner's dilemma' extends this line of reasoning: in terms of relative work effort and property values, any individual household gains most when it refrains from housing and environmental improvement, but others incur the costs of useful community organization and environmental improvement.

Once a community is organized with an appropriate assignment of responsibilities, costs and (possible) self-help labour, then the benefits can be substantial for the individuals and the community. Abelson (1996) has used comprehensive methods to show the source and volume of benefits for squatter upgrading in Visakhapatnam, India. The scope of his analysis included technical surveys of the social, health and tenure regularization improvements. Individual and social returns were evident in increased land values, raised incomes, enhanced skills from training schemes for women and others, and from improved health. In the 1988–91 period, average incomes rose by 50 per cent and the value of housing increased by 82 per cent, reflecting their increased economic efficiency and social effectiveness from reduced disease, death and other benefits. Some commentators writing about other contexts in Mexico (for example, Jones et al, 1994) claim to have found that land values decreased, but the studies were flawed because they did not allow for the separated and compensating effects of reduced demand, high rates of interest and other land cycle fluctuations which originated in Mexico's macro-economy (Pugh, 1997c). Once these factors are separated, it will generally be found that environmental benefits add to human welfare, these benefits being capitalized in higher land values which attend the effect of area-wide environmental and health improvements. This may or may not lead to 'gentrification' in favour of higher income groups depending upon the looseness or tightness of relevant housing submarkets. Tight markets can induce 'gentrification'.

POLITICAL ECONOMY, GOVERNANCE AND URBAN MANAGEMENT

Political economy is important. It can provide a guiding framework for urban and environmental policies, and it sometimes makes some social, ethical and economic principles explicit. Even when a political economy is unstated, it can more or less be inferred from some prevailing programmes and policies. However, political economy has some academic and policy risks. It can lead to excessive advocacy, for example, for state socialism, free markets, protected trade and import substitution, and social democracy. Excessive advocacy can allow ideology to canter on a free rein, unrestrained by empirical evidence or circumspect reason. In some periods – for example, in the 1970s and 1980s – ideological and contending advocacies characterized sections of urban studies including geography, sociology, political science and free market economics. Sometimes in a changing world, academics will modify their advocacies. The neo-Marxism of Burgess (1982) contrasts with a toned-down and less ideologically committed approach in the 1990s (see Burgess et al, 1997). In another example, Simon (1992) uses the language and some selected reasoning from dependency theory to evaluative general development and urban conditions in subSaharan African countries. Dependency theorists were concerned with two interacting exploitations, one between the developed and developing world and one within the structured inequality of developing countries. In a diluted form it has been used to describe the peripherality of the urban sphere in subSaharan Africa (Rakodi, 1997). The descriptions focus on relatively low growth, unfavourable terms of trade, large external debt (to GDP ratios) and largely deteriorating living conditions among large sections of African cities.

The ideological approaches and their derivatives are somewhat self-limiting. Various examples will clinch the point. In the early 1980s the (then) new macro-economic and micro-economic orthodoxies that underlay structural adjustment programmes ignored state incapacities and impacts on social development. The focus on the 'peripherality' of some countries in Africa ignores the sorts of policies in economics and governance that led to high performance in some Asian countries and how things might otherwise have been different in the urban environments in some African cities. And, in a final example, the statistical evidence in new housing construction was completely at odds with a Marxist theoretical assertion by Burgess that levels of construction varied inversely with increases and decreases in real wages (Strassman, 1982). Levels of construction are influenced, of course, by household formation, costs and state-market relations in land, finance and other urban development factors. Political economy can be derived in a more pragmatic way by studying the actual social and economic realities of developmental and urban conditions. This can still establish a principled theory. For example, for African contexts, Mamdani (1996) argues that failed development in some African countries is to be attributed to the colonial subordination of essentially African institutions to alien, imposed legal systems. The subordination led to bad governance, much patrimonial rule and the furtherance of preferentialism in politics rather than the general public interest. Mamdani speculates that the participatory aspects of some urban and environmental programmes could change Africans perhaps from subjects to citizens. He follows in the traditional political economy used by Adam Smith. It brings theory and evaluation in relationship to history, institutions and socio-economic relevance.

The foregoing suggests a number of points in the selection of political economies that are broad-based, relevant and conceptually significant for urban and environmental policies. First, an ideologically selected basis will often omit major elements in the changing real and operative forces of socio-economic and political development in urbanization. Second, a political economy of various environmental conditions may need some new ranges of theories, principles and concepts. For example, the laws, rules and institutions to improve insanitary squatter settlements or to effect curbs in the growth of CO_2 emissions would have to express much more than advocacies for increased public spending by social democrats, or *laissez faire* by free marketeers, or the eradication of exploitation by neo-Marxists and dependency theorists. The range of new theories, rules and institutions would open up new and shifting relationships between states, markets, society and households. Air pollution is not caused in any simple way by inequality and dependency between rich and poor countries. Special, complex forms of social cooperation are needed in both poor capitalist or socialist countries to reduce child mortality from diarrhoeal diseases in squalid settlements. Third, the choice of political economy would need to relate to fundamental economic, social and political changes that make old political economies either obsolete or requiring updating and reform. All the foregoing considerations may suggest the merit of scanning historical and modern political economies and theories to identify relevance and effectiveness in policy contexts. The next few paragraphs do this in a general and summarized way, bearing in mind that detailed environmental applications are discussed in other sections of this chapter and in Chapters 7 and 8.

Adam Smith wrote elaborately on development, the roles of the state and markets, law, ethics, urban agglomeration economies, governance and the cause for a reformed political economy for rapidly changing conditions in society (Smith, 1976, 1978, 1991; Raphael, 1985). His political and legal concerns ranged from the rules by which civil society should be governed, through rights and duties, infant mortality, the neglect of poverty and the development of institutionally loaded reform. Adam Smith's economics favours free trade for efficiency and growth, and the role of free markets in production and exchange. However, he added in 'political economy' for the state's roles in public finance and development policy. Urban areas were recognized for their characteristics as engines of growth and innovation, but with special needs of governance in the form of bye-laws and workable relationships among various landed and urban interest groups. Urban development was conceived and discussed as part of a wider economic development, reflected in trade, economic fluctuations and inequalities among towns. Adam Smith also perceived the internationalized aspects of urban development, with examples of British entrepreneurs imitating the qualities of Flemish cloth and French silks and velvet. Although he did not give urban social conditions much policy attention, he did record that 50 per cent of children died before the age of five, reflecting malnutrition and disease. For Adam Smith the ethics of social development and social justice centre on human feelings of sympathy and its relevance for discerning social wrongs.

One of the remarkable aspects of the previous paragraph is that, with some historical adjustments, it would usefully define large areas of modern developmental and urban policy. For example, the World Bank argues for the general growth roles of urban development, the necessity of redefining state and market roles and for improved governance (World Bank, 1991, 1994, 1997). It is straightforward to insert some aspects of modern economic and political research to construct a modern political economy of development and the environment. The task would commence with some observations about changing state–market–society relationships, some extended discussion of social justice and welfare, and some updating from the modern theories of institutions and property rights. Various authors who write on the revived interest in political economy (for example, Alt and Shepsle, 1990) comment on the conditions that are now giving rise to the rejoining of economics and politics, following the example of Adam Smith and other earlier classical economists. The reasons advanced for the increased modern interest in political economy centre around the greater complexities in modern state–market relations and the frequent need to blend these rather than to rigidly divide them. This then takes the focus to cooperative action and partnerships between states, markets and organized households in various pro-poor, housing and urban environmental policies.

Some post-1985 theories of political economy have been developed to bring the reconfiguration of state–market roles into account. One approach is the new political economy (NPE) which aims to achieve improved understanding of mutually useful roles between states and markets (Meier, 1991). The NPE originated as an extension of public choice theory which was developed in the 1955–90 period and as a reaction against various inefficiencies in some state roles. In Latin American, subSaharan and South Asian countries state roles had extended into market production and import substitution policies had curbed growth rates, aggravated structural poverty, and favoured formal sector incomes relative to the urban informal and rural sectors (Pugh, 1996b). Arguments from advocates of the NPE were towards rationalizing market–state roles on the grounds of efficiency and the pursuit of the general public interest rather than sectional preference. Clearly, in its origins the NPE was more cognizant of economics than politics, but from the late 1980s the political became more significant, reflecting the influence of pro-poor and environmental politics in national and international political agendas. Also, structural economic adjustment programmes reduced import substitution in favour of export-led growth, international economic integration and the gradual reconfiguration of state–market–society roles.

The NPE could not provide in itself significant theory, concepts and principles for the evolving reconfiguration of state roles and its practices in social and environmental programmes. What was required was an evolutionary modification of advocacies in reforming the inherited state–market roles in some developing countries in the 1970s. The theoretical requirement was for new theories of institutions and governance, and designing new multi-institutional and multi-organizational partnerships for social development and environmentalism, while retaining the arguments for growth and efficiency in the NPE and similar post-1980 economic orthodoxies. The social development and environmental emphases also required some modification of the conceptualisations of welfare and causes for egalitarianism in a rapidly changing political context in developing countries.

Advocacies for reformed social and political policies received great attention among governments and in the World Bank by the late 1980s. Some of this arose in response to adversities and omissions in the IMF's and the World Bank's structural adjustment programmes in Latin American and subSaharan countries in the early and mid-1980s. Structural adjustment programmes had commenced in the early 1980s, often based on the assumption that once fluctuating and badly managed economies were stabilized, investment would increase and economic growth would be restored. However, in some circumstances – for example, in subSaharan Africa (see the earlier discussions) – investment remained low and aggravated poverty and deteriorating environments remained unattended. By the late 1980s it was recognized that well designed social programmes should be inserted into structural adjustment (Grindle, 1997; Haggard and Kaufman, 1992; Nelson, 1990; Pugh, 1997c), and in the 1990s some commentators (for example, Munasinghe, 1996) advocated that environmental relevance should also be added. Although the results of structural adjustment programmes are controversial, the careful methodological studies (Jayarajah et al, 1996; Sahn, 1994) indicated that on average they reduced poverty and increased per capita income. Wide variations occurred in dispersions from the averages, inequality was scarcely altered, and the policies omitted a necessary theory of the state to bring competence to policy design and implementation.

Inequality was scarcely touched because reforms in this field would require long-term programmes in such factors as the redistribution of land

and the broadspread formation of human capital. Urban land and property rights in housing can be redistributed downwards in the distribution of household income. Examples can be found in the land, housing and urban policies of several countries. In the period 1977–90 Sri Lanka developed a mass small loans housing programme for new building and the rehabilitation of existing housing. Its subsidy arrangements and the design of the terms of the loans were advantageous to some low-income groups. In Chile in the years 1973–95 access to subsidized social housing was tilted in favour of low-income households; supplies grew more rapidly than increases in population; and one-off capital grants improved housing for some of the poor. Mandated social security funds were used to develop the housing finance system. With even greater effect, in Singapore housing wealth and price access has widened throughout most social groups over a long period, 1960–99. Some of this redistributed wealth is derived from the environmental improvement of pre-1990 constructed housing estates (for more details on these examples see Pugh, 1997a).

It is possible, of course, to extend the case for social justice and welfare beyond their inclusion in structural adjustment programmes. In fact, much that achieves improved social justice and welfare has longer developmental impacts than those contained in macro-economic stabilization and structural adjustment programmes. Lipton (1997) summarizes some of the policy and intellectual learning that has been accomplished since 1980, along with some remaining gaps. The positive lessons are that economic growth usually reduces the incidence and volume of poverty; that, within limits, growth can reduce inequality, as occurred in some Asian countries during 1950–85; and that the spreading of human capital reduces poverty. Furthermore, at technical levels, it is useful to add human performance indicators (including environmental indicators) in order to obtain a deeper view of welfare than head counts of poverty, standard Lorenz-type measures of income inequality and suchlike. As indicated above, social safety nets are required in the increasing circumstances of international macro-economic fluctuations and recovery programmes. In some circumstances, equalizing can increase growth, with importance in housing, health and environmental improvement (see the discussions of Fogel's research in the next section). The gaps in knowledge mainly refer to the sparse work on the long-term redistributive effects on the poor in various social, urban and environmental programmes. Also, it would be useful to know what institutional incentives would draw the poor towards lower fertility and a preference for quality in the human and social capital of children. This also has relevance to reducing adverse child labour which has sometimes increased in volume and intensity under the international integration of market economics during the 1990s.

A political economy of social justice and welfare also has significance for the conceptualization of welfare. Sen (1993; 1997) has a moralistic, Buddhist approach to economics, combining orthodox elements of theoretical efficiency with the position that economics is properly about moral and social ends. This can be applied readily to environmental conditions and policies. Humans face various opportunity sets with their endowments and entitlements. Their endowments can be improved in healthy environments, especially in urban squatter settlements. The entitlements refer to access and property rights in markets, in social and environmental programmes, and, for example, in participation in squatter upgrading schemes. For Sen, the ultimate way of understanding welfare is a capability of function in life, work and social interaction. One important aspect of functioning is that humans can choose more readily the values they pursue. In the context of this chapter, for environmental relevance this would mean healthier capacities in such areas as citizen participation, the rearing of children and the spreading of human capital among women and other groups. Again, this can be applied readily to the upgrading of squatter settlements and housing improvements.

Governance is an important element in sustainable urban development, deriving from wider development policies. It is essentially about state–market–society relations, where the state both influences socio-economic change and is itself influenced by the change. This perspective, although not completely new, was added to the development agenda in the mid-1990s. It comes in the form of both advocacy for 'good governance' and institutionally loaded reforms in state–market–society relations. As noted in earlier discussions, programmes for structural economic adjustment opened up questions of state capability and achieving coalitions of interests for effective implementation. This was all a part of the reconfiguration of state roles beyond public sector budgeting to various reforms in property rights, law, mobilizing communities for social and environmental improvement (for example, self-help in neighbourhood improvements), and in creating enabling frameworks for economic efficiency and social effectiveness. Various authors have put the historical reasons for the introduction of governance into development agendas. Grindle (1997) observes that in some senses governance was a reaction to states doing too much and too little. They did too much by engaging in economic production, often less efficiently than markets, and doing too little by neglecting the upgrading of capabilities in socio-economic change and the requirements for institutional reform. As Picciotto and Wersner (1998) argue, institutions, in principle, can be fitted to developmental objectives such as economic growth, social development and environmentalism. This can be regarded as creating 'institutional capital'. Other authors – for example, Rosenau and Czempiel (1992) – show that governance is a necessity in some international agreements on climate change: there is no such thing as a world government, and nations must negotiate agreements, develop institutions and create a context of persuasion in environmental ideas and programmes.

In urban and environmental contexts, governance has specialized relevance and significance. Earlier discussions referred to North (1990) who justified the cause for the enablement frameworks of legal, economic and social institutions. Closely related to North's reasoning, Coase (1960) demonstrated that both markets and states are limited where private costs and benefits diverge from significant social costs and benefits. Accordingly, he advocated appraisals of institutional–organizational forms for comparative advantage in reconciling the respective limitations of markets and states. For environmental applications Ostrom (1990) analysed actual institutions in common pool resources, aimed at the conservation, regeneration and the sustainability of environmental capital. Her essential precepts for sustainability include rules on appropriation, maintenance, the enforcement of rules, and the assignment of financial and economic responsibilities. In effect, multi-institutional and multi-organizational outcomes usually combined market, collective choice and participatory governance. It often developed civic association and pragmatically useful political economies fitted to the realities of social and economic conditions. The principles are relevant to such programmes as irrigation, infrastructure, forestry and the upgrading of squatter settlements. For relevance to structures of urban government and their relationship to governance, Judge and his co-authors (1995) emphasize that basic questions of theory and policy are significant. Urban politics and government has various theories ranging through democratic, Marxist, feminist, administrative-bureaucratic and economic. In its historical context of the mid-1990s, governance is often associated with regime theory. Regime theory places importance on agendas for institutional design, economic growth and restructuring, and building up supporting coalitions for reform programmes in these agendas. This is a policy context to attract investment and city roles in economic, political and civic entrepreneurship. The major issues revolve around creating networks for production and social development, and for achieving a development response. In another perspective, the emphasis on the socio-economic and political has implications either for reforms in town planning or sometimes for reducing its relative policy significance. The actual application of the theory is evolutionary and diffused. Shanghai, Singapore and other international cities are adapting policies and institutions for developmental and competitive regimes, including their approaches to governance and economic development.

All the foregoing has significance for the theory and practice of urban management, a subject that attracted attention in urban and environmental literature. In his general evaluative review, McGill (1998) attempts to give coherence and clarity to urban management which earlier commentators perceived as vague and poorly defined (for example, Stren, 1993). For McGill the content of urban management includes economic development, improved supplies of infrastructure, the upgrading of squatter settlements, and social sector development in education and health. At a conceptual level, urban management is seen as a requirement for agency coordination and for strategic purposes in patterning urban form and development. Institutional enablement and the appropriate governance for the socio-economic and environmental programmes have roles in urban management. Apart from McGill's perceptions, other aspects of principle and practice can be added. Essentially, urban management is a function that ought to link policy and operations in consistent ways, providing spatial expressions to development. In many countries urban management is not comprehensively developed and sustained. For example, in India senior administrators follow their career progression by transfer from function to function, seldom having long-term continuity in the urban sphere. This inhibits the growth of general urban and experiential knowledge. And modern environ-mentalism is not yet adequately embedded in urban educational and training courses. Modern World Bank courses include urban dynamics, municipal finance, state–market relations in infrastructure, housing and land markets, urban poverty and the urban environment. It is reasonably straightforward to set out educational content for urban management, but the major problem is that the educational prescriptions are largely new and at the present stage of development the operation is inadequate in scale and implementation.

Environmental Health

The burgeoning of literature on environmentalism during the 1990s has influenced some redirections in the central topics of significance in environ-mental health. For example, Moeller (1997) sets the context and aims for his revised edition of a basic textbook in terms of multi-disciplinary content and systems approaches which comprise clinical interventions, public health and environmental stewardship. He defines the field of study as the environmental impact on people and of people on the environment. Accordingly, the book has discussions on the socio-economics of health, water supply, susceptibility to toxic substances, to various elements in air pollution, and to the collection and disposal of solid and liquid wastes. In this context, prevention and risk reduction are often a matter of installing modern urban and environmental programmes, with monitoring require-ments and ongoing research into the spread of infectious and other diseases. Environmental health in its modern idiom has introduced the new concerns about sustainability, greenhouse gases, ozone depletion, and the improve-ment of housing and residential neighbourhoods.

Another indication of new significance in environmental health is the world health report for 1998 by the WHO (1998) which states:

> *Poor environmental quality is estimated to be directly responsible for 25 per cent of all preventable ill-health in the world today, with diarrhoeal diseases and acute respiratory infections heading the list* (WHO, 1998, p123).

Some 66 per cent of preventable ill health due to environmental conditions occurs among children, and is especially significant in developing countries. This is in a context that 1 billion people do not have ready access to safe water supplies and 60 per cent are without effective sanitation services. The world health report for 1998 also comments that urban environments are often hostile to children, with examples including low-quality housing and the increase in stressful and unhealthy conditions for child labour. Modern research (Swaminathan, 1998) demonstrates that some aspects of macro-economic reforms in India have increased adversities in child labour in diamond-cutting and ship-breaking industries. As would be expected, malnutrition is associated with poverty and vulnerability to consequent disease and death is associated with environmental quality along with other factors. Most premature births and low birth weights occur in developing countries, along with some 99 per cent of global deaths of mothers in pregnancy and childbirth.

Malnutrition has other adversities in developmental conditions. Fogel (1994) used the methods of economic history to combine medical and economic evidence to explore the human welfare and developmental significance of long-term improvements to nutrition and the work energy of people. Over long periods of time each new generation has less stunting and higher body mass, leading to increased participation rates in employment and increased productivity of labour. Fogel attributes this to advances in medical knowledge, reduced incidences of malnutrition and improved housing conditions. In developing countries in the 1990s, various studies indicate stunting and low body mass to be a problem among some sections of the population (WHO, 1998, p81). Housing has long-term developmental pay-offs, in this instance securing human retention of energy when cold air is shut out. Also, when environmental health risks are reduced, positive effects will occur in human thermodynamic energy and work. In modern policy contexts some of the self-help labour is significantly contributory to environmental improvement, including digging trenches for drainage and sewerage systems.

CONCLUSIONS AND PERSPECTIVE

The urban environmental problems in developing countries are enormous and growing. They are detrimental to health, production and social development. Many of the problems are visually evident in the conditions in squatter settlements, in fetid slums, in air pollution and in dirty rivers. Notwithstanding the grim realities, some progress has been made in the principles and practice of sustainable urban development. At the level of theory and principle, the idea of environmental capital has been elevated in intellectual significance, alongside economic, human and social capital. Environmental economists have developed concepts and some (limited) methods of measurement that can be used in project appraisal. In general terms, sustainable urban development is understood to be an interactive dialectic between the economic, the social and the political. This suggests that environmentalism becomes more coherent when it is seen in multidisciplinary perspectives. Abatement policies often require multi-institutional and multi-organizational solutions because any restriction to state roles alone, to market roles alone or to household and community roles alone would be inadequate. But in combination, abatement effectiveness depends on frameworks of governance and institutional design. This places environmental causes into the realms of theoretical and pragmatic political economy. In this, ideological preconceptions are much less useful than the exploration of concepts and ideas that are empirically related to the operative social realities. Such an approach can then give explanation to the relationships among poverty, urban living conditions, housing, residential environments and development.

Sustainable urban development also depends on professional developments, technology and the characteristics of political processes. Professional development is relevant to the improvement of squatter settlements, to designing and monitoring programmes to reduce air and water pollution, and in providing know-how for community-based environmental management and planning. Technological developments occur in research and market processes. Some innovations have impressive potential. One example is the Bintula port in Sarawak, Borneo. BP Shell has developed a huge gas-to-liquid reserve, achieving pollution-free jet fuel. In Norway biotechnology is used to convert methane, a greenhouse gas, into carbon dioxide, sugars and proteins. Greenpeace has become more involved in negotiations with business to limit the adversities from fossil fuels. None of this achieves perfection, but it does indicate important trends and some limited means of progress in sustainability. Politics can variously improve, retard or have neutral effects upon environmental improvement.

In closing this chapter, some general millennial reflections can be placed upon the theory and practice of sustainable urban development. Essentially, the major principle is to discern the implications of conceptualization and whether this admits of partial or fuller understandings. Partial understandings can be self-limiting, for example, giving advocacy and technical explanation in health, property rights, investment for economic growth or social rights for the poor, and so forth. However, the fuller and more systemic view has marked advantages, expressing interactions, the conservation of economic, social, environmental and human capital, and systemic adjustment from internal changes or exogenous shocks such as *El Niño*, 1997 or the Asian financial crisis of 1997–98. The systemic demands width and depth in cross-disciplinary appreciation, along with a challenge to elaborate relevant evaluative dialectics between the economic, the social and the political. Some of this was conveyed in the earlier sections on the relationships among environmental, economic, social and human capital. A similar systemic inference comes from the socio-economic conditions in the (systemic) financial crisis in some Asian countries in 1997–98.

The causes of the crisis were several, interactive and varied (see Pugh, 1999; Thomas and Belt, 1997; World Bank, 1998). In the first half of 1997 some US$35 billion (net) was invested into Asian countries, but in the second half a precipitous reversal occurred with a net outflow of some US$50 billion. In macro-economic terms the crisis was caused by a combination of massive short-term borrowing by the governments and corporate sectors, which was risky owing to hypermobile outflows when investors observed the scale of the liabilities and some over-valued exchange rates. The afflicted countries – Thailand, South Korea, Malaysia, Indonesia and the Philippines – also had fragile financial systems. They fell below good international standards in loan appraisal and being cautious in credit, liquidity and other risks. The urban and housing sectors were adversely affected both in the upswing and the downswing. One result was, for example, a year-on-year property inflation rate of 54 per cent in Indonesia from 1991 to 1996, with a subsequent collapse. More than this, the first-phase macro-economic austerity programmes, under IMF loan condition-alities, added cyclical poverty to longer-term structural poverty. This undermined housing markets and some social housing programmes. Accordingly, the second-phase recovery programme had to be designed for a triple crisis – financial, economic and social. Added to this was the heightened interest in reforming the environmental policies where failure was occurring in forestry, in air quality and in some sections of low-income living areas. As mentioned, the *El Niño* induced forest fires added relevance to significance. The recovery policies then, may adopt a systemic view of the dialectic of the economic, the social, the environmental and the political. Although the ultimate result is likely to fall short of fully successful comprehensiveness, it will have some of these features.

REFERENCES

Abelson P (1996) 'Evaluation of Slum Improvements: Case Study in Visakhap-atnam', India, *Cities*, vol 13, pp97–108

Alt, J and Shepsle, K (eds) (1990) *Perspectives on Political Economy*, Cambridge University Press, Cambridge

Anderson, D and Grubb, M (eds) (1997) *Controlling Carbon and Sulphur: Joint Implementation and Trading Initiatives*, Royal Institute of International Affairs, London

Baldwin, R (1995) 'Does Sustainability Require Growth?', in I Goldwin and L Winters (eds) *The Economics of Sustainable Development*, Cambridge University Press, Cambridge, pp51–78

Barbier, E (1998) *The Economics of Environment and Development*, Elgar, Cheltenham

Barry, J (1998) *Rethinking Green Politics*, Sage, London

Bohm, P (1997) *The Economics of Environmental Protection: Theory and Demand Revelation*, Elgar, Cheltenham

Boone, P (1996) *Political and Gender Oppression as a Cause of Poverty*, Discussion Paper 299, Centre for Economic Performance, London School of Economics

Burgess, R (1982) 'Self-Help Housing Advocacy, a Curious Form of Radicalism: A Critique of the Work of John F C Turner', in P Ward (ed) *Self-Help Housing*, Mansell, London, pp55–97

Burgess, R, Carmona, M and Kolstee, T (eds) (1997) *The Challenge of Sustainable Cities: Neoliberalism and Urban Strategies in Developing Countries*, Zed Books, London

Coase, R (1960) 'The Problem of Social Cost', *Journal of Economics and Law*, vol 3, no 1, pp1–44

Dasgupta, P, Mody, A, Roy, S and Wheeler, D (1995) 'Environmental Regulation and Development: A Cross Country Empirical Analysis', Research Paper 1448, Environment, Infrastructure and Agriculture Division, World Bank, Washington DC

Drakakis-Smith, D (1996a) 'Third World Cities: Sustainable Urban Development II: Population, Labour and Poverty', *Urban Studies*, no 33, pp673–701

Drakakis-Smith, D (1996b) 'Sustainability, Urbanization and Development', *Third World Planning Review*, no 18, ppiii–x

Drakakis-Smith, D (1997) 'Third World Cities: Sustainable Urban Development: Population, Labour and Poverty', *Urban Studies*, vol 33, no 8, pp673–701

Evans, P (1998) 'Government Action, Social Capital and Development: Reviewing the Evidence on Synergy', *World Development*, no 24, pp1119–32

Faucheux, S and O'Connor, M (eds) (1998) *Valuation for Sustainable Development*, Elgar, Cheltenham

Fogel, R (1994) 'Economic Growth, Population Theory and Physiology: The Bearing of Long-Term Processes on the Making of Public Policy', *American Economic Review*, June 1994, pp369–95

Goldin, I and Winters, L (eds) (1995) *The Economics of Sustainable Development*, Cambridge University Press, Cambridge

Grindle, M (1996) *Challenging the State: Crisis and Innovation in Latin America and Africa*, Cambridge University Press, Cambridge

Grindle, M (ed) (1997) *Getting Good Government: Capacity Building in the Public Sectors of Developing Countries*, Harvard University Press, Cambridge, Mass

Grubb, M, Koch, M, Munson, A, Sullivan, F and Thomson, K (1993) *The Earth Summit Agreement*, Earthscan, London

Haggard, S and Kaufman, R (eds) (1992) *The Politics of Economic Adjustment: International Constraints, Distributive Conflicts and the State*, Princeton University Press, Princeton, NJ

Haynes, J (1997) *Democracy and Civil Society in the Third World: Politics and New Political Movements*, Polity Press, Cambridge

Jayarajah, C, Branson, W and Sen, B (1996) *Social Dimensions of Adjustment: World Bank Experience, 1980–93*, World Bank, Washington, DC

Jones, G, Jiménez, E, and Ward, P (1994) 'Snapshot Analysis and the Impact of Public Policy on Land Valorization', in G Jones and P Ward (eds), *Methodology for Land and Housing Market Analysis*, UCL Press, London, pp214–35

Jones, G and Ward, P (1995) 'The Blind Men and the Elephant: A Critic's Reply', *Habitat International*, no 19, pp61–72

Jowsey, E and Kellett, J (1996) 'Sustainability and Methodologies of Environmental Assessment for Cities', in C Pugh (ed) *Sustainability, the Environment and Urbanization*, Earthscan, London

Judge, D, Stoker, G and Wolman, H (eds) (1995) *Theories of Urban Politics*, Sage, London

Lipton, M (1997) 'Poverty: Are There Holes in the Consensus?', *World Development*, vol 25, no 7, pp1003–7

Long, R and Hornburg, S (1998) 'What is Social Capital and Why is it Important to Public Policy?', *Housing Policy Debate*, no 9, pp1–16

Mamdani, M (1996) *Citizen and Subject: Contemporary Africa and the Legacy of Late Colonialism, 1964–71*, Princeton University Press, Princeton, New Jersey

Marris, P and Rein, M (1972) *Dilemmas of Social Reform*, second edition, Pelican, Harmondsworth

McGill, R (1998) 'Urban Management in Developing Countries', *Cities*, vol 15, no 6, pp463–71

McGranahan, G, Songsore, J and Kjellén, M (1996) 'Sustainability, Poverty and Urban Environmental Transitions', in C Pugh (ed) *Sustainability, the Environment and Urbanization*, Earthscan, London, pp103–34

Meadows, D (1972) *Limits to Growth*, Universe Books, New York

Meier, G (1991) 'The Political Economy of Policy Reform', in G Meier (ed) *Politics and Policy Making in Developing Countries: Perspectives on the New Political Economy*, Institute for Contemporary Studies Press, San Francisco, pp299–316

Moeller, D (1997) *Environmental Health*, revised edition, Harvard University Press, Mass

Mohan, R (1994) *Understanding the Developing Metropolis: Lessons from the City Study of Bogatá and Cali, Colombia*, Oxford University Press, Oxford

Munasinghe, M (ed) (1996) *Environmental Impacts of Macro-Economics and Sectoral Policies*, International Society for Ecological Economics, World Bank, UNEP, Washington DC

Myrdal, G (1968) *Asian Drama*, Penguin, Harmondsworth

Nelson, J (1990) *Economic Policy and Policy Choice: The Politics of Adjustment in the Third World*, Princeton University Press, Princeton, NJ

North, D (1990) *Institutions, Institutional Change and Economic Performance*, Cambridge University Press, Cambridge

Ostrom, E (1990) *Governing the Commons: The Evolution of Institutions for Collective Action*, Cambridge University Press, Cambridge

Ostrom, E, Schroeder, L and Wynne, S (1993) 'Institutional Incentives and Sustainable Development: Infrastructure Policies in Perspective', Westview Press, Boulder, Colorado

Ostrom, E (1995) 'Constituting Social Capital and Collective Action', in R Keohane and E Ostrom (eds) *Local Commons and Global Interdependence: Heterogeneity and Co-operation in Two Domains*, Sage, London, pp125–66

Ostrom, E (1996) 'Crossing the Great Divide: Coproduction, Synergy and Development', *World Development*, no 24, pp1073–87

Oxley, J and Yeung, B (eds) (1998) *Structural Change, Industrial Location and Competitiveness*, Elgar, Cheltenham

Patterson, M and Grubb, M (eds) (1996) *Sharing the Effort: Options for Differentiating Commitments on Climate Change*, Royal Institute for International Affairs, London

Picciotto, R and Weisner, E (eds) (1998) *Evaluation and Development: The Institutional Dimension*, Transactions Publishers, New Brunswick

Pugh, C (1996a) *Sustainability, the Environment and Urbanization*, Earthscan, London

Pugh, C (1996b) 'Methodology, Political Economy and Economics in Land Studies for Developing Countries', *Land Use Policy*, vol 13, no 3, pp165–79

Pugh, C (1996c) 'Urban Bias and the Theory and Practice of Development in Developing Countries', *Urban Studies*, no 33, pp1045–60

Pugh, C (1997a) 'Poverty and Progress? Reflections on Housing and Urban Policies in Developing Countries, 1976–96', *Urban Studies*, vol 34, no 10, pp1547–96

Pugh, C (1997b) 'The World Bank's Millennial Theory of the State: Further Attempts to Reconcile the Political and the Economic', *Third World Planning Review*, no 19, ppiii–xiv

Pugh, C (1997c) 'Methodology, Political Economy and the Economics in Land Studies for Developing Countires', *Land Use Policy*, vol 33, no 7, pp1045–60

Pugh, C (1999) 'The Asian Financial Crisis and its Urban Impacts', *Habitat International*, vol 23, no 2, pp157–65

Putnam, R (1993) 'The Prosperous Community: Social Capital and Public Life', *The American Prospect*, no 13, pp35–42

Putnam, R, Leonardi, R and Nonetti, R (1993) *Making Democracy Work: Civic Traditions in Modern Italy*, Princeton University Press, Princeton, NJ

Putnam, R (1998) Foreword, *Housing Policy Debate*, vol 9, no 1, ppv–viii

Rakodi, C (ed) (1997) *The Urban Challenge in Africa: Growth and Management of its Large Urban Cities*, United Nations University Press, Tokyo

Raphael, D (1985) *Adam Smith* Oxford University Press, Oxford

Rosenau, J and Czempiel, E-O (eds) (1992) *Governance Without Government: Order and Change in World Politics*, Cambridge University Press, Cambridge

Sahn, D (ed) (1994) *Adjusting to Policy Failure in African Economies*, Cornell University Press, Ithaca

Satterthwaite, D (1997) 'Sustainable Cities or Cities that Contribute to Sustainable Development?', in *Urban Studies*, no 10, pp1667–91

Sen, A (1993) 'Capability and Wellbeing', in M Naussbaum and A Sen (eds), *The Quality of Life*, Clarendon, Oxford

Sen, A (1997) 'Human Capital and Human Capability', *World Development*, no 25, pp1959–61

Simon, D (1992) *Cities, Capital and Development: African Cities in the World Economy*, Wiley, London

Smith, A (1976) *The Theory of Moral Sentiments*, Clarendon, Oxford

Smith, A (1978) *Lectures on Jurisprudence*, Clarendon, Oxford

Smith, A (1991) *The Wealth of Nations*, Campbell, London

Stone, P (1963) *Housing, Town Development, Land and Costs*, Estates Gazette, London

Strassman, W P (1982) 'Upgrading in Squatter Settlements: Test of a Marxist Hypothesis', *Journal of Economic Issues*, no 16, pp515–23

Stren, R (1993) 'Urban Management in Development Assistance: An Elusive Concept', *Cities*, no 9, pp125–138

Swaminatham, M (1998) 'Economic Growth and the Persistence of Child Labor: Evidence from an Indian City', *World Development*, vol 26, no 8, pp1513–28

Tendler, J and Freedheim, S (1994) 'Trust in a Rent-Seeking World: Health and Government Transformed in Northeast Brazil', *World Development*, no 22, pp1771–92

Thomas, V and Belt, T (1997) 'Growth and Environment: Allies or Foes?', *Finance and Development*, June 1997, pp22–4

Trostle, J, Sommerfield, J and Simon, J (1997) 'Strengthening Human Resource Capacity in Developing Countries: Who Are the Actors? What Are Their Actions?', in M Grindle (ed) *Getting Good Government: Capacity Building in the Public Sectors of Developing Countries*, Harvard University Press, Cambridge, Mass

United Nations Conference on Trade and Development (UNCTAD) (1994) *Combating Global Warming*, UN, Geneva

United Nations Conference on Trade and Development (UNCTAD) (1995a) *The Strategy of Joint Implementation in the Framework Convention on Climate Change*, UN, New York

United Nations Conference on Trade and Development (UNCTAD) (1995b) *Controlling Carbon Dioxide Emissions: The Tradeable Permit System*, UNCTAD, Geneva

United Nations Conference on Trade and Development (UNCTAD) (1997) *Combating Global Warming: Study on a Global System of Tradable Carbon Emissions Entitlements*, UN, New York

World Bank (1991) *Urban Policy and Economic Development: An Agenda for the 1990s*, World Bank, Washington DC

World Bank (1994) *Governance: The World Bank's Experience*, World Bank, Washington DC

World Bank (1997) *World Development Report 1997: The State in a Changing World*, World Bank, Washington DC

World Bank (1998) *East Asia: The Road to Recovery*, World Bank, Washington DC

World Health Organization (WHO) (1998) *The World Health Report 1998: Life in the Twenty-First Century: A Vision for All*, WHO, Geneva

3   SUSTAINABLE LEGAL MECHANISMS FOR THE PROTECTION OF THE URBAN ENVIRONMENT[1]

Amanda Perry

The law alone cannot protect the environment. In order to be effective, laws must be clear and enforced consistently. This is only possible in countries where the rule of law is supported. In developing countries, the rule of law is often not supported, with potentially damaging results for the protection of the urban environment. This chapter seeks to show how efforts to improve access to justice can create more sustainable methods for securing the rule of law and, in particular, protecting the urban environment. The chapter uses the case of the southern Indian city of Bangalore to illustrate how successes and failures in supporting the rule of law and access to justice have affected the urban environment.

THE RULE OF LAW AND THE PROTECTION OF THE URBAN ENVIRONMENT

Over the past decade, the role of law in the development process has received increased attention from international organizations (IOs), academics, bilateral aid donors and developing country governments (De Soto, 1989; World Bank, 1992).[2] In particular, the importance of the rule of law has been stressed – that is, it is widely agreed that unless the law is applied consistently to all, regardless of their status, then development, including the protection of the environment, will suffer.

'As important as what rules say . . . is what they mean in practice. A pristine statute . . . that is unknown, unadministered and unenforced is ineffective' (EBRD, 1996, p101). The rule of law is supported in two ways. First, laws must be properly drafted and publicized. If laws are to be effective, they must be known both to the public and to those charged with enforcing them. Funding shortages and institutional failures have restricted the extent to which laws are publicized in less developed countries. Second, laws must be properly implemented. The arbitrary, opaque or inconsistent application of environmental rules leads to uncertainty, inefficiency and a failure to achieve environmental goals. Before examining how these limitations on the rule of law arise in Bangalore, the institutions responsible for the environment in the city are outlined.

Institutions Responsible for the Environment in Bangalore

Bangalore has three levels of courts. At the lowest level are the Magistrates courts, which deal with non-serious offences and civil matters. At the next level is a District Court which deals with civil and criminal matters, including appeals from the Magistrates courts. The most important court is the High Court of the state which deals with civil and criminal matters of great importance, as well as appeals from the lower courts. Appeals from the High Court go to the Supreme Court in Delhi. The language of legal education and of the courts is English, and translators are provided where necessary (interviews 31 May 1995 and 19 April 1995).

The main institution responsible for governing the city is the Bangalore City Corporation (the Corporation). It is composed of an elected Mayor and Councillors and a state-appointed Commissioner. Some of the Corporation's responsibilities are: to build and maintain public areas, streets and buildings; deal with sewage and waste; to name and number streets and places; to regulate and abate offensive and dangerous practices; to reclaim unhealthy localities; to plant and maintain trees; to prevent the spread of disease and dangerous animals; and to provide parks and open spaces. The democratic validity of the Corporation is regularly called into question. It has been said that the mayor of the city is essentially a figure-head and that the real power is in the hands of the Commissioner who reportedly 'usually has little idea of what is going on in the city' (s 64(1) Karnataka Municipal Corporations Act, 1976; interview 22 June 1995).

The Bangalore Development Authority (the Development Authority) is the second most important institution responsible for the environment in Bangalore and is the local planning authority. Its members are appointed by the state government and perform the function of the Corporation in the new development areas. Once the streets and drainage have been provided for a new area of development, the Development Authority is supposed to hand control of the area to the Corporation. However, instead the Development Authority often maintains control over the land even after development and improvements, if any, have been completed. As a result, central 'old' Bangalore is controlled by the elected Corporation, while the ever-increasing outer circle of 'new' Bangalore is controlled by the unelected Development Authority (interview 6 May 1995; s 81(B) Planning Act; ss 29(1), 67 BDA Act).

The Development Authority and the Corporation are responsible to the state government in general and the Minister of State for Bangalore in particular. The municipal authorities have primary responsibility for most matters; larger projects require the financial and / or policy sanction of the Minister. Although the bodies are theoretically able to plan their own projects and obtain funding for them, in practice they tend to follow the state government even where they are not compelled to do so (interviews 6 May 1995; 24 June 1995).

The Karnataka State Pollution Control Board (the Pollution Board) is appointed by the state government and is responsible for enforcing the laws relating to water and air pollution, and the management and handling of dangerous chemicals and hazardous waste. It undertakes environmental awareness campaigns, educates and advises industry on compliance with laws, lays down law enforcement policies, inspects industries and local bodies, tests water for compliance with national and international standards, assesses the environmental suitability of proposed industrial sites, and monitors the quality of waste, effluent, ambient air and stack emissions (KSPCB, 1995, pp1–2; Water Act; Air Act and Environment Act).

Finally, the Bangalore Water Supply and Sewerage Board (the Water Board) is responsible for the supply of water and the treatment of sewage in Bangalore, and owns all facilities connected with water supply (s 15 Water Board Act, 1964).

The Rule of Law and the Environment in Bangalore

Some of the main obstacles to the consistent implementation of laws in developing countries are corruption, the improper exercise of bureaucratic discretion, ignorance of the law, the inadequate allocation of jurisdiction between government institutions and a lack of power and resources.

Corruption
Corruption can reduce the effectiveness of both courts and bureaucracies. Reisman classifies bribery into three types. Transaction bribes are used to get an official to exercise his or her discretion with greater speed. A variance bribe is paid to cause an official not to apply a particular rule to the bribe giver. As a variance bribe is easy to identify, it is more dangerous and therefore more expensive to obtain than a transaction bribe. Finally, the 'outright purchase' bribe allows for the purchase 'not of a service, but of a servant . . . who remains in place in an organization to which he appears to pay full loyalty while actually favouring the briber's conflicting interests' (Reisman, 1979, pp69, 75, 89).

Corruption is a popular explanation for environmental problems in Bangalore. A local politician said that 'corruption seems to have the better of pollution. To say that observance of the law is not up to scratch is an understatement. Laws are made only in order not just to sustain, but to provide for the growth of, corruption.' The Minister of State for Bangalore is reportedly 'only too willing to concede that there has been "deep rooted corruption" for the past 40 years.' The head of the Water Board was suspended from his post by the previous government for his alleged involvement in a scandal involving a computer company. As for the Corporation, several interviewees alleged that its elected members are mostly interested in making money during their term. Nor are the courts free from allegations, and in at least two cases citizens have brought legal proceedings against members of the judiciary who are accused of illegally acquiring land or planning permission (interviews 13 May 1995, 3 June 1995, 10 June 1995 and 22 June 1995; *Times of India*, 10 June and 1 July 1995).[3]

In Bangalore, corruption takes many forms, from land frauds to bus drivers who do not just keep the change, but keep the fare as well. For example, two large-scale land frauds were discovered in 1995, one involving collusion by tax officials in the illegal transfer of land owned by temples to developers, and the other involving the illegal sale of 200 sites by corrupt Development Authority officials (*Times of India*, 8 May, 20 May 1995 and 17 June 1995). One survey of Bangalore found that 21 per cent of respondents had paid an average of 656 rupees[4] in 'speed money' to the Corporation to facilitate transactions. Transport officials demanded an average of 648 rupees from 33 per cent of the respondents. Officials of the Development Authority valued themselves more highly and reportedly demanded an average of 1850 rupees from 33 per cent of the respondents in exchange for performing their statutory duties. Over 50 per cent of respondents reported that they would be willing to pay higher official charges for public services rather than have to pay bribes (Paul, 1995, pp23–4). The head of the Development Authority reportedly suggested that 'the public should deal only with senior officials' if they wished to avoid corruption (*Deccan Herald*, 29 April 1995).

Corruption of government officials is notoriously difficult to observe, document or study. There is a difference between actual corrupt practices on the one hand and on the other hand what may be called the 'folklore of corruption' whereby corruption is widely believed to occur, and is frequently invoked as an explanation for events, but where allegations are rarely accompanied by hard evidence. That some officials require 'speed money' to fulfil their ordinary duties or are willing to take bribes in return for inaction is no doubt true. That corruption is often alleged in the vaguest possible terms and without any substantiating evidence is also true. How much explanatory weight may be placed on corruption is difficult to gauge.

Bureaucratic discretion and the failure to enforce environmental laws

Where bureaucrats have discretion, there is the possibility of individual bureaucratic inconsistency (Trebilock, 1997, p41).This results in uncertainty for the public and the patchy enforcement of environmental laws. For this reason, it has been suggested that 'the less administrative discretion the better . . . for development prospects'. The negative effects of bureaucratic discretion can be limited by publishing clear criteria for decision-making and by reducing the number of bodies to which the public need to apply in order to get approval for their actions. But 'national policy can be interpreted inconsistently' by those bureaucrats who deal directly with the public. 'The cabinet or similar bodies may determine the menu, but it is the many officials, each reflecting departmental interests, who cook and may spoil the meal' (Stopford et al, 1995, pp1, 126 and 138). Thus, laws which could otherwise support the protection of the environment can be manipulated or ignored.

The Pollution Control Boards of India have been accused of viewing themselves as 'license giving authorities' rather than monitors and controllers of pollution (interview 15 May 1995). In Bangalore, an industry must obtain consent from the Pollution Board to pollute public waters. The penalty for failing to apply for consent is 18 months to 6 years' imprisonment and a fine. If no consent is sought by the industry, the Board can serve them with notice of the conditions that would have been imposed if they had applied for consent. Where no response is given to an application for consent, consent is deemed to be given after four months. This implies that consent to pollute will usually be given. The Board can order industries to stop polluting or to close down completely (s 33A Water (Prevention and Control of Pollution) Amendment Act 1988). In the year 1993–4, the Pollution Board successfully issued closure orders to 11 water-polluting industries in the state, but it also gave 1278 consents to pollute water supplies (KSPCB, 1995, pp3–4, 12).

In Bangalore, officials are deemed to be failing to follow environmental laws themselves 'either out of ignorance or out of callousness'. As one activist put it, 'how do you tackle a government which itself is violating laws?'. For example, it is alleged that the authorities have 'consistently turned a blind eye' or, more actively, 'subvert the planning procedure' by allowing land from parks and open spaces to be used for construction (interviews 6 May and 31 May 1995; *Deccan Herald*, 29 April 1995, *The Hindu*, 23 August 1993 and *Times of India*, 6 June 1995). Similarly, little notice is being taken by government bodies of their obligations to protect water tanks. It is reported that, of 127 tanks notified by the government as protected areas, 90 have gone to semi-permanent residential encroachers, 23 to agriculture, 8 to permanent residences or commercial buildings and 7 are 'untraceable' (*The Times of India*, 25 June 1995, quoting a report by ornithologist S Sridar, Centre for Science and Technology, Bangalore). Similar problems are reported in relation to the removal of sewage. It appears that 30 per cent of sewage created in Bangalore is not dealt with by the Water Board treatment plants and is unaccounted for. It is alleged that the raw sewage is diverted – illegally, of course – straight into tanks and lakes. Furthermore, the sewage released from Water Board drains into tanks and rivers is reportedly so noxious that the Water Board has to pay a substantial fine to the Pollution Board (interview 28 April 1995; *Indian Express*, 13 August 1994 and 29 April 1995).

A problem of equal significance to that of outright bribe-taking is the interference of politics in bureaucratic decision-making. Judges noted that 'big business ... can purchase ministers and officials' pressurize the government to change rules, such as those setting emission levels' and 'use their money and power to prevent effective action'. One judge said that 'the order of decisions is all wrong. Politicians decide on projects and then scientists simply concur. It should be the other way around, but no one has the guts to make an independent decision'. Furthermore, it is disconcerting to discover that when the Chief Minister of the state was replaced, the head of the Pollution Board felt it necessary to resign from his 'political' post (interviews 31 May 1995, 5 June and 22 June 1995).

Planning represents the most politically charged area of law in Bangalore. According to one leading activist, 'the politics of Bangalore is the politics of real estate' (interview 6 May 1995). Buildings are regularly built, either without planning permission or with planning permission provided illegally by authorities in areas that are reserved as parks. Authorities have the power to 'remove or pull down any such work and restore the land to its original condition or, as the case may be, take any measures to stop such use' and to charge the costs to the offender (ss 10, 14 and 15, Planning Act, 1961 and s 38A, BDA Act, 1976). However, 'once a building is constructed, it's hard to tear it down, because third party rights will already have been created'. As a result, the government usually tends to regularize unauthorized constructions instead, often at the time of elections in order to win votes. For example, in 1995 the Governor of Karnataka 'regularized' a substantial number of unauthorized constructions in the green belt area. In 1992, a Bangalore Court found that industrial units had, as a 'personal favour' been allowed to locate illegally in a residential area and had even managed to acquire electricity, water and sewage services (interview 10 June 1995; *V Lakshmipathy and others* v *State of Karnataka and others*, AIR, 1992, Kant 57; and *Times of India*, 3 June 1995).

Ignorance of environmental law

Environmental law will not be enforced if it is not known or if its importance is not acknowledged. In Bangalore, it was felt by interviewees that the government must be encouraged to have a greater interest in environmental issues generally. The former head of another state's Pollution Board 'regretted that there was no dedicated effort by the government to control pollution and to protect the environment'. Although monitoring and the study of environmental issues has increased, the Minister for the Environment was still using 1991 studies in order to brief Parliament on lead pollution in 1995 (*Times of India*, 3 May 1995 and 9 June 1995). The official responsible for providing information to elected representatives in the state revealed that not one of them had sought any information relating to the environment in 1994–95. Over the past decade, an emphasis on restrained growth has shifted to an emphasis on promoting foreign investment and fostering economic growth. Inevitably, environmental concerns are given a lower priority under the new regime (interviews 23 April, 4 May and 6 May 1995). For example, the head of the Pollution Board is quoted as saying that environmental standards must to some extent give way to industrialization since 'we cannot go back to the Gandhian era' (*Times of India*, 24 June 1995).

On a positive note, environmental training for staff from the Pollution Board, industry, NGOs and local government has been introduced by the Pollution Board, in association with the Danish government (KSPCB, 1995, pp20–1 and 26; *Times of India*, 6 June 1995).

Allocation of jurisdiction

The enforcement of environmental law is further hampered by the fact that 'the environmental issues facing the city . . . are strongly inter-linked, but the actions taken are fragmented, as each activity is the responsibility of a separate agency'. Failure to allocate clearly jurisdiction and responsibilities between government bodies causes inefficiencies and gaps in the implementation of law and policy, which can result in damage to the environment. Officials perceive themselves to lack power and members of the public who are keen to push for the accountability of those officials have difficulty in isolating the relevant official. The shuffling of bureaucrats makes even the allocation of individual jurisdiction difficult. Bureaucrats are reported to be constantly on the verge of, or recovering from, a transfer to another department or district, and this makes it difficult for officials to get into the spirit of more novel positions, such as those with an environmental angle. One activist claimed to have ceased to attend seminars organized by the government on environmental issues because by the time a programme is due to be implemented, the official responsible has been transferred and the money goes elsewhere (interviews 8 May and 22 June 1995, *Times of India*, 23 June 1995).

A 'fish kill' incident illustrates the problems that institutional overlap can cause for the protection of the environment. In June 1995, 70 per cent of the fish were killed in Sankey tank. The Forest Department claimed that the deaths were caused by 'poison' accidentally falling in to the water. The Fisheries and Horticulture departments claimed that the deaths were due to sewage which was the responsibility of the Water Board. The Corporation, which was said to be responsible for maintaining the tank, said that sewage could not be the cause because the tank had been cleaned recently. It said that a private fish breeder operating in the tank had caused the deaths by over-breeding. The fish breeder blamed it on sewage and therefore the Water Board. Theories circulated in Bangalore that the kill was caused by untreated factory effluent or the overuse of pesticides by the government in surrounding areas. A journalist attempting to investigate the incident was passed from the state Forest Department to the state Horticulture Department, to the Corporation Horticulture Department, to the state Tourism Department, to the state Fisheries Department and back to the state Forest Department, which finally acknowledged responsibility for the tank, but had not even heard of the fish kill (interview 24 June 1995; and *Times of India*, 15 June, 16 June, 24 June and 1 July 1995).

In another case, involving illegal industrial construction, the court noted that the land in question had become a 'virtual no man's land' due to 'inaction and abdication of power and control' by the ten authorities with jurisdiction over the matter, 'thereby resulting in betrayal of public interest on account of imperviousness to duty, callousness, nonfeasance and utter lack of supervisory, administrative and regulatory control over the area in question' (*V Lakshmipathy and others* v *State of Karnataka and others* AIR 1992 Kant 57). In a separate incident, the Minister for Large and Medium Scale Industries decided that three tanks were to be covered by a trade promotion complex. The Forest Department, which owns the land in question, had no idea of the decision. Nor did local residents, who had recently invested a substantial amount of money in desilting one of the tanks and had intended to create a park in the area (*The Times of India*, 25 June 1995).

There is also a good deal of overlap of responsibility in the supply of water. First, the Water Board blames its failure to provide water and remove sewage on the frequent power cuts, which are the responsibility of the electricity providers. Second, it is not clear who is responsible for the water and sewage infrastructure. The Water Board claims that the Corporation is responsible for infrastructure, but a former administrator of the Corporation claimed that this responsibility lay with the Water Board. In 1995, an official warned that in the absence of extensive repair, there was a real possibility that drains would burst, but it is difficult to imagine how a repair programme could be implemented in the context of these jurisdictional clashes (interview 24 June 1995; *Times of India*, 29 May and 4 July 1995; *Indian Express*, 1 April 1994; *The Sunday Times of India*, 7 May 1995).

The water and sewage services in Bangalore are extremely unsatisfactory, partly as a result of such jurisdictional clashes. Water supply is often unpotable and its supply is highly erratic. Some areas of the city go without water for over ten days, and water is frequently only available for three days a week. Many Bangaloreans fend for themselves using illegal connections to the water supply. When the Water Board 'decided to "condone" unauthorized water use for a fee, and asked for voluntary disclosure of unauthorized connections' the number of unauthorized connections suddenly increased. The Board eventually relinquished its amnesty plan and returned to ignoring illegal connections (interviews 6 May and 10 June 1995; *Indian Express*, 12 June 1981 and 20 November 1995, *Sunday Times of India*, 7 June 1995 and *Times of India*, 2 June 1995). The failure of the authorities to prevent such behaviour means that unauthorized connections pollute the water supply and force those with legal connections to bear the costs of the illegal.

The matter of jurisdiction is further clouded by the fact that the powers of local government institutions are regularly and legally usurped by other bodies at the request of the state government. For example, from the beginning of May until late July, the Corporation was run by the Mayor, the head of the Development Authority, the Mayor again, the head of the Development Authority again, the Housing and Urban Development Secretary (who gave up through sheer exhaustion), and finally, the head of the Development Authority again (who proved equal to his two tasks) (interview 24 June 1995; s 100 Corporations Act; *Times of India*, 13 May, 27 May, 29 May, 31 May and 23 June 1995). It is difficult to see how any constructive work can have gone on during this period. The Bangalore Metropolitan Region Development Authority (BMRDA) was set up to improve coordination between the various authorities responsible for governing Bangalore. The members of the BMRDA are appointed by the state government and the Development Authority, headed by a Commissioner who is a state civil servant (interview 24 June 1995; Bangalore Metropolitan Region Development Authority Act, 1983; and the President's Address 1989). However, the BMRDA is commonly perceived as a useless 'fifth wheel on the coach'. A former Administrator of the Corporation noted that 'to be very frank, the BMRDA has not taken off'. The 'proliferation of authorities always leads to confusion and a lack of coordination. One more body means more people can be accommodated. And of course, once you create a body, it is hard to kill it' (interviews 6 May and 24 June 1995; *Deccan Herald*, 29 April 1995).

Lack of power and resources

Governing bodies lack real power in some areas. Some authorities are weakened by inadequate fining powers. The illegal dumping of dangerous effluent into the sewage system is punishable with a commercially insignif-icant fine of 100 rupees and a daily fine of 50 rupees until the contravention ceases. The breaching of other requirements relating to the type and size of drain that must be built by an owner of a new building will result in a slightly more significant fine of 1000 rupees. Similarly, illegal attempts to build on or use the land are punishable by a relatively low fine of up to 1000 rupees, with a further fine of 50 rupees per day for continued breach of the provisions (ss 63(1), 68 and 85 Water Board Act, and s 73 Planning Act). Funding for environmental protection is also limited. In 1993–94, just 6 per cent of the annual budget was spent on environment-related projects, including forestry, wildlife, transport pollution, ecology and environment, urban development, and water supply and sanitation. Funds for the Pollution Board are provided by the state government, but these are often irregular and inadequate, resulting in serious resource problems. This may account for the limited legal expertise among the staff of the Pollution Board. In 1993–94, there were no law officers, although one position was sanctioned, and just two out of a possible six law assistant posts were filled (Government of Karnataka, 1995 F1–F6; and KSPCB, 1995, pp31–2).

Some would suggest that the laws 'are there, they are just not properly implemented'. It is the opinion of the head of the Pollution Board that it 'is one of the best in the country', and has 'the strongest [powers] in the world, stronger than the . . . powers of [its US equivalent]'. The Board claims that 'industries are being vigorously pursued to ensure that the pollution control systems are installed and commissioned within the stipulated time', and that consents to pollute are 'loaded with conditions'. But it is estimated by one academic that the industrial sector compliance rate with Pollution Board standards is about 40–50 per cent (interviews 26 April, 25 May and 5 June 1995; and KSPCB, 1995, p11). The Board's record for prosecutions of failures to comply is not particularly impressive. For example, in the year 1993–94, 87 complaints were lodged by the Pollution Board in the Karnataka courts for water pollution. Of that number, 44 have been resolved in the court and of those, 20 were in favour of the Board. Of those cases that the Board 'won', not one resulted in the imprisonment or fining of the defendant. Instead, restraint orders were passed against 19 of the industries and in the remaining case, the industry was given time to comply with pollution control requirements. In 1993–94, the Pollution Board had issued a total of 39 closure orders against industries in Karnataka. Out of that total, 19 industries were able to obtain stay orders from the courts, and five managed to get the closure orders revoked. Only five industries actually closed after the order was given. Of the remaining industries, two continued to operate even after the order for closure, a further two industries were shifted and seven were issued a warning after failing to comply with the closure order (KSPCB, 1995, pp52–4).

The court system appears to be a double-edged sword in the hand of the authorities. On the one hand, the court allows it to prosecute those who damage the environment. On the other hand, the more wily of its opponents are able to turn the legal process to their advantage. A former head of the Board felt the need to confirm at a recent conference that 'the Board was working and was not "dead"'. He defended the Board's poor record of convictions, asking how the Board could be expected to function when 'the court gives a stay to every other person who violates the law' (*Times of India*, 24 June 1995). For example, when the Pollution Board asked industries to recycle 50 per cent of their water, many failed to comply, even after prosecution orders were obtained. The industries simply obtained stay orders. As a senior judge remonstrated, the Board should not just give up, but should contest these applications for a stay. But 'it is not clear that their advocates are fast enough to do this'. According to one academic, the fact that the Pollution Boards are required, except in the case of an accident or an emergency, to resort to the criminal courts to force industries to stop polluting, 'defeats the very purpose' of the environmental laws, which were 'enacted specifically to overcome the procedural delays and technicalities of the regular criminal courts' (interviews 26 April, 10 June and 22 June 1995).

ACCESS TO JUSTICE AND ENVIRONMENTAL LAW

It has been shown that the government in Bangalore is failing to create and maintain a clean and safe environment, and is not preventing environmental degradation by individuals and government bodies. When the government fails to enforce the rule of law, the public may attempt to do so instead. But the ability of the public to involve itself in the enforcement of the rule of law can be restricted by financial, social, political and institutional factors. This is why it is said that the rule of law cannot be fully supported without support for its corollary, access to justice (Cappelletti, 1979; Galanter, 1975; Cranston, 1997). If it is important that the law should apply to all, it is also important, for reasons of efficiency and justice, that the law should be accessible to all. This section explains what gateways exist for citizens who wish to enforce the rule of law and what factors limit access to those gateways.

Legal Gateways to Environmental Justice

When government is unable, or refuses, to initiate legal action to prevent the infraction of environmental law, the public are able to use criminal, civil and public legal gateways to push for action. Criminal law gateways allow the public to force the government to prosecute on environmental damage caused by the private sector. Civil law allows individuals to prevent directly, or seek damages for, environmental damage caused by other individuals or the government. Public law gateways allow individuals to sue the government for its failure to prevent environmental damage by the government or other individuals.

Criminal law gateways

Criminal law is usually only available for use by the government. However, members of the public are able to use Indian criminal law in two ways for the purpose of protecting the environment.

First, under environmental legislation, citizens can lodge a complaint with the courts against illegal pollution of the environment, water or air, and thus place a duty on the relevant Pollution Board to begin a criminal prosecution against the polluter (s 43 Air Act, s 19 Environment Act and s 49 Water Act).

Second, the national criminal codes allow citizens to file complaints for public nuisance in order to stop smoke, smells and other noxious emissions, including water pollution, which cause 'common injury, danger or annoyance to the public or to people in general'. Depending on the type of pollution and whether it is ongoing or anticipated, complaints are made to the police or a magistrate, and offences can be punishable with a fine not exceeding 200 rupees, arrest and/or a notice to abate the pollution. Police can investigate the offence and, in some cases, Magistrates may conduct an inquiry and summon expert evidence. This allows for technical expertise produced as evidence, which is an important consideration in environmental matters (s 290 Indian Penal Code; ss 139, 154, 156, 173, 190, 202, 203 Code of Criminal Procedure).

Civil law gateways

In contrast to criminal procedures that seek to punish, civil law allows individuals to seek remedies such as financial damages from the person who has wronged them, or declarations and injunctions to affect the future behaviour of the wrongdoer.[5] Where a person has suffered injury or damage to property, the wronged party can sue the wrongdoer under the law of torts. It is up to the person who is suing to prove that the wrong occurred (ss 101–103, Indian Evidence Act). In environmental cases involving technical matters, it is sometimes difficult or exceedingly costly for an individual to provide such evidence for the court. In addition, civil law suits tend to be slow, costly and largely ineffective, especially when the remedy sought is financial rather than a mere injunction (Anderson, 1996, pp207–9). For this reason, while suits for civil injunctions may provide Bangalore's environmental litigants with an effective remedy, they are often less attractive than the public law remedies discussed below.

The utility of civil remedies is further reduced by laws that stop the courts from considering a matter which is covered by environmental laws. This means that citizens cannot sue each other over factual situations that the Pollution Boards are considering (s 58 Water Act, 1974, s 46 Air Act, 1981, and s 22 Environment Act, 1986; *Sreenivasa Distilleries* v *SR Thyagarajan* AIR 1986 AP 328). These provisions do not prevent citizens from challenging the procedural propriety of decisions taken by the Boards. But they do reduce the scope for tort actions considerably and undermine the authority of the civil courts to provide adequate relief to the public.

A separate system of courts exists for resolving consumer disputes. The quality of civic services, such as water supply, can be challenged in these courts, but only if they are paid for by a specific fee rather than a general tax. This means that in Bangalore, the quality of electricity, transport and water services can all be challenged in consumer courts; but services like road maintenance, garbage collection and sewage disposal, which are paid for indirectly through taxes, cannot be challenged (s 2(1)(d), Consumer Protection Act and s31 Water Board Act). The Bangalore consumer courts have a substantial number of cases pending that relate to the inefficiencies of the Development Authority. Cases have been filed by purchasers who have been unable to move into their new homes for over a year because no basic amenities have been provided; by victims of double allocations of the same plot; and by a customer who was forced to pay 5000 rupees in bribes in order to complete basic administrative steps towards buying a property (*Deccan Herald*, 29 April 1995 and *Times of India*, 30 June 1995).

Public law gateways

Under the Constitution, Indian individuals and groups can ask the courts to review the behaviour of government officials who have failed to perform their duty, including the duty to curb environmental damage. If the action is successful, the court can issue orders against the government official or authority concerned to force them to perform their duty. Such an action is known as judicial review (Articles 21, 32 and 226 of the Indian Constitution).

Actions can be brought against any government body since the definition of the 'state' under the Constitution has been interpreted widely. Where an individual alleges that an official's behaviour has resulted in a breach of fundamental rights, such as the right to life, the case can be heard directly in the Supreme Court in Delhi. Where any other legal right is to be enforced, the case is heard in the state's High Court. Judicial review actions are therefore dealt with more quickly than those that usually begin in the Magistrates courts. Individuals are often able to take environmental cases directly to the Supreme Court since the courts have decided that the fundamental 'right to life' guaranteed under the Constitution includes a right to a healthy and pollution-free environment.

The rules determining which members of the public may bring an action for review to the court have been expanded. Now any person who is acting in good faith may use this procedure, even if they have no individual interest in the outcome of the case, but are acting instead in the public interest. This means that environmental issues, which often affect the general public rather than just individuals, are more easily brought into the courts. Actions that are brought in the public interest are known as public interest litigations (PIL). The formalities usually associated with starting a legal case have been loosened for PIL and judges have been known to convert letters from the public into full petitions. As with all reform efforts in developing countries, questions of cost must affect which projects are considered to be viable. PIL provides a more efficient and accessible way of protecting the principles of access to justice and the rule of law. Relying on the combined power of public will and minimal institutional obstructions, PIL has given the Indian population an effective tool with which to battle against individual and government attacks on the environment (Anderson, 1995; Bakshi, 1993; Cottrell, 1992 and 1993; Rosencranz et al, 1991; Leelakrishnan, 1992; Singh et al, 1993; Hurra, 1993; Harding, 1992; Perry, 1998 and Peiris, 1991).

The prominent role of judicial review in general and of PIL in particular, is the most characteristic feature of Indian environmental law. As of March 1995, there were over 6000 cases and 2500 writ petitions pending against the Development Authority in Bangalore's High Court, mostly relating to allotments alleged to have been taken over by encroachers. In 1993–94, the Pollution Board reported that 65 PIL cases involving the Board had been filed, of which 24 had been decided and 41 remained pending. A total of 22 cases had been resolved in favour of the Board and two cases against it (KSPCB, 1995, p54; *Deccan Herald*, 29 April 1995).

The Thippagondanahalli Lake Case provides a good example of the power of PIL. In 1992, a public interest action was brought by concerned citizens in the High Court against the government and a private company, DLF. The petitioners claimed that a government order, which gave planning permission for DLF to build a housing development in the catchment area of the second major source of water for Bangalore city, was illegal (*Bangalore Water Supply and Sewerage Board* vs *Kantha Chandra*). The land concerned was originally designated as agricultural land. The petitioners claimed that the government 'yielded to the pressure of [DLF] on extraneous consider-ations, totally ignoring the interests of the citizens of Bangalore' which they were bound to consider under the Planning Act. The Court agreed, stating that the government 'acted totally without jurisdiction . . . and had done so only on collateral considerations yielding to the influence brought to bear on it by DLF. The Court described the behaviour of the government as 'amazing . . . most shocking . . . unfortunate . . . astonishing'. 'No argument is necessary to make out a case for quashing the impugned order, and no amount of argument can save it.' The judgment caused quite an impact. There were demands from the opposition members of Karnataka's assemblies for the chief minister to resign and newspapers were highly critical of the government. However, it is unfortunate that, although the petitioners' case was based largely on environmental and health grounds, the court found in their favour on administrative law grounds. The petit-ioners were concerned that the implementation of the scheme would 'adversely affect the interest of the residents of Bangalore city inasmuch as both the quality and quantity of water supply will be adversely affected' by the construction and introduction of borewells (High Court judgment, original copy, pp18–9, 28–9; interview 10 May 1995; and *Times of India*, 26 April 1992). While it is encouraging that the court saw fit to cause

Bangalore's water supply to be protected, a judgment on environmental grounds would have done more to contribute to an emerging environmental jurisprudence.

Improving Access to Environmental Justice

If the benefits to the rule of law which access to justice can afford are to be fully realized, a number of political and legal constraints must be eased. The main obstacles to access to justice are a lack of activism on the part of the public, a power imbalance between the government and the public, and inadequacies in the legal system.

The need for a culture of activism

Some interviewees reported having no memory of PIL cases being brought against Bangalore authorities. Although such cases have been brought, in fact, these impressions reflect the image of Bangaloreans as placid and inactive. While vehement letters appear weekly in local papers listing a myriad of failures on the part of the authorities and demanding that 'something be done', it is rare that the matters are taken to court, even by environmental activists. Many of those interviewed in Bangalore suggested that there is a 'low perception of environmental problems' in Bangalore and that PIL 'only occurs when there is a glaring environmental hazard'. An ex-chief justice of the Karnataka High Court expressed the opinion that 'people don't go to court for remedies although they could do, because they have no desire to spend the time and money. They are lethargic and there is no hope of a quick solution.'. However, he also suggested that Bangalore is probably a little more active than northern cities on environmental issues (interviews 9 May, 13 May, 10 June, 22 June and 24 June 1995). Others suggested that although a 'culture of resistance and inquiry are not yet deep rooted' in Bangalore, 'it is evolving'. Ten years ago such a culture would have been 'unthinkable, because people felt that law-making and enforcement were the role of the executive, legislature and judiciary' (interviews 23 May, 31 May and 5 June 1995).

Over 50 organizations in Bangalore were identified as having some interest in environmental issues. These included groups focused on environmental and animal welfare issues, civil rights, residential areas, consumer issues and social welfare, as well as service clubs, labour unions and individuals. They attempt to increase the public's awareness of the effects of pollution, the responsibilities of various government officials and the powers that the public have to change things. NGOs also take direct action to deal with government failures. For example, when four years of residents' complaints to government officials about noise and air pollution caused by a private diesel generator resulted in no action, a local environmental NGO complained to the Pollution Board. The Board issued a notice, which was not complied with, and then did nothing. The NGO went to the owner directly and resolved the issue in six months, without further government involvement. Examples of legal activism do exist, including one local lawyer who has taken part in at least three PIL actions relating to the planning and infrastructure of Bangalore. Also, in June 1995, a PIL petition was launched by individuals against the state government, asking that they be ordered to remove debris that it had dumped for five years in a local park (interviews 8 May and 10 June 1995; *Times of India*, 20 June 1995).Other examples have been noted throughout this chapter.

However, there are questions as to whether the public, and NGOs in particular, are acting with the best possible motives. One lawyer said that, at a conservative estimate, 'about 25 per cent of all PIL actions filed are direct personal vendettas'. It has been suggested that activists in Bangalore sometimes tend to protest both late and falsely against infractions of environmental law. The implication is that activists protest for publicity rather than to demonstrate a sense of injustice. However, this allegation was refuted by one judge who claimed that 'there are very few PIL cases in Bangalore anyway. In my opinion they are valid'. According to a local judge, 'some NGOs are really honest. Others are [just] happy if they get the money'. The head of the Pollution Board agreed that 'some NGOs have a rather negative approach' with 'no technical or scientific support', but others are 'quite helpful', bringing important issues to the attention of the Board, and giving 'a true account of the facts'. A senior bureaucrat noted that 'NGOs come up like mushrooms in this country. Some have no idea about environment, ecology – what it means. They also get foreign funding. They give glossy reports based on our [government] statistics and then wither away' (interviews 28 April, 25 May, 5 June, 10 June, 17 June and 22 June 1995). For example, it was recently discovered that as much as 20 million rupees was spent on NGOs fraudulently purporting to carry out an innovative programme for children's environmental education (*Times of India*, 18 June 1995).

The power imbalance between the government and the individual
Some feel that India's 'patriarchal system of government' leaves a 'dichotomy between the values of freedom and the welfare state demands'. On the one hand, individuals have strong legal rights to challenge the government; on the other hand, both the government and the public expect the government to have the final word. This attitude of superiority has been accepted with gusto by the municipal institutions of Bangalore. A senior bureaucrat stated that 'most NGOs think that we are not transparent enough. Most of us are very opaque'. Activists reported varying degrees of difficulty in interacting with government officials responsible for Bangalore and made the following comments on the subject: 'If you know how the government works, then you can get things done. It requires a certain amount of follow up.' 'Government officials respond and are pleasant, but they have limitations. They talk a lot.' 'Access to information is very difficult. Government officials are polite but substantively unhelpful.' 'You have to really bash them.' (interviews 6 May, 8 May, 15 May, 1 June, 10 June and 17 June). A survey of Bangaloreans found that most government institutions in Bangalore 'are not "citizen friendly.". They do not seem to view the citizen as a client to be served'. For example, criteria

used by the Corporation for assessing taxes 'are not explicit and are not known by many taxpayers. The public has accepted it as a negotiable tax'. Some institutions even treat their Annual Reports 'as internal documents and are not readily accessible to the public'(Paul, 1994, pp26–7).

The availability of information is a significant determinant of the quantity and quality of public attempts to enforce environmental laws. For example, by refusing to make information available to the public or by keeping the details of 'public' consultations secret, 'the government has rendered public participation [in environmental impact assessment procedures] a farce' (interview 6 May 1995; *Sunday Times of India*, 11 June 1995). It remains true that 'political expediency makes a virtue of secrecy in official information gathering. Accessing [the government's] data is difficult as a journalist, let alone as an ordinary citizen'. Environment laws provide the concerned citizen with 'no right to information. Thus [s/he] is at the total mercy of the government authorities'. In addition, the Government can declare many relevant documents and places to be 'secret' under the Official Secrets Act and thus prevent public access (*Times of India*, 9 June 1995). As a result, NGOs are often limited to small, inaccurate studies, such as counting buses or literally looking at lakes to confirm that they appear polluted. Until information becomes more readily available, much of the discussion surrounding environmental issues will continue to be based on speculation and activists will continue to be in danger of being misguided in their protests. On the other hand, the Pollution Board publishes an Annual Report which is clear, comprehensive and available in both English and Kannada. The reports, which were obtained easily upon request, detail the composition of the Board, its powers, its major achievements and decisions, and expenditures.

The imbalance between the government and the individual is worsened by the fact that many government institutions are protected from unan- nounced attacks through the legal system. For example, two months' notice must be given to the Water Board before any suit, except one merely claiming an injunction, can be brought against it. The notice must detail the specific cause of action, the nature of relief sought, the amount claimed and the complainant's name and address (s 126(1) Water Board Act, 1964). Also, a person who wishes to file a complaint in order to trigger a criminal prosecution of an individual by the government must give 60 days' notice to the relevant authority of his or her intention to file the complaint, along with the details of the alleged polluter.[6] The notice provision was intended to allow the polluting company and/or government body to mend its ways, thus promoting an amicable dispute resolution over prosecution. However, the 60-day requirement can be criticized on three grounds. First, it allows the authority to secure the prosecutorial initiative, thereby excluding the concerned public from the process, and possibly allowing the authorities to cut a deal with the polluter. Second, it provides the polluter with ample time to conceal polluting activities and to destroy evidence of past pollution. Third, it introduces unnecessary delay into the process, thereby frustrating concerned citizens and robbing them of political momentum.

Problems in the legal system

The three aspects of the legal system that most seriously restrict access to environmental justice are delays, costs and a lack of qualified lawyers.

'In 1987, the Supreme Court of India noted that even if no new cases were subsequently filed, it would take 15 years to dispose of all pending cases. In 1993, it was taking between 12 and 15 years for a case to be tried before the Bombay High Court, with an additional period of 10 to 12 years before all appeals would be exhausted'(Cranston, 1997, p235). Environmental cases 'don't get special priority in the court lists. They have to wait their turn. This can mean up to three years,' although injunctions 'can be obtained more speedily.'. The exact number of cases in arrears in the Karnataka legal system appeared to be unknown. However, an estimate of around one million was made. It was said that the speed with which a case is heard depends greatly upon the seniority of the lawyers involved, whether the government attempts to obstruct matters, and whether the judge 'is environmentally conscious or not' (interviews 6 May, 8 May, 5 June and 22 June 1995). Since the authorities have to use the courts to enforce environmental law and PIL cases are able to proceed directly to the higher courts, it is possible that a PIL action could offer a speedier solution than government prosecution. Of course, that would result in the costs of enforcement being transferred to the public.

It cannot be denied that PIL itself 'requires a lot of money and a lot of effort'. Although it is reputed to be cheaper and quicker than many forms of litigation, PIL actions still require funds up front before a case can be brought. Funds can be reclaimed as costs, but only in the event that the petitioner wins the case. One activist also described the risks of arrest while protesting issues which may become the subject of PIL actions (interviews 6 May and 5 June 1995).

Finally, it is important that 'the legal profession tends to gravitate towards the most lucrative work – in a developing society, the rapidly growing commercial work – with a resultant decrease in legal services available for purchase at the lower margin'(Cranston, 1997, p234 quoting Barry Metzger). Interviewees reported that advocates in Bangalore do not generally take up environmental cases on their own initiative and there are very few lawyers who have either the experience or the interest in environmental cases at all. None of the activists interviewed who had taken part in PIL cases or were considering doing so, had chosen their lawyer on the grounds of relevant experience. Indeed, judges, activists, journalists, academics or scientists interviewed could not name one lawyer who specialized in environmental law. According to one lawyer, 'a lawyer can file any case on the environment, but [she or he] has no time to collect data for the case. If an NGO or public spirited individual takes up an issue and researches it, then the lawyer can pursue it, even without remuneration.'. However, there is always the risk that 'the legal profession will not tolerate deviation' and a lawyer's career will suffer if they pursue environmental cases (interviews 31 May, 10 June and 22 June 1995).

CONCLUSION

If the urban environment of Bangalore is to be protected, the rule of law must be enforced, both by the government and by the public. While the government continues to fail to enforce the rule of law, the public can provide an important and sustainable check on the worst excesses of the failure of the government. The public will only be able to play its full part in supporting the rule of law if it has access to justice. But access to justice in turn requires the financial and active support, and genuine participation, of both the public and the government. An increased culture of activism, a redressing of the balance of power between the government and the public, and a resolution of the inadequacies in the legal system would all contribute to improving access to justice. If these improvements are made, and if the government and the public increasingly act in concert, the law can provide an effective and sustainable method of protection for the Indian urban environment for the next century.

NOTES

1   This chapter is based in part on material collected and personal interviews conducted in Bangalore by Amanda Perry in April–June 1995. Funding was provided by the Ford Foundation and the Economic and Social Research Council, UK, under the School of Oriental and African Studies (SOAS) (University of London) Law Department project 'Access to Environmental Justice in Asia and Africa'. Initial conclusions were published in Amanda J Perry and Michael R Anderson (1996) 'Access to Justice in Bangalore: Legal Gateways in Context', SOAS Law Department Working Paper No 12, SOAS, London. The author gratefully acknowledges the intellectual contributions of Michael Anderson, the time given by interviewees and the financial contributions of the aforementioned institutions.
2   For current projects in law reform see http://www.worldbank.org; www.oecd.org; www.adb.org; www.ebrd.org and www.un.org.
3   All newspapers are Bangalore editions.
4   At that time one British pound was worth roughly 50 Indian rupees.
5   Civil law procedures are governed by the Code of Civil Procedure, 1908.
6   See section on criminal gateways.

REFERENCES

Books, Papers and Reports

Anderson, Michael R (1995) 'Public Interest Perspectives on the Bhopal Case: Tort, Crime or Violation of Human Rights?', in D Robinson and J Dunkley (eds) *Public Interest Perspectives in Environmental Law*, Wiley Chancery, London

Anderson, Michael R (1996) 'Individual Rights to Environmental Protection in India', in A Boyle and M R Anderson (eds) *Human Rights Approaches to Environmental Protection*, Clarendon Press, Oxford pp201–2, 207–9

Bakshi, P M (1993) *Environmental Law: The Procedural Options*, Indian Law Institute, New Delhi

Cappelletti, Mauro (1979) (ed) *Access to Justice: Volumes 1–3*, Sijthoff, Milan

Cottrell, J (1992) 'Courts and Accountability: Public Interest Litigation in the Indian High Courts', *Third World Legal Studies*

Cottrell, J (1993) 'Third Generation Rights and Social Action Litigation', in S Adelman and A Paliwala (eds) *Law and Crisis in the Third World*, Hans Zells Publishers, London, p102

Cranston, Ross (1997) 'Access to Justice in South and South-East Asia' in J Faundez *Good Governance and Law: Legal and Institutional Reform in Developing Countries*, Macmillan, London, p234

De Soto, Hernando (1989) *The Other Path*, Harper & Row, New York

EBRD (1996) *Transition Report 1996*, EBRD, London

Galanter, Marc (1975) 'Why the Haves Come Out Ahead: Speculations on the Limits of Legal Change', *Law and Society Review*, vol 9, pp95–160

Government of Karnataka (1995) *Draft Annual Plan 1995–96*, vol 2

Harding , A (1992) 'Public Interest Law and Development in Malaysia', *Third World Legal Studies*, pp231–43

Hurra, S (1993) *Public Interest Litigation*, Mishra, Ahmedabad

KSPCB (1995) *Annual Report of the Pollution Board, 1993–94*, Bangalore

Leelakrishnan, P (1992) (ed) *Law and Environment*, Eastern Book Co , Lucknow

Paul, Samuel (1994) 'Public Services for the Urban Poor: Report Card on Three Indian Cities, *Economic and Political Weekly*, vol 29, no 50, December

Peiris, G L (1991) *Public Interest Litigation in the Indian Subcontinent: Current Dimensions, International Comparative Law Quarterly*, vol 40, pp66–90

Perry, Amanda J (1998) 'Law and Urban Change in an Indian City' in E Fernandes and A Varley (eds) *Illegal Cities: Law and Urban Change in Developing Countries*, Zed Books, London

President's Address, Karnataka United Urban Citizen's Federation Decennial Anniversary Celebration, 15 July 1989, Bangalore

Reisman, Michael W (1979) *Folded Lies: Bribery, Crusades and Reforms*, The Free Press, London

Rosencranz, A, Divan, S and Noble, M (1991) *Environmental Law and Policy in India: Cases, Materials and Statutes*, Tripathi, Mumbai

Singh, G, Anklesaria, K and Gonsalves, C (1993) *Environmental Activists Handbook*, Gonsalves, Mumbai

Stopford, John M and Strange, Susan S (1995) *Rival States, Rival Firms: Competition for World Market Shares*, Cambridge University Press, Cambridge

Trebilock, M J (1997) 'What Makes Poor Countries Poor? The Role of Institutional Capital in Economic Development' in Edgardo Buscalglia, William Ratliff and Robert Cooter (eds) *The Law and Economics of Development*, JAI Press, Connecticut

World Bank (1992) *Governance and Development*, World Bank, Washington, DC

Newspapers

Deccan Herald
The Hindu
Indian Express

The Sunday Times of India
Times of India

Legislation

Air Prevention and Control of Pollution Act, 1981 (Air Act)
Bangalore Development Authority Act, 1976 (BDA Act)
Bangalore Metropolitan Region Development Authority Act, 1983
Bangalore Water Supply and Sewerage Act, 1964 (Water Board Act)
Code of Civil Procedure, 1908
Code of Criminal Procedure, 1973
Consumer Protection Act, 1986
Environment Protection Act, 1986 (Environment Act)
Indian Evidence Act, 1872
Indian Penal Code, 1860
Karnataka Municipal Corporations Act, 1976
Karnataka Town and Country Planning Act, 1961 (Planning Act)
Water (Prevention and Control of Pollution) Amendment Act, 1988
Water Prevention and Control of Pollution Act, 1974 (Water Act)

Cases

Bangalore Water Supply and Sewerage Board v *Kantha Chandra,* ILR 1987 (I) Karnataka 1617
Sreenivasa Distilleries v *SR Thyagarajan* AIR 1986 AP 328
V Lakshmipathy and others v *State of Karnataka and others* AIR 1992 Kant 57

4 ENVIRONMENTAL HEALTH OR ECOLOGICAL SUSTAINABILITY? RECONCILING THE BROWN AND GREEN AGENDAS IN URBAN DEVELOPMENT[1]

Gordon McGranahan and David Satterthwaite

This chapter describes the conflicts that can occur between those who prioritize environmental health issues (often called the brown agenda) and those who prioritize ecological sustainability (often called the green agenda) when considering urban development in Africa, Asia and Latin America. It then maps out areas of agreement between these two agendas and discusses the measures that help to encourage the simultaneous achievement of improved environmental health and more ecologically sustainable urban development.

INTRODUCTION

Urban environmental problems can be divided into two sets of issues or two agendas. First, there are the items on the conventional 'sanitary' or environmental health agenda (often termed the 'brown' agenda) which have long been familiar to urbanists (Bartone et al, 1994; Leitmann 1994). These include unsanitary living conditions, hazardous pollutants in the urban air and waterways, and accumulations of solid waste. Such problems have many immediate environmental health impacts that tend to fall especially heavily on low-income groups (see, for instance, Bradley et al, 1991; McGranahan, 1991; Hardoy et al, 1992a). Secondly, there are the items within the more recent 'green' agenda promoted by environmentalists (mostly from high-income countries): the contribution of urban-based production, consumption and waste generation to ecosystem disruptions, resource depletion and global climate change. Most such problems have impacts that are more dispersed and delayed, and often threaten long-term ecological sustainability.

Conflicts arise between the proponents of these two agendas in regard to which environmental problems should receive priority.[2] The conflicts can be especially acute in the urban areas in Africa and in much of Asia and Latin America, where environmental health problems are particularly serious and where the capacity for environmental management is generally weak. However, provided both agendas are taken seriously, these conflicts can be minimized.

This chapter argues that:

1   Many of the approaches traditionally used to improve urban environmental health – such as subsidizing piped water and water-borne sewerage systems and conventional solid waste collection systems – can undermine sustainability, and often fail to reach those whose health is most at risk.
2   Some of the new approaches promoted by those concerned with ecological sustainability – such as restrictive water use regimes – can undermine the environmental health of the poor.
3   There are approaches and frameworks more directly supportive of the needs and priorities of low income urban dwellers that can improve environmental health while also achieving progress within the green agenda. There is also some practical evidence that these can work, as discussed in the final section of this paper.

THE BROWN AND THE GREEN AGENDAS

Table 4.1 highlights some of the contrasts between these two agendas. From a radically 'green' perspective, a focus on the 'brown' agenda is short-sighted: what about future generations? What about the impact of city-based consumption on rural resources and ecosystems? And might not a focus on improving environmental health conditions in cities encourage more people to move there?[3] From a radically 'brown' perspective, emphasizing the new concerns on the 'green' agenda is élitist: what about the needs and priorities of the poor? What about the very high environmental health burdens suffered by those lacking adequate provision for piped water, sanitation, drainage and garbage collection? Environmental hazards remain among the main causes of ill-health, injury and premature death among lower income groups in most urban centres in Africa, Asia and Latin America; in urban centres with the least adequate provision for basic infrastructure and services, they remain among the main causes of ill-health, injury and premature death for the whole urban population (Bradley et al, 1991; Hardoy et al, 1992a; WHO, 1992; WHO, 1996).

Although there are very real conflicts between the proponents of the 'brown' and the 'green' agendas as to which problems should receive priority, it is important not to create a false dichotomy. Some environmental improvements serve both agendas. Equally important, a concern for greater equity is central to both agendas – it is just that each chooses to emphasize different aspects of this equity.

Table 4.1 *Stereotyping the Brown and Green Agendas for Urban Environmental Improvement*

	The 'Brown' Environmental Health Agenda	The 'Green' Sustainability Agenda
Characteristic features of problems high on the agenda:		
Key impact	Human health	Ecosystem health
Timing	Immediate	Delayed
Scale	Local	Regional and global
Worst affected	Lower income groups	Future generations
Characteristic attitude to:		
Nature	Manipulate to serve human needs	Protect and work with
People	Work with	Educate
Environmental services	Provide more	Use less
Aspects emphasized in relation to:		
Water	Inadequate access and poor quality	Overuse; need to protect water sources
Air	High human exposure to hazardous pollutants	Acid precipitation and greenhouse gas emissions
Solid waste	Inadequate provision for collection and removal	Excessive generation
Land	Inadequate access for low income groups to housing	Loss of natural habitats and agricultural land to urban development
Human wastes	Inadequate provision for safely removing faecal material (and waste water) from living environment	Loss of nutrients in sewage and damage to water bodies from the release of sewage into waterways
Typical proponent	Urbanist	Environmentalist

Note: The entries in this table are only indicative. In practice, neither the agendas nor the issues they address are so clearly delimited. For example, while the table refers to lower income groups as the worst affected by 'brown' environmental problems, in most urban centres there is considerable variation even within lower income groups in the extent and nature of environmental health risks in the shelters and neighbourhoods in which they live. Each person or household makes their own trade-off between, for instance, cost, locations with good access to employment or income-earning possibilities, space, tenure (including the possibility of home ownership) and the factors that influence environmental health (eg, quality and size of the accommodation, and the extent of the basic infrastructure and services).

EQUITY

Graham Haughton has identified five interconnected equity principles that can apply to environmental problems in urban areas (Haughton, 1999) and these help to clarify the different perspectives from which the proponents of the brown and the green agendas work.

For the proponents of the brown agenda, the main priorities are:

- *intragenerational equity* (as all urban dwellers have needs for healthy and safe living and working environments and the infrastructure and services these require); and
- *procedural equity* (to ensure that all person's legal rights to, among other things, a safe and healthy living and work environment are respected, that they are fairly treated and that they can engage in democratic decision-making processes about the management of the urban centre in which they live).

For the proponents of the green agenda, the priorities are:

- *intergenerational equity* (which includes a concern that urban development does not draw on finite resource bases and degrade ecological systems in ways that compromise the ability of future generations to meet their own needs);
- *transfrontier equity* (to prevent urban consumers or producers transferring their environmental costs to other people or other ecosystems – for instance, disposing of wastes in the region around the city); and
- *interspecies equity* (with the rights of other species recognized).

Working from this recognition of the different aspects of equity that the two agendas prioritize allows a better understanding of how progress on both the brown and the green agendas can proceed, and how potential conflicts can be minimized. It provides a common language for addressing both sets of concerns and potentially a common goal (reducing inequity). It helps to identify the conditions under which pursuing one agenda is likely to undermine the other – if, for example, the needs of low income groups are ignored, they are likely to bear a disproportionate burden of any efforts to protect future generations and vice versa. Moreover, by framing the problem in terms of equity, it is easier to see why in some cities (where intragenerational and procedural inequities dominate) the brown agenda deserves more attention, while in others (where the other inequities predominate) the green agenda should prevail.

CONTRASTING BROWN AND GREEN PRIORITIES

Both green and brown proponents have reason to criticize many existing approaches to urban environmental management, even if their priorities differ. At a superficial level, the brown and green agendas are in direct opposition to each other. For example, the brown agenda would seem to call for more water use, more sewerage connections, more waste collection, more urban residential land and more fossil fuel use (to replace smoky biofuels). By way of contrast, the green agenda would seem to call for water conservation, less water-borne sewerage, less waste generation, less urban expansion and less fossil fuel use. While these potential contradictions should not be ignored, a review of existing policy problems indicates that the trade-offs need not be as sharp as such generalizations seem to imply.

Water

Urban water supply planning has been preoccupied historically with how to increase supplies to meet growing demand, given the physical and financial constraints of the city. By and large, demand has been assumed to be beyond the influence of water sector policies. For those households and businesses connected to piped water systems, water is generally provided far below its full cost. For example, there is little incentive for users to conserve or encouragement to the industries that are the largest water users to recycle waste water or seek less water-intensive systems of production.

In some of the wealthier cities, subsidized water supply systems have brought major benefits to most of their populations, including a high proportion of their lower income populations. For instance, there has been a considerable expansion in the proportion of the population with piped water supplies in many of the wealthier Latin American cities. In cities such as São Paulo, Belo Horizonte, Curitiba and Pôrto Alegre, most of the population receives piped water supplies to their homes (Jacobi, 1994; Mueller, 1995).

However, the proponents of the green agenda can rightly point to the serious consequences this often brings. The emphasis on increasing supply and keeping the price of water 'affordable' has resulted in major cities throughout Africa, Asia and Latin America overexploiting local water resources. For instance, in many coastal cities local aquifers have been overpumped, resulting in saltwater intrusion. Overexploitation of underground water has also caused serious problems of subsidence for many buildings and sewage and drainage pipes in many cities (Damián, 1992; Postel, 1992). As local ground and surface water sources are overused (or polluted), meeting rising city demands generally means having to draw on ever more distant and expensive water resources. This can be to the detriment of the populations (and often ecosystems) in the areas from which the water is drawn and with the higher water costs rarely reflected in higher prices for the largest city water users.

Proponents of the brown agenda often share this green agenda concern for unrealistically low water prices. They can point to how the discrepancy between water utilities' costs and revenues (from water sales and public subsidies) often inhibit expansion to low income areas and help to ensure that high proportions of the population in most cities remain unconnected to piped water systems. Indeed, a combination of price controls and very limited public funds is a recipe for intragenerational inequities, with the subsidies that do exist flowing, along with the water, to those who least need them. Even for those low income groups who have access to connections, water supplies are often irregular or of poor quality or difficult to access – for instance, as dozens of households share each standpipe. At least 300 million urban dwellers in Africa, Asia and Latin America remain without piped water supplies (WHO/UNICEF 1993) and tens of millions of those whose governments include in their statistics as having access to piped supplies still face inadequate, irregular or unsafe supplies which are often difficult to obtain (Satterthwaite, 1995; WHO, 1996).

While the water-related priorities of the green and brown agendas are different, their goals are not inherently incompatible. The often unmet minimum daily needs for health (about 30 litres per capita) amounts to about two flushes of a conventional toilet or one slowly dripping faucet. The international standard of 150 litres per capita per day is only a small fraction of the typical usage in affluent cities in the North. Providing sufficient water for health needs is not the reason that many cities are overtaxing their water supplies; indeed, in many cities programmes encouraging water conservation and ensuring the better management and repair of piped water systems can often free up sufficient 'new' supplies to allow regular piped water supplies to be extended to unserved households with no overall increase in water use (see, for instance, Connolly, 1999 who discusses this for Mexico City). Intragenerational water inequities need not be solved by creating intergenerational or transboundary water inequities or vice versa. It is politics and policy instruments, not physical imperatives, that create a stark trade-off between environmental health and ecological sustainability. Moreover, for most cities it is relatively clear whether environmental health or ecological sustainability ought to be the more pressing concern.

Sanitation

Proponents of the green and brown agendas can also point to problems in provision for sanitation, although, as in water supplies, they emphasize different problems. Here the conventional approach has been to promote water-borne sanitation systems, or steps in that direction, with the ultimate aim of providing all households with a flush toilet connected to a sewer. Again, households obtaining connections receive considerable benefits, often at subsidized prices. But in most urban centres, sewerage systems are characterized by significant inequities, relevant to both the brown and green agendas.

There are some cities in Latin America, Asia and parts of Africa where most of the population is adequately served by sewers. These are also generally the cities with low infant mortality rates and high life expectancies. However, the (generally) high unit costs of such systems also means that these cities are in the minority and very few cities have sewerage systems that serve most of their residents. In many cities, sewers only serve a small proportion of the population (generally those in the more centrally located and wealthier areas). Most small urban centres have no sewer system at all. Estimates suggest that close to one-half the urban population of Africa, Asia and Latin America lack adequate provision for sanitation. Tens of millions of urban dwellers have no access to any form of sanitation or have only such poor quality, overcrowded public facilities that they have to resort to defecation in the open.[4]

Proponents of the green agenda point to the environmental costs that conventional sewer systems can bring, especially the large volumes of water used to flush toilets and the problem of disposing of large volumes of sewage. In Latin America, Asia and Africa only a small proportion of sewage is treated before disposal (WHO/UNICEF, 1993; WHO, 1996; Bartone et al, 1994). Untreated sewage is a major contributor to highly polluted water bodies in most cities, although it is generally difficult to determine its contribution relative to that of untreated industrial wastes and storm and surface run-off. Fisheries are often damaged or destroyed by liquid effluents arising from cities. Thousands of people may lose their livelihood as a result as some of the largest cities are close to some of the world's most productive fishing grounds.[5] Sewage systems also require large volumes of water to function and, as such, help to build into city sanitation systems high water demands. And although there are many examples of cities where some of the sewage is used for crop or fish production, the proportion of sewage used in such a way is limited by the sheer volume of such wastes and the difficulties (and costs) of transporting them to areas where they can be used productively. Proponents of the green agenda often point to alternative sanitation systems that do not require sewers. These include many that bring ecological advantages such as requiring no water at all and some that are designed to allow the conversion of human wastes into safe fertilizers, allowing the recycling of nutrients in the food system. These limit water demand and remove the problem of sewage disposal. Simple sewerless sanitation systems are also generally much cheaper than sewered systems, especially when account is taken of the cost of sewage treatment.

But here there is a serious potential conflict between the brown and the green agenda. Proponents of the brown agenda can point to the hundreds of millions of urban dwellers who currently rely on sanitation systems that do not use water – for instance, pit latrines – which bring serious health risks and often contaminate groundwater. They often contaminate piped water supplies too, as inadequate maintenance of the piped water network means many cracks and leaks and water pressure is not constant (many city water supply systems have irregular supplies, with water available in many districts for only a few hours a day), so sewage seeps into the pipes. Pit latrines can be particularly hazardous in areas that regularly face floods as the pits become flooded and spread human excreta everywhere. There is also the problem in many cities of the lack of services to empty them (or the high price that has to be paid for doing so – see, for instance, Muller,

1997), while space constraints inhibit provision for solutions which limit this problem – for instance, twin vault systems or larger pits. There is also the question of cost; in many cities, even a good quality pit latrine within their home (or plot) is an unattainable luxury for many low income households. This includes the large proportion of low income groups who rent accommodation and for whom there is no rented accommodation that they can afford with adequate provision for sanitation. A stress on sewerless latrines may mean that the importance of adequate water supplies are forgotten (the latrines may need no water, but the households who use them certainly do, including the water needed for washing and personal hygiene). A stress on dry latrines may also mean that the problem of removing waste water is forgotten; one of the key advantages of a sewer system is that it also conveniently and hygienically removes waste water other than sewerage after its use for cooking, laundry or washing. Brown agenda proponents can also point to instances where the unit cost of installing sewers was brought down to the point where they were no longer far beyond the price that low income households could pay (Orangi, 1995) and to community level sewer systems that do not require high levels of water use and with local treatment which greatly reduces the ecological impact of the effluents on water bodies (see, for instance, Gaye and Diallo, 1997; Schusterman and Hardoy, 1997). In assuming that all waterborne sanitation systems have unacceptable ecological impacts, there is a danger of promoting 'alternative sanitation systems' that bring inconvenience, higher maintenance costs and greater environmental risks to the users, or of simply producing latrines that the population do not use.

In short, an excessive reliance on conventional water-borne sewerage intensifies the discrepancies between the brown and green agenda: as a tool of urban environmental management it can reduce intragenerational inequities, but typically at the cost of transboundary and intergenerational inequities. Undoubtedly there are many instances where extending water-borne sewerage systems is justified, especially in high-density residential areas. There are also the measures that can be taken to reduce greatly the ecological disadvantages of such systems, as noted above. However, proponents of both the brown and the green agendas can take issue with measures that subsidize sewerage systems for relatively affluent urban dwellers, diverting public funds from low income dwellers and imposing environmental costs on those living downstream and even future generations.

Other Urban Environmental Issues

In most other areas of urban environmental management, it is possible to identify conflicts between brown and green priorities. As with water and sanitation, the extent of the conflict depends as much on the socio-economic context and the policy instruments applied as on any underlying physical trade-offs.

For the solid wastes that households generate, a priority to improving environmental health includes ensuring a regular and efficient collection of such wastes. In most urban centres, 30 to 50 per cent of the solid wastes generated are not collected, although this percentage is over 90 per cent for some urban centres (Grieg-Gran, 1998; Cointreau, 1982). Many households who in theory are served by garbage collection systems in practice have no more than a communal skip or collection point at some distance from their home with unreliable and irregular collection. Uncollected wastes bring serious environmental health problems as wastes accumulate on open spaces, wasteland and streets. These include the smells, the disease vectors and pests attracted by garbage (rats, mosquitoes, flies, etc) and the overflowing drainage channels clogged with garbage (Cointreau, 1982; Hardoy et al, 1992). Leachate from decomposing and putrefying garbage can contaminate water sources (ibid; UNCHS, 1988). In urban districts with the least adequate provision for sanitation, the uncollected solid wastes usually include a significant proportion of faecal matter.

But from an ecological perspective, the critical concerns are the promotion of waste reduction or waste reuse or recycling and addressing the environmental impacts of waste dumps. Most solid wastes that are collected are deposited in open dumps, many of them unauthorized. Even for those that are authorized, rarely is there careful environmental management (as in a well-managed sanitary landfill site). This gives rise to many environmental problems, including the contamination of ground and surface water, methane generation and air pollution from uncontrolled burning.

Crude measures to reduce the ecological burden of waste can create an environmental health burden and vice versa. Moreover, policies appropriate to one city may be entirely inappropriate to another. In affluent cities, for example, higher waste-disposal fees are often an effective means of reducing waste generation and have no adverse environmental health impacts. In a low income city where environmental controls are lax and large sections of the population have inadequate incomes, these same waste-disposal fees are likely to encourage the illicit dumping, burying and burning of waste in residential neighbourhoods, creating environmental health problems without reducing ecological burdens.

Even air pollution priorities vary from brown and green perspectives, and between cities. Some of the worst environmental health problems are related to the residential use of smoky but potentially renewable fuels such as fuelwood and charcoal. Green agenda proponents may object to the transition to cleaner fuels because they increase fossil fuel use, but this can bring major health benefits, especially to those who spend most time in the smoky environments, typically women and girls cooking and undertaking other household tasks (WHO, 1992). Some measures to reduce air pollution exposure, such as chimneys for households using smoky fuels can reduce indoor air pollution but increase outdoor air pollution. Higher chimneys for industrial polluters can reduce air pollution within the city but create transboundary environmental burdens even as they improve local environmental health. Alternatively, some measures to reduce greenhouse gas emission, acid precipitation and other ecological damage can exacerbate local environmental health problems. This even applies to interventions in low income neighbourhoods where, for example, efforts to improve the efficiency of biofuel stoves are likely to increase the emissions of health-threatening pollutants. All measures that seek to reduce air pollution or, more generally, greenhouse gas emissions, need to be assessed for their effects on intragenerational as well as intergenerational equity. For instance, recent measures in Mexico City to allow the newest automobiles that match higher standards in terms of polluting emissions to be exempt from restrictions on their use obviously advantage higher income groups and disadvantage those who are unable to afford such automobiles (Connolly, 1999).

One final example of potential conflict between brown and green agendas is over land use management. Proponents of the green agenda rightly point to the way in which most growing urban centres encroach on high-quality agricultural land and damage or disrupt rural ecosystems. Peri-urban forests, wetlands and other ecologically important sites are often lost to urban developments or recreational facilities serving (generally high income) urban dwellers, such as golf courses. Other urban demands can also mean the loss of land with valuable ecological functions – for instance, from the demand for building materials, fuelwood and landfill.

While proponents of the brown agenda share a concern for the impacts of such developments, they will highlight the extent to which low income households need cheap, well-located land to allow them to develop better quality homes. Or, from a citywide perspective, the extent to which increasing the supply and keeping down the cost of well-located land for housing helps to improve housing conditions, and provides many lower income households with more secure and better serviced alternatives to illegal subdivisions or illegal land occupation. Allocating large areas of land around a city to parks or ecological 'belts' can restrict the supply and increase the cost of land for housing (Bartone et al, 1994) and undermine the livelihoods of those who depend on agricultural or forest lands for their livelihoods (see, for instance, Kelly, 1998 and Douglass, 1989). Middle and upper income groups often claim to be promoting the green agenda to defend the maintenance of large 'green areas' in or around their homes when their real priorities are maintaining their privileged access to open space and ensuring that no lower income residential developments take place in their vicinity.

DRAWING TOGETHER THE BROWN AND GREEN AGENDAS

The discussions above concentrate on potential disagreements between proponents of the brown and the green agendas. But there are also many areas where there is more agreement and where both brown and green agenda proponents work together – for instance, in the movement against what is generally termed 'environmental racism' (the location of the more dangerous or unsightly factories and waste management facilities in low income areas) and in the campaigns by citizens, community organizations and NGOs against industrial pollution and its effects – for instance, the destruction or damage of local fisheries – or, more generally, against air pollution.

Reconciling the brown and green agendas means recognizing that different cities and even different neighbourhoods within cities should have different priorities. For example, the environmental agenda of affluent cities, where everyone has water piped into their home, good sanitation, door-to-door waste collection and clean fuels is clearly not the same as that of a city where a sizeable share of the population lacks these basic services.

In any given city, however, the overlap between brown and green concerns is likely to be substantial. For instance, a brown agenda concern for the needs of low income groups for health, air quality and good public transport can overlap with a green agenda concern to reduce fossil fuel use (and thus also greenhouse gas emissions) and the air pollution that can contribute to ecological damage 'downwind' of the city – for instance, through acid precipitation or ozone plumes. Both concerns are likely to be served by high-quality public transport, good traffic management (including appropriate provision for pedestrians and cyclists), land use management that encourages public-transport oriented city expansion, and controls or financial disincentives on excessive private automobile use.

Similarly, a recognition of the importance of urban agriculture for the livelihoods of significant sections of the low income populations in many urban centres can combine a brown agenda perspective through supporting low income groups' access to land with green agenda perspectives regarding the ecological advantages of increased local production (Smit et al, 1996). A commitment to improved solid waste collection and management can combine green and brown perspectives – for instance, in waste management systems supporting waste reduction and the reclamation and reuse or recycling of materials from waste streams which also generate many jobs. Improved provision for water supply and sanitation, which is so central to the brown agenda, can be done within a framework that recognizes green concerns – for instance, through water tariffs that ensure the price per litre rises with per-capita consumption,[6] or community sewer systems that reduce the volume of water needed and have local treatment systems allowing the nutrients in the waste waters to be used for fish farming or crops (see, for instance, Gaye and Diallo, 1997; also Smit et al, 1996).

There are also many complementarities that tend to be overlooked. For example, hygiene education is central to improved environmental health, and demand management is central to water conservation, but there have been few, if any, attempts to combine hygiene education with improved demand management. There is a serious danger that one agenda will come to be manipulated in the interests of the other: that an ostensible concern for health will mask a drive for conservation or vice versa. But both health and, in the long run, water resources, would benefit if people knew how to use water more effectively to protect themselves from disease. The tools of demand management could easily be adapted to serve both ends, as described in the following section. This serves as one example of a tool that can promote greater complementarity between green and brown agendas. After this section, some of the broader institutional issues about how to reconcile the two agendas are discussed.

The Example of Demand Management

In essence, demand management advocates a shift away from the 'supply-fix' approach to water, energy and urban infrastructure provision generally. Instead, attention is paid to 'providing the same services with less' by enabling improvements on the demand side – traditionally considered beyond the purview of the institutions that provide infrastructure and services. In many instances it has proved less expensive for utilities to promote energy and water conservation (through, for example, more efficient lighting, low flush toilets or time-of-day metering) than to engage in costly supply expansion. Moreover, the environmental benefits can be considerable.

The almost exclusive focus on resource conservation is inappropriate in many southern cities where environmental health issues are more pressing. Indeed, there is a serious danger that resource-oriented demand management will leave many environmentally deprived urban households even worse off than with the conventional supply-fix approach. But many of the same insights apply to situations where the priority problems involve environmental health. Here too there is a bias towards 'supply fix' – put in more pipes and fill them with water; extend the electricity grid in the hope that people will switch from smoky fuels, etc.

Water demand management need not focus only on conservation. It is also a problem for health that water utilities stop being concerned once the water has left the pipes (at least until it becomes a drainage problem). They do not pay sufficient attention to how the water is used; how the quality of water declines between tap and the mouth (especially where water has to be collected from communal taps and stored within households); how an understanding of the demand side could increase access for the groups that need water most, and so on. Hygiene education is, in effect, a form of demand management and many argue that it should accompany supply provision. So is finding connection arrangements that low income groups can afford – for example, shifting the often high cost of connection to a piped water supply or sewers on to a monthly bill, providing cheap bulk supplies to a neighbourhood for a single payment with the inhabitants organizing the collection of individual household payments, negotiating with resident groups to find the best means of providing water, helping to develop in-house storage systems that will not allow dengue-bearing mosquitoes to breed there or the water to become faecally contaminated.

In the energy sector too, demand management need not be restricted to conservation. It could include offering consumers (or settlements) a wider range of demand-side electricity options, including, for example, pre-payment meters, boards containing the circuitry for households for whom house wiring would be prohibitive, or the possibility of paying capital costs (potentially for electric stoves) through the electricity charges. To the extent that urban consumers switch from smoky fuels, environmental health should be improved and, depending on the local energy system, the broader environmental impacts as well.

In relation to solid waste, comparable possibilities range from improved storage systems, both for households and communities, to systems to promote recycling. Again, some of these measures could improve health by reducing pollution from waste burning, reducing pest infestation, and reducing the mixing of recyclable waste and faecal material. In this case, it is generation rather than demand that is being managed, but many of the principles remain the same.

WHAT BROADER INSTITUTIONAL PROCESSES HELP TO RECONCILE BROWN AND GREEN AGENDAS?

Reconciling the brown and green agendas in urban development requires institutions and processes that:

- reduce the inequities that are of concern to both the brown and green agendas;
- enable collective and democratic responses to the public aspects of both brown and green environmental problems; and
- provide a better understanding of the environmental issues that different cities face.

There are at least three important areas where action is needed.

The first is open and participatory processes within each city that allow environmental problems to be discussed and agreements reached over priorities for action and investment. It is worth noting how green and brown agenda components have been integrated in various cities. These include the environmental action plans modelled on Local Agenda 21s (as recommended by the UN Earth Summit in 1992) developed in cities such as Manizales in Colombia (Vélasquez, 1998) and Ilo (Díaz et al, 1996; López Follegatti, 1999) and Chimbote in Peru (Foronda, 1998). These Local Agenda 21s were developed by a variety of groups, including community organizations, environmental NGOs, local academics and government agencies – and, in the case of Manizales and Ilo, with strong support from municipal government. Pôrto Alegre in Brazil, which is well known for its successful 'brown agenda' and its pioneering role in developing more transparent and participatory government structures, also has a strong green component to its environmental policy.[7] All of these examples happened within countries with democratic local governments and with decentralization programmes that had allowed city authorities more scope for environmental investment and management. In effect, the governance systems allowed citizens and their community organizations and NGOs to have more influence on development plans and investment priorities, and this increased the incorporation of green and brown agenda priorities. Most of the innovations also took place soon after the decentralization and the democratic reforms, and they need to be understood within the context of these broader national-level reforms (see Vélasquez, 1998; also Miranda and Hordijk, 1998; Foronda, 1998).[7]

This highlights the second area where action is needed – national policies that encourage and support urban development that takes account of ecological sustainability but within an understanding of potential conflicts with brown agenda priorities and other social and economic priorities. This is, in effect, the legislative, fiscal and managerial framework that allows 'good' city and municipal governance that in turn includes green and brown agenda priorities. For green agenda issues to be included within urban development, this will need national governments to support and then respect the appropriate international agreements that seek to protect sites of particular ecological importance, and limit the generation of greenhouse gas emissions and stratospheric ozone-depleting chemicals or limit the generation of toxic or otherwise hazardous wastes (or their inappropriate disposal). Elected city governments are accountable to the populations living within their boundaries, not to those living in distant ecosystems on whose productivity the city producers or consumers may draw. It is also difficult to ensure that the needs and rights of future generations and of other species receive adequate attention in urban policy and practice without the appropriate framework and support from higher levels of government. For instance, it is difficult for local authorities to include systematically a concern for protecting biodiversity or for keeping down greenhouse gas emissions without a clear national policy. Although there are examples of cities whose Local Agenda 21 or other environmental action plans have included components to reduce the transfer of environmental costs outside city boundaries or into the future, the scope for such action will be limited by the need for all cities to be competitive in attracting new investments. For instance, no city can promote large reductions in greenhouse gas emissions if this encourages many enterprises to move to another city where no such measures are taken. Without supportive national policies and international agreements, it is difficult to realize fully the potential that cities have for combining safe and healthy living environments with resource conservation and waste reduction.

The third area where action is needed is a stronger basis for mutual understanding between the brown and green agenda proponents and this depends on a good knowledge of the environmental issues within and around each urban centre. Developing 'state of the environment' reports that draw on the knowledge and resources of citizen groups, NGOs, private business and local educational institutions are often valuable underpinnings for this. Involving all such groups in developing such reports can also be a valuable way of allowing each group to understand better the priorities of other groups. It is also worth noting the strong commitment by the different groups developing the Local Agenda 21 within Manizales and the municipal government in Pôrto Alegre to environmental education as a key part of their environmental policies. A well-informed public debate about environmental priorities backed up with good documentation of local and regional ecology also provides the best defence against the misuse of brown or green agenda arguments by powerful commercial, industrial and real-estate concerns. New developments that primarily benefit middle and upper income groups or major industrial or commercial concerns often use 'green' or 'brown' agenda arguments to justify public support and even subsidy.

The cities and regions that are pioneering more ecologically sound, pro-poor and democratic development models deserve international as well as local attention. Historically, the most successful urban environmental initiatives, from sanitary reform to cleaner technology, have drawn on international experience and support. The inequities underlying both the green and brown agendas have international dimensions. Allowing international priorities to dominate local environmental initiatives would further reinforce some of these inequities. But better rather than less international engagement can help to encourage innovative solutions.

NOTES

1   Gordon McGranahan and David Satterthwaite are with the Human Settlements Programme at the International Institute for Environment and Development (IIED). The authors are grateful to Cedric Pugh for his comments on an earlier draft.
2   There are also two other areas of disagreement that are beyond the scope of this chapter that have been discussed elsewhere. The first is the disagreement over the extent to which the concept of sustainability can be usefully taken to include non-environmental goals such as poverty alleviation – see, for instance, McGranahan et al, 1996 and Marcuse, 1998. The second, related to this, is the scale of the urban poor's contribution to environmental degradation; many green agenda authors assume that urban poverty in general or the urban poor in particular contribute much to environmental degradation. But in general, levels of consumption and waste generation among low income urban house-holds are very low so it is difficult to see how this is the case. Green agenda proponents often confuse high levels of environmental risk (which most low income groups face) with large contributions to environmental degradation (which are far more associated with higher income groups and larger industrial and commercial concerns). See, for instance, Hardoy et al, 1992b; Hartmann, 1998 and Satterthwaite, 1998.
3   Within this is an implicit assumption that an increased concentration of people in cities is necessarily bad environmentally. However, this assumption has been shown to be invalid in many instances, especially in well-managed compact cities with good quality public transport – see, for instance, UNCHS, 1996.
4   Discussions with municipal employees and NGOs in many cities have pointed to the large number of people who have to defecate in the open or in bags that are then disposed of in garbage, open sites or ditches because they have no toilet facilities or else communal or public

provision is so inadequate that they often cannot get access to them. But there is not much detailed documentation of this. For some documented examples, see CSE, 1982; Robotham, 1996 and Hardoy et al, 1992a.

5   See Hardoy et al, 1992a, op cit, for summaries of many case studies of this.

6   This can create serious problems for households that rely on communal taps as they are charged higher rates per litre of water than those with individual household connections.

7   For details of the participatory budgeting, see Abers, 1998. The commitment to green issues can be seen in the major investment programme in ecological tourism and sewage treatment, and the extensive programme of environmental education that includes the production and dissemination within schools of a very detailed environmental atlas of the city and its surrounds (Menegat, 1998).

8   Obviously, not all urban environmental innovation happens in democratic societies, as can be seen in the fact that much of the environmental innovation in Curitiba (Brazil) preceded the return to democracy in Brazil. The brown agenda is likely to be more strongly associated with local democracy than the green agenda, especially where the green agenda serves the interests of higher income or otherwise politically powerful groups. In addition, the low-consumption and waste-generation levels of most low income urban dwellers also serves to keep down the ecological impact of the urban centres in which they live, which means that care is needed to avoid potential conflicts between reducing consumption as part of the green agenda and the increased consumption implied by poverty reduction. But as various examples given in this chapter suggest, there is rarely much conflict between consumption levels that meet health needs and ecological sustainability.

REFERENCES

Abers, Rebecca (1998) 'Learning democratic practice: distributing government resources through popular participation in Porto Alegre, Brazil', in Mike Douglass and John Friedmann (eds) *Cities for Citizens*, John Wiley & Sons, West Sussex, pp39–65

Bartone, Carl, Bernstein, Janis, Leitmann, Josef and Eigen, Jochen (1994) *Towards Environmental Strategies for Cities: Policy Considerations for Urban Environmental Management in Developing Countries*, UNDP, UNCHS and World Bank Urban Management Program No18, World Bank, Washington, DC

Bradley, David, Stephens, Carolyn, Cairncross, Sandy and Harpham, Trudy (1991) *A Review of Environmental Health Impacts in Developing Country Cities*, Urban Management Program Discussion Paper No 6, The World Bank, UNDP and UNCHS (Habitat), Washington, DC

Cointreau, Sandra (1982), *Environmental Management of Urban Solid Waste in Developing Countries*, Urban Development Technical Paper No 5, The World Bank, Washington, DC

Connolly, Priscilla (1999), 'Mexico City: our common future?', *Environment and Urbanization*, vol 11, no 1, April, pp53–78

CSE (1982) *The State of India's Environment 1982: A Citizen's Report*, Centre for Science and Environment, Delhi

Damián, Araceli (1992) 'Ciudad de México: servicios urbanos en los noventas', *Vivienda*, vol 3, no 1, January–April , pp29–40

Díaz, Doris Balvín, Follegatti, José Luis López and Hordijk, Micky (1996) 'Innovative urban environmental management in Ilo, Peru', *Environment and Urbanization*, vol 8, no 1, April, pp21–34

Douglass, Mike (1989) 'The environmental sustainability of development – coordination, incentives and political will in land use planning for the Jakarta metropolis', *Third World Planning Review*, vol 11, no 2, May, pp211–38

Forondo, Maria Elena F (1998) 'Chimbote's Agenda 21: supporting its development and implementation', *Environment and Urbanization*, vol 10, no 2, pp129-47

Gaye, Malick and Diallo, Fodé (1997) 'Community participation in the management of the urban environment in Rufisque (Senegal)', *Environment and Urbanization*, vol 9, no 1, April, pp9–29

Grieg-Gran, Maryanne (1998) *The Waste Hierarchy: Recycling and Solid Waste Management in Developing Countries*, prepared for DFID, IIED, London

Hardoy, Jorge E, Mitlin, Diana and Satterthwaite, David (1992a) *Environmental Problems in Third World Cities*, Earthscan, London

Hardoy, Jorge E, Mitlin, Diana and Satterthwaite, David (1992b) 'The future city', in Johan Holmberg (ed), *Policies for a Small Planet*, Earthscan, London, pp124–56

Hartmann, Betsy (1998) 'Population, environment and security: a new trinity', *Environment and Urbanization*, vol 10, no 2, pp113–27

Haughton, Graham (1999) 'Environmental justice and the sustainable city', *Journal of Planning Education and Research*, vol 18, no 3, pp233–43

Jacobi, Pedro R (1994) 'Households and environment in the city of São Paulo; problems, perceptions and solutions', *Environment and Urbanization*, vol 6, no 2, April, pp87–110

Kelly, Philip F (1998) 'The politics of urban-rural relationships: land conversion in the Philippines', *Environment and Urbanization*, vol 10, no 1, pp35–54

Leitmann, Josef (1994) 'The World Bank and the brown agenda: evolution of a revolution', *Third World Planning Review*, vol 16, no 2, pp117–27

López Follegatti, José Luis (1999) 'Ilo: a city in transformation', *Environment and Urbanization*, vol 11, no 2, pp181–202

Marcuse, Peter (1998) 'Sustainability is not enough', *Environment and Urbanization*, vol 10, no 2, October, pp103–11

McGranahan, Gordon (1991), *Environmental Problems and the Urban Household in Third World Countries*, The Stockholm Environment Institute, Stockholm

McGranahan, Gordon, Songsore, Jacob and Kjellén, Marianne (1996) 'Sustainability, poverty and urban environmental transitions', in Cedric Pugh (ed) *Sustainability, the Environment and Urbanization*, Earthscan, London, pp103–34.

Menegat, Rualdo (main coordinator) (1998) *Atlas Ambiental de Pôrto Alegre*, Universidade Federal do Rio Grande do Sul, Prefeitura Municipal de Porto Alegre and Instituto Nacional de Pesquisas Espaciais, Pôrto Alegre

Miranda, Liliana and Hordijk, Michaela (1998) 'Let us build cities for life: the National Campaign of Local Agenda 21s in Peru', *Environment and Urbanization*, vol 10, no 2, October, pp69–102

Mueller, Charles C (1995) 'Environmental problems inherent to a development style: degradation and poverty in Brazil', *Environment and Urbanization*, vol 7, no 2, October, pp67–84

Muller, Maria S (ed) (1997) *The Collection of Household Excreta: The Operation of Services in Urban Low-income Neighbourhoods*, WASTE and ENSIC, Gouda

Orangi Pilot Project (1995) 'NGO Profile: Orangi Pilot Project', *Environment and Urbanization*, vol 7, no 2, October, pp227–36

Postel, Sandra (1992) *The Last Oasis: Facing Water Scarcity*, Worldwatch Environmental Alert Series, Earthscan, London

Robotham, Don (1994) 'Redefining urban health policy in a developing country: the Jamaica case', in S Atkinson, J Songsore and W Werna (eds) *Urban Health Research in Developing Countries: Implications for Policy*, CAB International, Wallingford, pp31–42

Satterthwaite, David (1995), 'The underestimation of poverty and its health consequences', *Third World Planning Review*, vol 17, no 4, November, ppiii–xii

Satterthwaite, David (1998) 'Cities and Sustainable Development: What Progress Since Our Common Future?', in Softing, Guri Bang, George Benneh, Kjetil Hindar, Larse Walloe and Anders Wijkman, *The Brundtland Commission's Report – 10 years*, Scandinavian University Press, Oslo, pp27–39

Schusterman, Ricardo and Hardoy, Ana (1997) 'Reconstructing social capital in a poor urban settlement: the Integrated Improvement Programme, Barrio San Jorge', *Environment and Urbanization*, vol 9, no 1, April, pp91–119

Smit, Jac, Ratta, Anna and Nasr, Joe (1996) *Urban Agriculture: Food, Jobs and Sustainable Cities*, Publication Series for Habitat II, vol 1, UNDP, New York

United Nations Centre for Human Settlements (UNCHS) (1988) *Refuse Collection Vehicles for Developing Countries*, HS/138/88E, UNCHS (Habitat), Nairobi, Kenya

United Nations Centre for Human Settlements (UNCHS) (1996), *An Urbanizing World: Global Report on Human Settlements, 1996*, Oxford University Press, Oxford and New York

Vélasquez, Luz Stella (1998) 'Agenda 21; a form of joint environmental management in Manizales, Colombia', *Environment and Urbanization*, vol 10, no 2, pp9–36

World Health Organization/United Nations International Children's Emergency Fund (WHO/UNICEF) (1993) *Water Supply and Sanitation Sector Monitoring Report 1993*, WHO/UNICEF Joint Monitoring Programme, Geneva

World Health Organization (WHO) (1992) *Our Planet, Our Health*, Report of the WHO Commission on Health and Environment, WHO, Geneva

World Health Organization (WHO) (1996), *Creating Healthy Cities in the 21st Century*, Background Paper prepared for the Dialogue on Health in Human Settlements for Habitat II World Health Organization, Geneva, reprinted in Satterthwaite, David (ed) (1999) *Sustainable Cities: A Reader*, Earthscan, London, pp137–72

5 INEQUALITIES IN URBAN ENVIRONMENTS, HEALTH AND POWER: REFLECTIONS ON THEORY AND PRACTICE

Carolyn Stephens

INTRODUCTION

Nuestras vidas son los rios que van a dar en la mar, qu'es el morir: alli van los señorios derechos a se acabar y consumir; alli los rios caudales, alli los otros, medianos y más chicos, allegados son yguales, los viuen por sus manos e los ricos . . . Este mundo bueno fuë si bien vsisemos del como deuemos . . .[1]

Jorge Manrique (1460), Coplas por la muerte de su padre

Aristotle once pointed out that 'when some people have a large amount and some people have nothing, the result will be either extreme democracy, or an unmitigated oligarchy, or despotism will come from either of these two excesses' (Aristotle, 335BC). Many centuries later, in 1460, Jorge Manrique wrote one of Spain's most well-known and beautiful poems which described the relationship of wealth, poverty, power and ethics through the examination of death.

Both men believed that over-concentration of wealth brought earthly riches to a few, but gave them only specious gains in terms of current or future well-being. Such views are echoed by those today who advocate the reduction of over-consumption and materialism in the wealthy and the pursuit of 'sustainable' lifestyles and policies (for example, LaTouche, 1993). Also, like many other writers in periods with strong value systems, Aristotle and Manrique pointed out the futility of the process of exploiting others for personal gain. At the end of the 20th century, we have moved through a period where personal gain is rarely judged for its unfair impact on others – at least in the sense that we move through a period where such gain is not often curtailed through policy.

This chapter starts, then, with a philosopher and a poet – both from distant European history – to discuss the issues of inequalities in the environment, health and power at the end of the 20th century, in a book focused on urban sustainability. Why? This chapter draws on the distant past of the so-called developed world to reflect on the lessons that history could teach us if we were not living in such a profoundly arrogant and ahistorical time. This chapter also reflects on the need for those with education and influence to use all disciplines and forms of knowledge to create a future in which equitable urban sustainable development is an achievable reality, not just an idealistic vision – as both Manrique and Aristotle argued. History should not teach us to accept that inequality is perennial. History should be used to show the ways to avoid going in circles of inevitability. Disciplines should not struggle independently to achieve sustainability. Disciplines should unite and collaborate in the pursuit of sustainability.

This chapter aims to make four points, each related to inequality and health. First, there will be a discussion of the international policy context in which this book is written – one of extreme resource and power inequality with concurrent health and social impacts that are concentrated increasingly in urban areas. Second, the development of the theories of sustainability and globalization and their links to inequality will be discussed. Third, the ways forward towards equity, including the need for the development of more ethical professional behaviour by those with education and positions of influence and power will be described. Finally, the opportunities for more involvement in the policy processes of those without power or influence – those who bear the brunt of health and environment inequalities – will be reviewed. Throughout, a discussion of policy processes will be the main priority.

THE CONTEXT – UNEQUAL, UNHEALTHY AND URBAN

There is clear evidence that this chapter is written during a period when the world is, as Aristotle defined it, in a state of 'oligarchy'. It is an oligarchy in which the poor and unhealthy majority, increasingly concentrated in the urban areas of the world, exist in a context of powerlessness over their lives, their opportunities and their deaths (UNCHS, 1996). Evidence shows that the powerful in the world live in the Northern countries, with no less power over the lives of the powerless in the South than during the periods of overt colonial control in the last centuries (Post and Wright, 1989; UNDP, 1999). Even the actual depiction of the lives of the poor majority is in the hands of 'others', others with influence over the very conceptualization of the problems of disempowerment and lack of opportunity, and yet often with no understanding of the experience of poverty (Chambers, 1995; Wratten, 1995).

The Unequal Future

More acutely, this chapter is written at a time when the world is not only in the hands of the wealthy countries, it in the hands of a tiny minority of wealthy people in all countries, most of whom control power from the world's major urban financial centres (Castells, 1997; Cohen, 1998a; Krugman, 1999). Thus, the United Nations Development Programme (UNDP) reports that the value of the combined assets of the 200 richest persons in the world now exceeds the combined incomes of 41 per cent of the world's population. Figure 5.1, using data drawn from the UNDP, shows that the wealthiest 20 per cent of the world's population have now increased their ratio of wealth to 74:1. The future, in this context, is one of inequality.

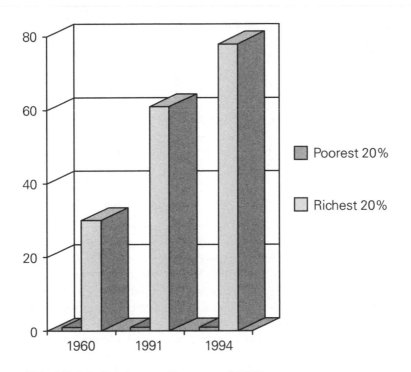

Source: United Nations Development Programme (UNDP)

Figure 5.1 *The Unequal Future*

Does inequality matter? It is argued that some increases in inequality can correlate with declines in levels of some types of poverty. The share of the poorest 20 per cent of the world's people in global income is 1.1 per cent, down from 1.4 per cent in 1991 and 2.3 per cent in 1960 (UNDP, 1999). Therefore, income poverty cannot be on the decline. This begs the question of definitions – of poverty, inequality and wealth, for example. Other papers have tackled these issues, particularly for urban areas, some in terms of health (see Wratten, 1995; Chambers, 1995; Stephens, 1996; UNCHS, 1996). Most definitions, including those in urban areas, still grapple weakly with the relationship of poverty to wealth and inequality – traditional definitions of poverty relate typically to the identification of the measurables of 'absolute' poverty, the basic means to survival (Stephens, 1996; Wratten, 1995). Thus, we can identify physical 'poverties' that affect health and survival directly, such as food poverty, water poverty, housing or shelter poverty (which could include parameters of space, crowding, design and facilities such as sanitation), or transport poverty. Furthermore, other parameters of poverty affect health indirectly: thus, it is the poverty of 'opportunity' that underpins access to the physical means to survival. For example, income poverty often predicts the lack of the physical means to survive. Income poverty then stems from opportunities in education and occupation. Education and employment opportunities form the more profound forms of poverty that determine current and intergenerational traps for the 'poor'.

Fundamentally it is argued that all these forms of measurable material poverty can be linked to 'poverty' in terms of access to information and decision-making. The poor often cannot use information or affect the decisions that determine their access to any facility or opportunity. Terms such as 'vulnerability' attempt to capture all facets of poverty, including the ability of people to influence decisions over them (see Wratten, 1995; Chambers, 1995). Vulnerability lies in the poverty of power.

The Urban Future

There is also clear evidence that this unequal, vulnerable future is increasingly urban. A key aspect of the international policy context is that of population movements and macro-economic policy shifts (UNCHS, 1996; Cohen, 1998a). Movements into urban areas are a major part of the equation. The urban movement has taken place in the context of the gross polarization in wealth and assets between the rich and the poor people introduced above.

Inequality, poverty and urbanization are closely linked. By the year 2025, three out of five people will live in urban areas, the majority in Southern 'developing' countries where 40–70 per cent of the population will live in low income settlements (UNCHS, 1996). Figure 5.2 shows the distribution of urban peoples in the world, demonstrating that the highest proportion of urban people will be in the poorest regions in the world. It has been argued that poverty – and vulnerability – has also become an increasingly urban phenomenon (UNCHS, 1996). Furthermore, the rural poor rely increasingly on urban opportunities for their current and future needs.

The Unhealthy Future

The latest UNDP report repeats once more the statistics of health inequality (UNDP, 1999). In fact, the report documents increases in inequalities. There

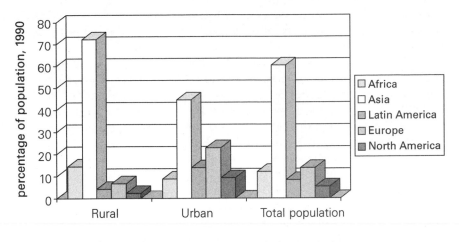

Source: United Nations Centre for Human Settlements (UNCHS), 1996

Figure 5.2 *Our Urban Future*

have been gains in life expectancy for all. Yet, despite our scientific knowledge of what is needed to give sustained health improvements to the majority, the UNDP reports again that in gross terms, the peoples of the most powerful countries of the world experience the best quality of life, measured in terms of health, basic environmental standards and opportunity (UNDP, 1999). Thus, North America and Europe rank highest and the African and Asian states are lowest in quality of life terms.

Furthermore, there is considerable evidence that the most powerful people in each nation experience the best social, environmental and health conditions (Wilkinson, 1997). Teased apart further to look at the urban context, evidence shows that the most powerful in each city also experience life favourably compared to the less powerful (Stephens et al, 1994; Stephens, 1996; Benneh et al, 1993; Jacobi, 1994).

Common understanding has been that urbanization would bring the same long-term health gains to the South as the cities of Europe seemed to deliver. In other words, it is thought that perhaps there is an inevitable 'satanic mills' or dirty phase of urban development, which once over delivers economic prosperity and health (Smith and Lee, 1993). But evidence implies that it has been a fallacy to think that the process of urbanization in the developing world would bring long-term health and wealth to the majority (Satterthwaite et al, 1990; Stephens et al, 1996). As Cohen has pointed out recently, macro-economic shifts have been instrumental in population movements towards towns and cities, but they have not been shifts towards healthy lives for the majority: 'the metropolitan areas of the world are, above all, marked by their differences; differences in access by individuals, households and communities to services, resources, opportunities, and most of all, quality of life' (Cohen, 1998c). In fact, urbanization has brought more clear evidence of health inequalities between peoples, masked before as an issue of urban/rural power, but now revealed to be an issue of power between wealth and poverty within cities, within nations and between nations.

There are two points to be made here: evidence now shows inequalities in health from cities as diverse as London, Washington, Accra, Cotonou, Cape Town, São Paulo and Belo Horizonte (Stephens et al, 1996; UNCHS, 1996). It was clear decades ago that the urban poor in the South were not benefiting from urban development in terms of health. However, it was not until the 1980s that the health of the urban poor began to be documented in contrast to the health of the urban wealthy in developing country settings (for example, Stephens et al, 1994; Benneh, 1993). Furthermore, history shows the necessity of unpicking even the apparently simple stories of urban health. History suggests the fallacy of using 'urban' as the definition of relative health for the majority – the poor in cities have always borne ill health and the wealthy have evaded most illness, even in epidemics as far-reaching as the plague that hit London in the 17th century. As Daniel Defoe in 1645 explains:

> *It is true a vast many people fled, as I have observed, yet they were chiefly from the west end of town, and from that we call the heart of the city: that is to say, among the wealthiest of the people, and such people that were unencumbered with trades and business. But the rest, the generality stayed, and seemed to abide the worst . . .*

The people of the two wealthy cities of Washington and London should now be beyond much of the burden of those health inequalities linked to the basic access to water, food, sanitation and shelter. Yet, health inequalities persist in patterns of deaths from violence; social inequalities have impacts on health and the infectious disease profile persists among the homeless (Wilkinson et al, 1998). Evidence suggests that patterns of inequality exist in cities such as London or Washington, just as they do in São Paulo or Delhi today. In all of these contexts the wealthy and powerful can find ways to avoid poor conditions even when they create them in part themselves (see, for example, Stevenson et al, 1999, who document car ownership and pollution injustice in London). Are these health inequalities the avoidable consequences of the poverty of power, over decisions and resource allo-cation, among certain groups in otherwise wealthy cities?

In addition to this evidence, Figure 5.4 shows, perhaps, the most important issue of urban health inequality: that of the urban development paradox. This is the paradox of the so-called 'double burden' of urban health (Harpham et al, 1990). In other words, the urban poor suffer both the problems of 'under-development' (infectious diseases associated with lack of basic means)[2] and the problems of 'development' (chronic diseases associated usually with industrial development, including increased vehicle use – see, for example Smith and Lee, 1993). But what does urban develop-ment mean in these terms?

Does the double burden imply an inevitable *industrial* development in some form, or at least a *chemical* urban development with inevitably

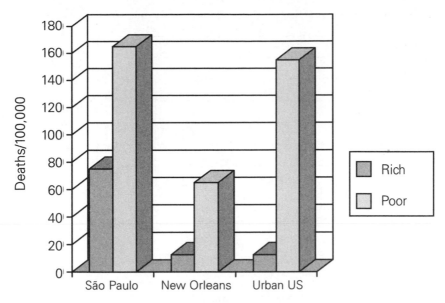

Source: São Paulo (age 15–44): Stephens et al, 1994; New Orleans (age 15+): Brandan and Caterwall, 1995; Urban US (age 15–24): Cohen and Swift, 1993

Figure 5.3a *Violence – the New Disease of Urban Poverty*

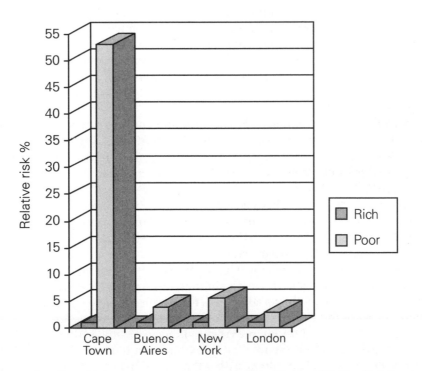

Source: Cape Town: Yack and Harrison, 1996; Buenos Aires: Bianco, 1983; New York: Drucker et al, 1994; London: Landon, 1994

Figure 5.3b *Tuberculosis – Classic Disease of Poverty Returns*

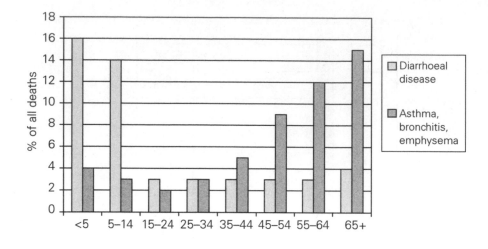

Source: CEMSAP, 1997

Figure 5.4 *Double Burdens in Calcutta*

unhealthy air, water and ambient space? Data from Calcutta shows the double burden clearly: put bluntly, even if the people of Calcutta survive the traditional diseases of urban poverty they soon feel the impacts of the diseases of an urban development characterized by 'dirty' industrialization. Deaths from conditions associated with chronic exposure to air pollution[3] occur even in under five-year-olds. They rise, as a proportion of all deaths, in adults and the elderly. Evidence of the double burden is clear for all age groups.

Calcutta is a metropolis with over 12 million people – evoked by many as an extreme example of the urban development crisis. Up to 50 per cent of Calcuttans live in extreme poverty, with a higher figure in the central municipalities of Calcutta and Howrah from where these data were drawn (CEMSAP, 1997). The people in Calcutta rely currently on 'dirty industrialisation', as do the people in many other urban centres internationally. The crux of the urban development crisis is how to move these people out of material poverty without resorting to dirty industrialization.

The reality of the urban experience as felt by many people internationally is not one of health. The reality is the experience of the urban environment as ill health, lowered abilities and sometimes death. Calcutta provides evidence of the paradox, in health terms, of dirty urban development. Washington provides evidence of the paradox of socially unequal urban development. London provides evidence of both, as do many other cities in the world. But the final paradox for Calcuttans, and many urban people in the poorest countries, is that there is evidence that even the pact of dirty industrialization will not achieve health for the majority. For the majority of urban citizens internationally there is constant tension between the benefits and disbenefits of urban living. This tension must be related to the proximity of those experiencing the disbenefits of urban living to those experiencing the benefits. The proximity is that of the urban powerless and the urban powerful.

This chapter does not simply outline the extent of inequalities in life and death experienced by the majority of urban peoples. It is a discussion of why and how unequal power influences these experiences. It attempts to argue that shifts towards increased poverty of power, in terms of information and decision making, underlies the unsustainable and poverty-laden context.

Why would poverty of power – of information and decision making – be so important, if the 'poverty' that leads to unequal life chances can be alleviated despite growing inequality in the control of information and decisions? First, Wilkinson refutes the idea that improved life chances can be bought through material wealth alone. Using data from countries that have material wealth for the majority, he argues that unequal power over decisions in people's lives affects their health directly (Wilkinson, 1997). In other words, control or power over life – at individual or group level – affects the impact of material conditions on an individual or group.

History shows that there is a deeper reasoning for the inclusion of the poverty of power in discussions of urban sustainability and health – reasoning that underpins this chapter and book – and that it is always worth defining the process of power that allows wealth as well as poverty in any period. It is helpful to look at the powerful and how they achieve health. Logically, then, and in contrast to 'vulnerability', wealth must now mean 'invulnerability'. At the very least, invulnerability must mean access to the material means for survival and, for the future, access to opportunity. Evidence now suggests that wealth in all countries means much more than basic needs achieved and opportunity fulfilled. Invulnerability must mean also the access to disproportionate and ill-used power – to accrue more than is needed (or to give away excess) and to resist changes in opportunity (or to change). It does not need a modern academic to repeat the replete historical evidence that poverty (vulnerability) has always been related to wealth (invulnerability). Yet, so many modern theorists attempt to separate 'absolute' poverty and its alleviation from its roots in the processes of power that create wealth (see the World Bank *World Development Reports* of *1990*, *1992* and *2000* on poverty for examples of this). Perhaps the *descriptions* of poverty could remain forever, in the absolute. Yet, as Aristotle and Manrique, among many more recent philosophers, have pointed out, the *alleviation* of poverty, when poverty is poverty of power as well as material poverty, and when poverty is controlled by the wealthy, demands discussion of power. It requires discussion of the roles of both the vulnerable and the invulnerable in the creation of the context.

The next section introduces a discussion of the processes and actors that create the context, and the processes needed to change these inequalities.

The Processes Underlying the Context: Globalization and Sustainability in Theory and Reality

Into this period of urbanization and inequality have come concepts that attempt to explain or change the reality of our unequal, unhealthy, urban world: globalization and sustainability. These concepts contrast radically. Globalization theories attempt to explain, post hoc to reality, the 'inevitable' processes assailing the world. Sustainability, in advance of reality, attempts to envision and develop a whole new world. Both are key concepts for understanding the context in which we live and for the future that we must develop. Yet, they are also concepts that few people utilize explicitly in the development of most urban policies at present. The following sections outline their relevance to the development of equitable environmental and health policies in cities.

Globalization and Inequality

The context of inequality internationally can be seen as driven by the process known as 'globalization'. An increasing number of analysts, including health professionals, have commented on the potential impacts on public health of this process (Castells, 1997; Stephens et al, 1999; Coates, 1998).

The term 'globalization' has come to mean many things to many people, but tends overall to imply forms of 'integration' – for example, in economic and information terms (termed by Castells as 'informational capitalism'). Thus the Human Development Report of 1999 suggests that the spread of new technologies such as the Internet have concentrated power still further into the hands of educated, young, white males who live in the North principally, benefiting from improved information and contacts (UNDP, 1999). These young men operate from the financial centres of the world, moderating the movement of capital and affecting millions of people with each action they take (Castells, 1997; Krugman, 1998; Krugman, 1999). Furthermore, these men work within transnational organizations, unaccountable to the peoples of the world in the sense that they are unelected, answerable to shareholders rather than citizens, and are more powerful than national governments (Korten, 1995). Of the world's largest economies, over one-half are now not countries but companies. Increasingly, transnational business is the provider of a whole range of public essentials – transport, utilities, welfare, health services.

Furthermore, it is transnational corporations that have the power to decide on foreign investments, forcing countries to compete their peoples against each other, in what has been described as a 'global race to the bottom' in terms of environmental, health and social conditions (Coates, 1998). Clearly, this must have a strong influence on urban people in each country, with the poor competing against each other for jobs under circumstances that may not alleviate the central problems they face – economic poverty and disempowerment.

The positive aspects of globalization could include social and political integration, as the world's systems show apparent convergence in these terms too (Castells, 1997). As the peoples of the world move into the urban areas of the world, there is also more potential for connection and communication across ethnic, social, gender and religious divides. Information could be turned into knowledge and learning about each other and our diverse positive values.

It can be argued, and is, that the current process of connection, in terms of power concentration, in a globalized world can be used to alleviate poverty in any one area. It is argued that investment, moved around the planet by the wealthy towards the less wealthy countries, will achieve development for all, benefiting rural and urban peoples in both wealthy and poor countries (Fitzgerald, 1998). Yet evidence suggests that poverty and the health of the poor will only be improved if the conditions of foreign or local investment are designed and managed with this mutual benefit in mind. At the very least, it seems logical that health will not improve and poverty reduce if all investment benefits simply return to the powerful agents responsible for investing. Furthermore, and in urban areas, to alleviate poverty, investment must provide employment and opportunities for the poor that will help them in their current dilemma and not undermine their future. Evidence suggests that this power of investment, to date, has not delivered solutions for the 'double burden' and rarely secures a future. Urban development based on foreign or local investment, without conditions, may be both dirty and unable to deliver the economic development to lift people out of the conditions that they experience currently.

The positive and negative aspects of integration between countries in economic and social terms were discussed in the past. Globalization, in terms of economic and political integration, is not a new story (Castells, 1997). Yet there are two features of integration that may be important now: it is occurring both in the context of huge movements into urban areas and of the reliance of these new urban dwellers on cash economies and unstable opportunities (UNCHS, 1996). These opportunities are managed in a globalized economy, where decisions made far from a city can deeply affect policies for sustainability and equity in any context. Further, these changes are occurring in a context of information expansion, where people in cities across the world can see each other's lives more clearly than ever before. Their aspirations and opportunities converge and are manipulated increasingly by forces beyond the control of the nation states in which urban peoples live.

Many academics, non-governmental analysts and activists in the fields of environment and development question the process of globalization (for example, Coates, 1998). They note that globalization in its current form has a number of features that bode badly for people's health and the environment. The sharp increase in global inequality has coincided with the acceleration of the process of globalization, and increasing economic integration and growing inequality appear closely related, although further research on inequality is necessary in its global context. Such inequality is linked to continued poor health for the majority in the South, to rapid deterioration in health in the former Soviet Union (Bobak et al, 1998), and to the re-emergence of the classic diseases of deprivation, such as tuberculosis, in the North (Porter and Ogden, 1998).

While globalization is argued by some to have produced increases in wealth for the 'world', evidence suggests the need to disentangle the aggregate picture and ask 'whose world is wealthier; whose world is healthier?'. As the earlier sections have shown, the urban world is unhealthy and unequal. Yet the urban world is also the employment base and often home of the wealthiest people of the world: the UNDP's young (and old) white males are concentrated in the financial markets of the powerful nations and in the multilateral corporations that operate out of them (UNDP, 1999). The process of global integration – economic, informational and social – appears to be facilitating the concentration of power into the hands of a tiny urban minority who control the share of wealth, information and health for all.

Sustainability and Inequality

There is now a surfeit of theories of both the concept of sustainable development and how to achieve it (Pugh, 1996a). 'Health' for the majority has become a central challenge of the sustainable development conundrum. Figure 5.5 shows a WHO model of sustainable development, in which the dual goals of health and sustainability are achieved through a convivial, viable and equitable mix of environment, economy and social values. Sustainability in these terms is a theoretical paradigm at extreme odds with

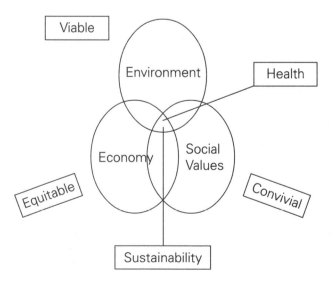

Source: WHO, 1997

Figure 5.5 *The Utopian Image of Sustainability*

some of the current processes of globalization, including global and regional macro-economic fluctuations.

In addition, it does not need an academic reflection to observe that in practice there appears to be a substantial mismatch between visions such as that of the WHO and the political reality of the world. Sustainability, defined as it has been to mean that we meet the needs of those today without compromising the needs of those tomorrow, is far from an imaginative grasp, let alone evidence's reality.

This chapter looks briefly at both theory and practice, but it is worth making an overall observation on the eternal interaction of academic and conceptual theory, and the practice of actions in political reality. The contrast of the theories of globalization and sustainability is telling. Globalization is a process in political reality, in search of theories to explain it – the theories have been slow to catch up with the forces now being termed globalization (Castells, 1997). In contrast, sustainability is largely a vision in search of political reality (Pugh, 1996b).

Although we have much to learn from history, we must acknowledge also that the practice of sustainability, in terms of health for the majority of cities in the 'developing countries', will be new territory. The development of the urban centres of the so-called developed world have never been based on the principles of sustainability as we now see it (ie, on visions of environmental, health and social sustainability). We have few models of actions for urban sustainability overall that have worked in terms of the criteria of health and environmental sustainability. Indeed, the development of urban Europe and, to a lesser extent, North America, has relied historically on unsustainable practices when seen in the light of long-term health and environmental degradation. Europe's urban peoples have been pulled into 'development', if it is defined as access to material means for survival, by drawing on the resources and wealth of the countries of the South, as well as developing environmentally unsustainable industrial and agricultural processes within European countries (Luckin, 1986). It requires that analyses of urban sustainability employ neither naïve utopianism nor prophecies of doom. It is probably most useful that analyses employ Gramsci's principles of 'pessimism of the intellect and optimism of the will' (Gramsci, 1996). And, as Pugh notes, new forms of knowledge must be developed acknowledging more historical input, more disciplinary diversity and more interaction of pragmatism and vision – or theory and practice (Pugh, 1996b).

It could be argued that the process of globalization is moving quickly, while that of sustainable development, urban or otherwise, is slow or non-existent. In terms of the goals of equity in health and sustainability, urgency and radical change is needed. Sustainability is related profoundly to equality, just as globalization and inequality seem closely related.

What are the kinds of radical changes that are needed? The last section discusses two approaches: the development of professional and personal ethics among all those with power or influence; and a new kind of participation – that of participation in setting agendas, as well as implementing them.

WAYS TOWARDS EQUITY: SHIFTS IN THE USE OF POWER AND PROCESS

This chapter discusses a limited set of themes out of a large debate on equity, health and sustainability in urban areas. But in suggesting ways forward, this chapter will not discuss what actions or what interventions are needed to achieve a healthy, equitable and sustainable urban context. We now have centuries of scientific evidence testifying that long life expectancy and health can be achieved by a set of relatively simple interventions: they include adequate potable water, clean and ample food, adequate shelter, including waste-disposal facilities, and safe, remunerative work. Such conditions presage health and long life. We also know what actions can achieve equal distributions of such health – equally shared food, water, shelter and environmental resources, and equal access to opportunity.

These facts are so well accepted as to need little more scientific proof to be seen as truth. As the minister for international development in the UK has put it:

> *what we want is a global society in which people everywhere are entitled to live in peace and security with their families and neighbours ... they need fresh air to breathe, clean water to drink, uncontaminated food to eat, and livelihoods that allow them to earn their keep and raise healthy educated children.*[4]

Along with these truths, evidence suggests that we know a great deal about the content and impact of policies, but far less about the processes that are needed to achieve real change (Grindle and Thomas, 1993). Thus, for example, there have been many discussions in the 1990s about how to achieve urban sustainability through shifts in policy interventions. These discussions suggest the use of intersectoral and participatory policy processes such as Local Agenda 21s and Healthy Cities (Dooris, 1997; Harpham and Werna, 1996). Both policies have goals of equity and sustainability, the ideal that was set out in the earlier section on sustainability. There is now evidence that these approaches have very mixed success in the face of existing policy structures (Dooris, 1997). Too often, the new policies are superimposed on existing structures and ignore existing power bases within urban management.

Setting the chapter in the context of globalization opens the discussion still further to one in which the processes in cities must change to tackle more than just power distribution within individual urban areas. Processes must develop that will change profoundly the behaviour of the powerful. The final sections will discuss this briefly.

The Role and Power of the Educated

Here we are in the same place as seventy years ago . . . you people
with all the education – what are you doing with it? Are you just
using all that education for making profits?

Ga Mantse Elders, Accra, Ghana, in Songsore and
Stephens, 1999

Castells has identified a key element in the power of those who control the
world's wealth which he terms 'informational capital' (Castells, 1997).
Information has always been known to be a highly important source of
power. In the urban context, if there is an information myth that suggests
that urbanization is healthy, the urban poor can be ignored in policy.
Furthermore, if there is no divulgence of the evidence of the distributional
impacts of policies, there is no justification or means to advocate for
distributional changes. It is the educated and influential in cities, countries
and internationally who control information. As the Ga Mantse chiefs of
one of the poorest areas of Accra in Ghana ask: what do they, or indeed all
those who write and read such books as this, do with power?

Certainly, since the 1980s there has been much more work on using
information to identify the scale and processes of inequality in cities, and
pushing an agenda based on environmental justice and rights (Cohen,
1998c; SOAS, 1996; Stephens, 1996). International meetings of United
Nations agencies now highlight inequality and social exclusion, and not
simply material poverty, suggesting a shift in conceptual thinking at
international level (Cohen, 1998a; Wolfe, 1995). At an international level,
information is put forward to confront the process of globalization, challenging it to become more equitable (UNDP, 1999). Internationally, work that
makes explicit the disaggregated health impacts of macro policies, within
nations, within cities and between individuals starts the policy process. It
begins to make the 'problem' of inequality visible, and is a step towards
shifts in the process of inequality.

At every level of policy, the divulgence of data on inequality can create
an advocacy pressure and, more importantly, can improve policy transparency. For example, in 1994, following a study of health inequalities in
São Paulo, a council woman stood for election using the research methods
and results to sponsor a bill to monitor and publicize inequalities routinely,
commenting: 'It is essential to have access to data and information to
construct a just society . . . I would like to draft a bill which enforces the
municipal authorities to divulge data related to quality of life in a systematic
way.' (Aldaisa Sposati, personal communication, June 1994.) Similarly, the
more evidence we garner of the impacts of the process of globalization on
the urban poor, the more we can make explicit the 'global race to the
bottom'.

But who acts on this information, however transparent? It would be
true to say that the evidence of urban inequalities that reaches light currently

tends to be presented as advocacy to a powerful policy élite in each relevant context – whether it is London, Washington, Calcutta or São Paulo. This local policy élite are themselves under pressure from an international élite, as the section on globalization discussed.

There is little evidence that information on inequalities is changing distribution in cities today, when the poor exist, ignored, alongside the wealthy, with little sense of commitment on the part of one group towards the rights of another or their own responsibilities in that context. As importantly, they are also mostly arguments made by those who control and consume resources about those who do not.

Transparency can move the policy debate forward in terms of high-lighting environmental and health inequalities and advocating policy debates among all those with influence and education within cities. But it is argued increasingly that the willingness to be transparent can only really be facilitated by higher levels of ethical professional and personal behaviour of those with power (Chambers, 1995; Cohen, 1998c).

The policy élite of the 19th century faced both inequity and globalization in terms of economic and political integration when dealing with the urban poverty they faced (Luckin, 1986). In this context a technical élite argued in allegiance for the value of change to a political élite. The arguments of the technical élite were complemented by those of the political élite who advocated the entire reformation of political structures in favour of the poor. Even in this period the changes that occurred were initiated and defined by a rarefied group of decision makers who defined the problems and the solutions to their own advantage (Luckin, 1986).

The policy context differs today. The allegiance of many across the policy élite to advocate equity is being rediscovered, but there is little in the way of new political theory towards equity to complement it. Indeed, evidence suggests that the current force of globalization is exacerbating inequity. There is conceptual confusion, most notably in the use of the theories of individual and collective rights. How long will individual freedoms be allowed to dominate collective rights? For example, acknowledging the collective rights of the urban poor will eventually (or immediately) involve changes in the individual rights of the powerful. This provides a further justification for the appeal that many now make to shifts in the values and ethical positions that people with power and education hold (for example, Chambers, 1995).

Higher levels of ethical behaviour will not solve inequality alone. There is still an assumption that those in control of the decision-making process will somehow make decisions in favour of the unjustly treated, once they rediscover how unfair the current process is. The discussion by the Chief Executive Officer (CEO) of the Accra Metropolitan Assembly regarding the distribution of resources between over 1 million people highlights one dilemma that would be recognized by any government in any city. Asked whether he could use an analysis of environmental and health inequalities in his city to advocate resource allocation to the deprived areas which are home to over 600,000 people (47 per cent of Accra's population), he replied, 'What would I say to the people of "Airport" [a rich residential area with

1.6 per cent of Accra's population] who knock on my door?' (Stephens, 1998). Unless the poor can 'knock on the doors' of the policy élite with the same pressure as the wealthy, the policy élite rely on their fragile ethics alone.

There is a further assumption, that ethical information and policy will be constructed in a way that mirrors the perceived needs of those without power. This assumes that both the information gatherers and the inform-ation disseminators will act ethically. Yet, as many recent authors have noted, academics are confined to narrow, parochial questions defined by the powerful (Muttit, 1999); and disseminators of the evidence in the United Nations are being drawn into greater and greater involvement with the globalizing agents who are currently key in undermining sustainability and equity (Karliner, 1999). This section has covered briefly the role of the educated, but it is with the next section that change can really occur. Thus, the final section discusses the need for participation in policy processes by those with the most direct experience of the problems.

Reinforcing Equity through Participatory Decision-making Processes – the Role and Power of the Majority

The idea of participation has become a common mantra in some senses. Mitlin and Thomson discuss the use of participatory processes as a tool to change the ways in which community improvements in urban areas are undertaken (Mitlin and Thomson, 1995). At another level entirely, the international non-governmental environmental movement has proposed participation in the agreements on trade and international investment as a way of developing more ethical standards for the operations of trans-national corporations in the face of globalization (Coates, 1998).

Participation is one of the solutions, but it is no accident that the solution is hard won. There is now considerable evidence that the participation of poor individuals and communities in the development of urban policy has been successful in improving conditions, but often has reinforced the status quo in terms of who benefits and how (Mitlin and Thomson, 1995). Furthermore, participation at all levels of policy tends to be confined to the stages of the policy process where interventions are implemented, not at the stage of problem identification or agenda setting.

Yet, it is at the stage of problem identification that the power over defining solutions is held. Evidence suggests that so far few Local Agenda 21 projects have managed to incorporate participation beyond a narrow group of actors in urban areas and rarely to achieve participation in major problem identification (Dooris, 1997).

Enhancing the participation of all those affected by the unequal distrib-ution of power and resources in cities may change the entire nature of the policy content. It does not make the policy process easier – in fact, it makes it much harder, but it does create another form of transparency, one which reveals that the perceptions of those who control decisions are often very different from those who experience problems. Changing the balance of power in problem identification can change the policy interventions considerably and radically.

Enhancing participation in the decision-making process within cities from an outset point of problem identification will not mean validating the view of the élite on priorities. It means challenging them and broadening them, but it may strengthen the advocacy of those lobbying for greater equity. For example, in Calcutta, an innovative environmental strategy (CEMSAP, 1997) was designed with a partial mandate to identify the relative health importance of air and water pollution, narrowly defined as ambient air pollution and toxic chemicals in water. The strategy would have been narrow also had the perceptions of the poor been excluded from the problem identification phase. However, in a problem identification process, the perception of those affected by problems was given equal weight to the perception of those with technical and political power. The poor in Calcutta reinforced a broad public health perspective that basic water and sanitation, rather than air quality, were key problems for the majority.

In addition, as Figure 5.6 shows, the poor highlighted employment and education above the physical determinants of their health. In other words, they reinforced an emphasis on the policy process determinants of their health disadvantage. Finally, Figure 5.6 reveals the final reason why participation at the outset of policy is important. It is the wealthy people in Calcutta who prioritize air pollution over problems prioritized by the poor. There are similar findings on these different priority perceptions from São Paulo, Accra and London (Jacobi, 1994; Benneh et al, 1993; Dooris, 1997).

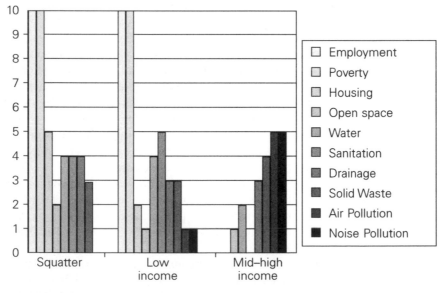

Source: CEMSAP, 1997

Figure 5.6 *How the Vulnerable and the Invulnerable Perceive Priorities in Calcutta*

As the poor noted, the 'double burden' of Calcutta will not be solved without addressing the need for standards of employment and education that allow them to address their own physical conditions. Work that is dirty, dangerous and poorly paid both pollutes the overall environment and fails to alleviate the problems of the poor. The poor understand this better than most of the policy élite who define problems on behalf of others.

Enhancing participation in the decision-making process within cities does not simply mean empowering the poor to assist the powerful in advocating for physical rights. It also includes the responsibility of the powerful to accept their ethical responsibility to devolve power over decision making to those with the right to decide – those most affected by problems.

Initiatives that hold promise of this do include Local Agenda 21s and the Healthy Cities initiatives, which emphasize local participatory planning towards equity and stronger local processes generally (Dooris, 1997). But until such innovative urban strategies are devised that address power in decision making transparently and identify the responsibility of the powerful and the rights of the powerless, they may remain theories for policy content shifts in search of evidence in political reality.

CONCLUSIONS

> ... *with education camouflaged,*
> *I do not see, but must pretend I see*
> *I do not feel, but must pretend I feel ...*
> *the only few that can make it,*
> *Keep dragging the rest for ransom*
> *To the utopian land of progress*

Agbenyega, 1996

Inequality in resource use and life chances has become a perennial, unnecessary human outcome between those with too much and those with too little. Inequality dates from so far in our evolutionary past and has become so perennial a problem that we have come to accept its inevitability. Yet the urban areas of the world today provide the most vivid images of our need for greater equity now. They are concurrently the locus of power and home to the majority of the powerless in the world.

The process termed globalization is being driven by the cities of the world. Urban sustainability can be achieved, but only if its proponents start to deal with the concepts and debates of globalization and power. The poor peoples of urban areas may be among the most vulnerable to the processes of globalization; and, ironically, the wealthy peoples of the urban centres may be the engines for the process. For example, it was the urban people who felt the most pain as the Asian 'Tigers' crashed owing to the economic movement of capital. The same has been true in Latin America. Both macroeconomic shifts were engineered from the financial urban capitals of the world. New trade agreements are being negotiated in these powerful urban centres that will affect the lives and opportunities for all urban people. They are currently negotiated in secret among only the most powerful people in the world, negotiating in the wealthiest cities of the world (Stephens et al, 1999; Coates, 1998).

The needs of the current poor and the needs for the future in terms of sustainability are complementary. They imply both a renewal of ethics in the powerful and, perhaps, that the need for more profound forms of participation by the powerless has never been so urgent. As senior economists have noted of the 1998 financial market movements, there is increasing concern that the management of the world's economic systems are in the hands of people described by those in their own discipline as agents as 'moral as great white sharks' (Krugman, 1998) and as people who will 'on the flimsiest pretext, unconstrained by ethical considerations, abandon the unwary in a heartbeat' (Friedman, MIT, 1998). Krugman has commented further that we are all the victims of a 'global intellectual scam' that tells us that competition and the mechanisms to enhance it is the only route to the achievement of public well-being for all people. The scam is clear when we consider that it is the urban poor competing against each other across the world for jobs that will not alleviate their poverty, in industries and workplaces that are unprotected and polluting, with economic rewards that are often meagre. All this for the advantage of the rich who live alongside them.

Inequality is an issue of deep historical importance – one we have never resolved. It has always been an issue of ethics, power and, in terms of logic, the futility of excessive wealth for human happiness. Ironically, with the rich and the poor alongside each other in cities, the aspirational model of the selfish accumulation of wealth is part of the globalizing information. The poor in cities everywhere see the lives of the wealthy, while they can barely, and badly, stay alive. Perhaps never before have we been aware that if this pattern continues it is not just the poor who will be racing to the bottom in this scam, but all of us. Perhaps the pursuit of urban sustainability is the new political theory that will achieve equity. Conversely, the pursuit of equity could enhance the development of sustainability.

Ethics in the use of power and resources by the rich may be a long way off in this historical moment. However, in the face of current processes, participation has already started. For example, it was in part the use of informational power by environmental and anti-poverty non-governmental organisations (NGOs) and their worldwide coalition that derailed the latest trade agreement, the Multilateral Agreements on Investments (MAI). This agreement would have shifted more power into the hands of transnational corporations to control the way that all governments were able to work for their people (Coates, 1998).

Urban areas may be home to the most powerful people, but they may also be the locus of the visible, connected struggle against the inequitable processes of globalization, as the 1999 demonstrations in many of the world's cities showed (Labes, 1999). These same coalitions are starting to bring pressure for ethics to the operations of the United Nations (Karliner, 1999) and to the behaviour of academics (Muttit, 1999).

If the future is urban and destined to perish unless we make it sustainable, then we must develop the means to make global integration a process towards urban equity and sustainability. We have to hope and make sure that the macro-economic theorists who see the inevitability of inequality are proved wrong. They must be proved wrong by the millions of urban people who can now see each other, understand each other and act better or worse on the basis of that understanding. We have never needed more to demonstrate our human capacity to act ethically, responsibly and openly towards each other.

ACKNOWLEDGEMENTS

The perspectives in this chapter were developed during a longitudinal policy study to develop conceptual understanding of the use of information in policies for urban environmental equity. This was based on evidence from Accra, São Paulo and Calcutta, and interviews with members of the World Bank, the WHO and bilateral donors. The study was supported by the Global Environmental Change Programme of the UK Economic and Social Research Council. I would like to acknowledge the excellent support of this programme. I would also like to thank Ben Doe, Jacob Songsore, Marco Akerman, Amelia Cohn, Pedro Jacobi, Mike Cohen, Romulo de Sousa, Simon Lewin, Steve Wing, David Richardson, David Satterthwaite, Richard Wilkinson, Dela Attipoe, and Nii-Akwei Allotey for feedback on these ideas.

NOTES

1 *Our lives are the rivers that flow out into the sea, which is death. There, lordships go straight to their ends to be consumed. There the great rivers, and there the others, of middling size and smaller, are equal when they arrive: those who live by their hands and the rich . . . this world would be good, if we made the good use of it that we ought . . .*
2 Defined routinely to include food, water, shelter, sanitation, waste disposal and additionally minimum income and primary education.
3 Using routine data and ICD9 coding for asthma, bronchitis and emphysema.
4 Speech on taking up her ministry: Right Honourable Member of Parliament, Claire Short, Secretary of State for International Development, May 1997.

REFERENCES

Agbenyega, C (1998) 'Blinded by education' in *Poverty Alleviation in Ghana – Reality*, Ada, Press, Ada Ghana

Aristotle (335BC) (1992) *The Politics 4 129c* (translated by T A Sinclair 1962), Penguin Books, London

Benneh, G, Songsore, J, Nabila, J S et al (1993) *Environmental Problems and the Urban Household in the Greater Accra Metropolitan Area (GAMA) – Ghana*, Stockholm Environment Institute, Stockholm

Bianco, M (1983) *Health and Its Care in Greater Buenos Aires*, paper for the WHO meeting on PHC in urban areas, Geneva, 25–29 July

Bobak, M, Pikhart, H, Hertzman, C, Rose, R, Marmot, M (1998) 'Socioeconomic factors, perceived control and self-reported health in Russia. A cross-sectional survey.' *Soc Sci Med*, vol 47, no 2, pp269–79

Brandan, S and Caterwall, M D (1995) 'Race, socio-economic status and domestic homicide', *Journal of the American Medical Association*, vol 273, no 22, pp1755–58

Castells, M (1997) *The Information Age: Economy, Society and Culture: Volume I The Rise of the Network Society*, Blackwell Publishers, Oxford

CEMSAP (1997) 'Calcutta Environmental Management Strategy and Action Plan' Department of Environment, Government of West Bengal, India

Chambers, R (1995) 'Poverty and livelihoods: whose reality counts?', *Environment and Urbanization*, vol 7, no 1, pp173–205

Coates, B (1998) *The Developmental Implications of the MAI: WDM Critique of the Fitzgerald Report to the UK Department for International Development*, World Development Movement, UK

Cohen, M (1998a) *The Impact of International Economic Change on Cities: Implications for Local Forms of Governance*, remarks presented to the National Congress of the Royal Australian Institute of Planners, Brisbane, 7 July

Cohen, M (1998b) *Crystal Balls and Rear View Mirrors: Redefining Urban Practice at the Turn of the Century*, proceedings of 25th Anniversary Conference of DHV Amersfoort, The Netherlands

Cohen, M (1998c) *The Contradiction of the Metropolitan Imperative or 'Vive la Difference ou Survive les Differences?'*, Paper presented to the International Colloquium: Cities in the 21st Century: Cities and Metropolises – breaking or bridging, La Rochelle, France, October 1998

Cohen and Swift, (1993) 'A public health approach to the violence epidemic in the US', *Environment and Urbanization*, vol 5, no 2, pp50–66

Defoe, D (1667) (1995) 'A visitation of the plague' in *A Journal of the Plague Year 1665*, Penguin Books, London

Dooris, M (1997) 'Health and Local Agenda 21: integrating strategies in local government to achieve action', in *Sustainable Development Background Paper for UK National Roundtable of Local Governments*, Bristol: The Create Centre

Drucker, E et al (1994) 'Childhood tuberculosis in the Bronx, New York', *Lancet*, vol 343, no 8911

Gramsci, A (1996) in Q Hoare, G Nowell Smith (eds) *Selections from the Prison Notebooks of Antonio Gramsci*, Lawrence & Wishart, London

Grindle, J and Thomas, M (1991) *Public Choices and Policy Change*, Johns Hopkins University, Westview Press, Colorado

Harpham, T, Vaughan, P and Lusty, T (1990) *In the Shadow of the City: Community Health and the Urban Poor*, Oxford University Press, Oxford

Harpham, T and Werna, E (1996) 'The Idea of Healthy Cities and its Application' in C Pugh (ed) *Sustainability, the Environment and Urbanization*, Earthscan, London

Jacobi, P (1994) 'Households and environment in the city of São Paulo: problems, perceptions and solutions', *Environment and Urbanization*, vol 6, no 2, pp87–110

Karliner, J (1999) 'Co-opting the UN', *The Ecologist*, vol 29, no 5, pp318–21

Korten, D (1995) 'Sustainability and the global economy: beyond Bretton Woods', *Forests, Trees and People*, Newsletter 29

Krugman, P (1998) 'Rashomon in Connecticut: what really happened to long-term capital management', *internal Internet document MIT*, 1 October

Krugman, P (1999) *The Return of Depression Economics*, Allen Lane, The Penguin Press, London

Labes, L (1999) 'June 18 Reports in News and Campaigns', *The Ecologist*, vol 29, no 5, p300

LaTouche, S (1993) *In the Wake of the Affluent Society: An exploration of Post-development*, Zed Books, London

Luckin, B (1986) *Pollution and Control. A Social History of the Thames in the Nineteenth Century*, Adam Hilger, Bristol, pp1–198

Manrique, J (1460) 'Coplas por la muerte de su padre' in Cohen, J M (ed) (1988) *The Penguin Book of Spanish Verse*, Penguin Books, Harmondsworth

Mitlin, D and Thompson, J (1995) 'Participatory approaches in urban areas: strengthening civil society or reinforcing the status quo?', *Environment and Urbanization*, vol 7, no 1, pp231–51

Muttit, G (1999) 'Degrees of involvement', *The Ecologist*, vol 29, p326

Porter, J D and Ogden, J A (1998) 'Social inequalities in the re-emergence of infectious diseases' in Strickland, S S and Shetty, P (eds) *Human Biology and Social Inequality*, Cambridge University Press, Cambridge, pp96–114

Post, K and Wright, P (1989) *Socialism and Underdevelopment*, Routledge, London

Pugh, C (1996a) 'Introduction' in Pugh, C (ed) *Sustainability, the Environment and Urbanization*, Earthscan, London

Pugh, C (1996b) 'Conclusions' in Pugh, C (ed) *Sustainability, the Environment and Urbanization*, Earthscan, London

Rosen, N (1998) 'The truth about trade: a conversation with Professor Noam Chomsky', *The Boulder Weekly*, Colorado, 14 May

Satterthwaite, D, Cairncross, A and Hardoy, J (eds) (1990) *The Poor Die Young: Housing and Health in Third World Cities*, Earthscan, London, pp1–309

School of Oriental and African Studies (SOAS) (1996) *Claiming our future environmental justice workshop*, Law Department, University of London (unpublished)

Silver, H (1995), 'Reconceptualizing social disadvantage: three paradigms of social exclusion', in G Rodgers, C Gore and J B Figueiredo (eds) *Social Exclusion: Rhetoric, Reality, Responses*, International Institute for Labour Studies/United Nations Development Programme, Geneva, pp57–81

Smith, K and Lee, Y (1993) 'The environmental risk transition' in J Kasarda and A Parnell (eds) *Third World Cities: Problems, Policies and Prospects*, Sage Publications, London

Stephens, C (1996) 'Healthy cities or unhealthy islands? The health and social implications of urban inequality', *Environment and Urbanization*, vol 8, no 2, pp9–30

Songsore, J and Stephens, C (1999) *Baseline Social Impact Study of the Accra Waste Project*, Report for engineering teams on behalf of the UK Department for International Development

Stephens, C, Timaeus, I, Akerman, M et al (1994) *Environment and Health in Developing Countries: An Analysis of Intra-urban Differentials Using Existing Data. Collaborative Studies in Accra and São Paulo and Analysis of Urban Data of Four Demographic and Health Surveys*, London School of Hygiene & Tropical Medicine, London

Stephens, C, McGranahan, G, Leonardi, G, et al (1996) 'Environmental health impacts' in UNEP/UNDP/World Bank/WRI (1996–97) *World Resources Report World Resources Institute*, Washington, DC

Stephens, C, Leonardi, G, Lewin, S and SanSebastian Chasco, M (1999) 'The multilateral agreement on investment: public health threat for the 21st century', guest editorial, *European Journal of Public Health*, vol 9, pp3–5

Stevenson, S, Stephens, C, Landon, M et al (1998) 'Examining the inequality and inequity of car ownership and the effects of pollution and health outcomes such as respiratory diseases', *Epidemiology*, vol 9, no 4

United Nations Centre for Human Settlements (UNCHS) (1996) *Global Report on Human Settlements*, Oxford University Press, Oxford

United Nations Development Programme (UNDP) (1994) *Human Development Report 1994*, Oxford University Press, New York

United Nations Development Programme (UNDP) (1998) *Human Development Report 1998*, Oxford University Press, New York

United Nations Development Programme (UNDP) (1999) *Human Development Report 1999*, Oxford University Press, New York

Wilkinson, R (1997) *Unhealthy Societies. The Affliction of Inequality*, Routledge, London

Wilkinson, P, Landon, M, Walls, P et al (1998) *Wide Socio-economic Variation in Tuberculosis in London and the South East*, proceedings of the Madrid Conference on Urban Environment and Health

Wolfe, M (1995) 'Globalization and social exclusion: some paradoxes', in Rodgers, G, Gore, C and Figueiredo, J B (eds) *Social Exclusion; Rhetoric, Reality, Responses* International Labour Organization, Geneva, pp81–103

World Health Organization (WHO) (1997) 'Sustainable development and health; concepts, principles and framework for action for European cities and towns', *European Sustainable Development and Health Series 1*, WHO Regional Office for Europe, Copenhagen, Denmark

Wratten, E (1995) 'Conceptualizing urban poverty', *Environment and Urbanization*, vol 7, no 1, pp11–37

Yack, D and Harrison, D (1996) *Inequalities in health determinants and status in South Africa*, MRC, Durban, Pretoria

6 HEALTH, GOVERNANCE AND THE ENVIRONMENT

Trudy Harpham and Maria Allison

Debates about governance in the health sector have largely stemmed from urban settings where the role of local government is sometimes being strengthened through decentralization and where attempts at community involvement – for example, through the formation of neighbourhood health committees – have been more active and, arguably, more successful than in rural areas. Within the health sector itself, it is environmental health activities, rather than curative health services, which have been prioritized by community members and which lend themselves most readily to the principles of governance. In this chapter, a conceptual framework of governance is presented, followed by highlights of current thinking about sustainable development and environmental health; then a case study from South Africa is used to illustrate the link between governance and health.

DIMENSIONS OF GOVERNANCE

The term 'governance' is given a variety of meanings and is used in many different contexts. Governance does not merely refer to the exercise of governmental authority, but is rather an expansion of the notion of government to include forms of collective decision making, formal and informal, participatory and representative, and national as well as local (Harpham and Boateng, 1997). Issues of governance have emerged at key international meetings and in the conditionality clauses of the multi- and bi-lateral funding agencies over the last few years. The prominence of 'governance' in the literature from such agencies marks a significant shift in the approach to development assistance. Kooiman (1993) and Swilling (1997) refer to a 'new responsive mode of governance' which has replaced three 'outdated' modes of governance, namely the traditional hierarchically organized state; the large institutionalized corporatist state; and the autonomous welfarist state where services are delivered uniformly to all as a basic right. As is often the case with post-modern concepts, it is difficult to discern what this new responsive governance means beyond being complex, diverse and dynamic. It certainly implies 'third way' language (Giddens, 1998) such as new partnerships between the state, private sector, non-governmental organizations (NGOs) and community-based organizations (CBOs), and an emphasis on decentralization. However, this language is not new either to the health sector or the urban development sector (for example, see Harpham and Tanner, 1995 and Werna et al, 1998).

Harpham and Boateng (1997) reviewed current literature on governance in terms of the three dimensions of governance identified by Boeninger (1991): technical, political and institutional. Harpham and Boateng (1997) then took this further to include a fourth, cultural, dimension. The technical dimension of governance is defined by Boeninger (1991) as the constraints imposed by natural resources, levels of education, human resource skills and installed industrial capacity of a given society. The technical dimension of governance is biased towards the performance rather than the representation side of governance and has been dominated by debates on economic growth. The United Nations Development Programme (UNDP) (1992) and Holmberg et al (1993) point out that it is not so much about how much economic growth, but rather what kind of economic growth takes place. This brings in the issue of environmental sustainability with regard to the processes that are currently being pursued to achieve economic growth. Most developing countries, and especially cities, cannot hope to sustain the same patterns of growth that have been associated with previous growth patterns of urban areas in developed countries. An example of the widening disparity between nations is in the access to technology and information systems that expose the inadequacies of urban areas to deal technically with problems.

The technical dimension of governance reveals the imbalance between economic and human development. Within the technical dimension of governance, decision makers have a responsibility to address human development and to ensure that there is a more equitable allocation of resources. A balance must be struck to present development in a holistic manner that encompasses the needs of all groups in society. This is magnified in the cities of developing countries and is reflected in the operations of environmental health services such as environmental health promotion and the disposal of waste.

Closely related to the technical dimension of governance is the political dimension. This dimension refers to the establishment of objectives and the exercise of leadership (Boeninger, 1991). It moves away from viewing economic and social policy in isolation from decision-making processes. The World Bank (1994) attempts to draw a clear distinction between the political and technical dimensions of governance by stating that its mandate is the promotion of sustainable economic and social development. The Bank's Articles of Agreement explicitly prohibit the institution from interfering in a country's internal political affairs and requires it to take only economic considerations into account in its decisions. This approach, however, is counter to the 'just development' approach suggested by Clark (1991) which emphasizes popular participation of all sections of any society.

Hirst (1993) argues that in developed countries, where democratizing and empowering civil society has attempted to place political responsibility and governmental tasks more in the hands of citizens, a mature democracy is required. His debate is relevant to urban governance in that it links the political and technical dimensions. The political dimension of urban governance has to be examined within a social milieu that provides a setting in which the relationship of the state and groups in civil society allows debate and the exchange of ideas without the fear of persecution or discrimination.

The question of whether civil society has the opportunity to organize around specific interests relates to the institutional dimension of governance. This dimension refers to the ability to manage and implement projects (Boeninger, 1991). The structural adjustment programmes designed by the World Bank and implemented in developing countries in the 1980s were indirectly the processes of institutional reform (Messkoub 1992). The attempts at institutional reform gave governments which were implementing these packages the legitimacy to modify economic and social institutions to the advantage of the private sector. The institutional dimension of governance addresses the failure of existing mechanisms to provide services equitably to all groups. Clark (1991) and Midgley (1986) both argue that the community sector has evolved into a sophisticated sector and to some extent combines practices that are normally associated with the private and public sectors in imaginative ways. Established institutions of the private and public sectors are changing gradually, but still present forces that attempt to keep the status quo intact through the forces of hierarchy, inertia, subversion, degeneration and corruption in the organizational sphere. McAuslan (1993) demonstrates that the dynamic nature of the process of governance requires a legal framework that is flexible enough to accommodate change, yet relevant to the context of where this planned intervention occurs. The legal framework should right the present imbalance that favours the élite in most development processes in cities.

In addition to the above three dimensions of governance identified by Boeninger (1991) and Harpham and Boateng (1997) include the cultural dimension identified by Martin (1991) whose premise for including the cultural dimension is that different societies will have different bases on which they conceptualize governance. The state does not operate in a vacuum. It operates, according to Martin (1991), in an environment in which people share certain beliefs and values, compete for some objectives and associate for others, and differ in ideas about power and how it should be exercised. The state cannot be separated from culture nor can governance be considered without reference to its cultural context. The definition of culture given by Leiris (1969) proposed that 'Culture must be understood as including the whole of a more or less coherent ensemble of ideas, mechanisms, institutions and artefacts – explicitly or implicitly – guide the behaviour of people belonging to a given group'. In pursuing what one society has agreed to be 'good' governance, it must be appreciated that there must be some agreement as to what is considered 'good'. This will bring into focus what that society is prepared to do to reach this objective. This might appear simplistic initially, but the notion of the 'ensemble of ideas' included in cultures essentially constitutes a code through which the ethical orientation of a particular society relates to its institutions and its structure of authority. This ensemble is not static or closed. Amselle (1990) illustrates that culture is best understood as a loose and evolving framework that establishes the bases on which groups act and interact in society. Cultures are dynamic and change in response to the external influences on them and the interplay between groups in any given society. In other words, the quality of governance derives from one culture in the society to another and from one period to another. Martin (1991) states that 'If there is an indispensable and irreducible prerequisite for good governance, it would appear to be the need for all social and political actors to refer to – not necessarily to comply with – a shared ensemble of ethical values'.

From their review of the literature supporting a four-dimensional framework of governance, Harpham and Boateng (1997) concluded that the promotion of 'good' governance is one of the strongest 'competitors' to sustainable development in the development field in the 1990s. Banuri and Holmberg (1992) demonstrate that the relationship between institutional development and environmental issues arises from the increasing acceptance that the environment is common property and therefore requires mechanisms for collective action. There is a growing recognition that a major cause of environmental degradation is the breakdown of governance. There is a need to reinforce this link and to capitalize on the fact that the principal obstacle to sustainable development is not so much the absence of laws as the absence of institutions through which laws can be implemented effectively and consistently. The above four-dimensional framework of governance is applied to a case study of South Africa below.

SUSTAINABLE DEVELOPMENT AND ENVIRONMENTAL HEALTH: CURRENT THINKING

Sustainable development has certainly received more attention by the World Health Organization (WHO) since Gro Harlem Brundtland was appointed Director General in mid-1998. In the previous regime, under Dr Nakajima, environmental health played handmaiden to health services. Most health sector reform that dominated national ministries of health and which was supported by multilateral – for example, the WHO – and bilateral agencies – for example the Department for International Development, UK (DFID) – was health services reform and totally neglected environmental health. The restructured WHO has nine technical programme 'clusters', one of which is 'sustainable development and healthy environments' which will focus on the major determinants of health at a global and national level and will highlight the importance of addressing poverty, macro-economic and physical environmental factors that influence human health (Yach, 1998). The degree to which the restructured WHO will be able to articulate with ministries of health in developing countries, which rarely have these issues on their agenda, remains to be seen. A preliminary challenge is to assist ministries to restructure in a similar vein. In many countries there may be a political will for such restructuring. For example, in Zambia health sector reform has included the formation of community/neighbourhood health committees which communicate needs to the local primary health centres. Most of the needs expressed to date concern environmental health improvements such as water supply and sanitation. This has prompted, for example, the Lusaka district health team to allocate money for such community initiatives within the devolved financial planning process. This local shift of priorities has yet to be reflected at the central, ministry of health, level. What we have then is support for a more sustainable environmental view of health at international and local levels. Health ministries will need collaboration and assistance from other ministries – for example, environment, housing, finance and public works – to tackle environmental health effectively and this is the focus of the Healthy City movement (for a general description, see Werna et al, 1998 and for its relevance to sustainable development, see Harpham and Werna, 1996).

LINKING ENVIRONMENTAL HEALTH AND GOVERNANCE: A CASE STUDY FROM SOUTH AFRICA

There is a growing acceptance that the social-political context is a determinant of health. It has been argued that governance is a useful framework for exploring the social-political context of environmental health (Stuttaford, 1998). However, the limits of governance as an approach towards implementing environmental health policy requires further exploration and is considered here in the context of South Africa (Stuttaford, 1998).

The environmental health risk factors, such as poor housing and inadequate sanitation, that are encountered everyday by the majority of South Africans are to an extent a consequence of apartheid policies. Under the apartheid government, the state aimed to dominate civil society. Reciprocal actions and influences between government and civil society were inhibited from materializing. With the overthrow of the apartheid government, largely as a consequence of the organization of civil society into a mass movement to force change, the nature of the relationship between government and civil society has changed. In the current transformation of South Africa, new means of interaction between government and civil society are being sought to address problems of sanitation provision and its effect on people's right to a healthy living environment.

Although criticized for being idealistic and difficult to measure (Head, 1996; Nutbeam, 1986; Zwi and Mills, 1995) the WHO's definition of health is the most widely accepted: a state of physical, mental and social well-being, and not merely the absence of disease or infirmity (WHO, 1948). Such a holistic definition of health requires a similarly holistic definition of the physical factors that influence environmental health. For example, housing is not taken simply to mean the physical structure of a dwelling, but encompasses the surrounding physical and social environmental impacting on the dwelling and its occupants. Sanitation is also taken to refer to a broad range of processes: planning, designing and developing sanitation; managing and financing sanitation, and maintaining sanitation.

The existing means of sanitation provision through central and local government institutions and through households are not keeping pace with the demand for environmental health services. A number of studies have discussed the need for institutional reform in terms of urban environmental management (Eberhard and Quick, 1995; Hamza, 1989; Hardoy and Satterthwaite, 1986). However, as Schteingart and de Mexico (1989) demonstrate from Mexico City, institutional reform is insufficient on its own. Rather, there needs to be a process of democratization at national and local levels to open the way for civil society participation in decision making. The importance of communities having a role in decision making in development has been well documented and a number of benefits identified (Boshielo et al, 1996; Espinosa and Rivera, 1994; UNCHS, 1995).

In addition to the practical advantages of community participation in sanitation projects, it also assists outsiders in obtaining a better understanding of the cultural norms and beliefs of the residents involved in the project. Culture influences community identity, gender roles, forms of authority and concepts of how power should be exercised (Franceys et al, 1992). Culture influences human behaviour and shapes the way in which people interpret the environment. As such, culture will also influence the way in which people regard environmental health behaviour such as sanitation (Franceys et al, 1992; Gilbert and Gugler, 1982; Yacoob and Whiteford, 1995).

The international epidemiological literature, while admitting to the difficulty of establishing a link between a particular illness and an individual causal factor, demonstrates the now well-accepted complexity of the technical, political, institutional and cultural facets of environmental health. Rapid urban growth in itself does not necessarily have a detrimental impact on the environment. Hardoy et al (1992) explain that urban populations in developing countries have expanded faster than the provision of services necessary for a healthy environment. This is particularly the case where there are 'forms of urban governance which cannot begin to meet their responsibilities' (Hardoy et al, 1992, p17).

In South Africa, the importance of focusing beyond the physical environment is recognized. As Chetty (1992, p226) observes, addressing the shortage in infrastructure and the inequalities in service provision requires 'political will' and 'a drastic restructuring of South African society. Until such time any interventions will be addressing the symptoms and not the root cause of the problem, and will prove to be ineffective'. Indeed, South Africa provides a clear example of the extent to which the social-political environment influences health. In South Africa, environmental health has been influenced by apartheid laws that have had an impact on the spatial outcome of urban areas and on the processes and patterns of urbanization. Medical officers played a key role in encouraging local authorities to engage in the destruction of slums. Intrinsic to the concern for public health was a desire for control over the urbanizing African population (Robinson, 1996). The inequalities in environmental health parallel the societal divisions imposed by apartheid. Ways now need to be found to overcome past inequalities as well as to keep abreast of the naturally increasing demand of an urbanizing population. One way is to recognize people as the solution to environmental health problems rather than as the source of problems (Seager, 1992).

In reviewing international policy – for example, WHO, 1995; World Bank, 1997; UN, 1996) on issues pertaining to urban environmental health, a shift from a project-based approach to an interest in developing policies and recommending broader social-political reforms has been identified. The emerging policies are based on adopting an intersectoral approach that will facilitate the formation of partnerships between government and civil society. Such an approach is commonly referred to as governance. Although the need for government institutional reform is recognized, local government may be slow to respond. Moreover, while the technical and institutional capacity of the local government side of partnerships has been considered, the technical ability and cultural willingness of civil society has not been considered in environmental health policy. The case study, using the example of sanitation provision, shows how the lack of consensus on governance and insufficient consideration of the factors affecting the role of civil society in environmental health-related policy is hindering the formation of equal partnerships in environmental health.

The Bill of Rights contained in the Constitution of South Africa (section 24) (RSA, 1996) states that: 'Everyone has the right (a) to an environment that is not harmful to their health or well-being; and (b) to have the environment protected, for the benefit of present and future generations, through reasonable legislative and other measures'. The principle of sustainable development is thus embodied in the declaration of the right to environmental health. Achieving this right requires an intersectoral approach and a cooperative approach to government is outlined in the Constitution (RSA, 1996). This is partly recognized by the fact that the Department of Housing, the Department of Health, the Department of Environmental Affairs and Tourism, and the Department of Water Affairs and Forestry, all make provision for health in their respective act and white papers. However, while the various departments recognize the importance of environmental health and the role of governance in implementing policies, consensus has not been reached on the actual meaning of governance. The white paper on health defines governance as 'the processes used by governing structures to make and implement laws and provide services' (RSA, 1997, p224). The environmental management white paper defines governance as 'setting policy to guide activity and then making sure that the money, people and institutions to do the work are in place. It also means making sure that people are accountable for the work that they do, monitoring what happens and making new plans to carry the work forward' (RSA, 1997, p83). These narrow definitions can be contrasted to the definition of governance adopted by the Department of Housing (1995, p32): 'governance refers to the interactive process between the government, civil society and the private sector'. The latter definition accommodates the goals of a cooperative, intersectoral government involving partnerships with civil society as laid down in the Constitution. In line with this approach, the Urban Development Framework (UDF) is to be implemented through the formation of partnerships between different government departments, the private sector and community interest groups (Department of Housing, 1997). The goals of the UDF aim to develop urban areas that will be spatially and socio-economically integrated, centres of economic opportunity, centres of governance managed by democratic and efficient local governments, environmentally sustainable, planned for in a participative way, characterized by good housing and infrastructure, integrate a range of urban resources such as industry, commerce, housing and education, and be financed by government subsidies and private sector partnerships (Department of Housing, 1997).

The concept of governance has been adopted by policy makers as a means to incorporate the social-political determinants of environmental health. The four-dimensional framework of governance is used to explore the application of governance in sanitation policy because it incorporates the recognized interaction between: increasing physical and technical access to services; reforming responsible institutions; and being aware of the diversity in the political and cultural understanding of sanitation. South Africa provides an example of where the government, following the deposition of an autocratic regime, envisages adopting governance to address environmental health. However, there is not a common understanding of what is meant by the term governance, nor are the actual mechanisms by which governance is to be implemented expanded on. In order to understand better the application of a governance framework to environmental health policy, a number of factors were identified and explored as potentially impacting on the involvement of CBOs in sanitation provision.

Method

The research question posed in the case study was: what factors may promote or inhibit the involvement of CBOs in the sanitation provision process? An exploration of these factors was conducted in Cape Town during 1997. The case study approach used intensive, multiple sources of data, including in-depth interviews, semi-structured open-ended interviews, focus groups, direct observation and document review. The principal unit of analysis and therefore the case were CBOs. It was anticipated that a number of outside actors would influence the CBOs. These included the public sector, NGOs, other CBOs, researchers from tertiary education and the private sector. It was therefore decided to interview key informants from each of these in order to contextualize fully the operations of the CBOs.

The selection of CBOs was purposive and Masiphumelele and Victoria Mxenge were selected for their theoretical replication. The main selection criterion was the manner in which the government housing subsidy was applied for. The Housing Subsidy Scheme (HSS) is central to the type of development that takes place. In terms of the subsidy, each application must have a clearly identified community-based partner (CBP) to share the responsibility of development with other partners.

Masiphumelele is located approximately 30 kilometres from Cape Town on the Cape Peninsula. The estimated 2766 people will be accommodated on site and service schemes once the development is complete. Victoria Mxenge is located approximately 8 kilometres inland from Cape Town. The completed development will comprise 148 houses and a community centre. The majority of respondents at both sites were women. All spoke isiXhosa as the home language. Education levels varied but few had completed high school. In both cases the majority of residents were unemployed. At the time of the research respondents at Victoria Mxenge and from the informal section of Masiphumelele used communal toilets and taps, while those in the formal section of Masiphumelele lived on serviced sites. Residents of Victoria Mxenge have security of tenure, while at Masiphumelele residents were waiting to receive the title deeds to their properties. Links with outside organizations were high in both instances. However, the nature of these relations varied and has led to different patterns of interaction. Funding in both instances is mainly from the housing subsidy, although the means for accessing it differ. At Victoria Mxenge all residents are also members of the CBO acting as the CBP. At Masiphumelele, there was initially a CBO which then ceased to function.

How do CBOs Interact with Funding Bodies?

The way in which CBOs interact with funding bodies varies and this may create new inequalities in the access to a health-promoting living environment. If a governance approach is to be effective, the state needs to act to ensure that partnerships are equal. However, partnerships may not be equal in terms of resource allocation where the private sector is involved due to goals of profit maximization. The housing subsidy has failed to take account of the tensions or dynamic nature of interactions between the private sector and CBOs. While the four-dimensional framework of governance includes a cultural dimension in order to examine the shared objectives between partners, the framework does not make room for instances where there are conflicting objectives. Where partnerships are unequal, the aims of the government to facilitate housing delivery to the poorest of the poor through governance does not lead to a sanitation provision process that is accessible to everyone.

In a pluralist system, CBOs are seen to be able to hold the state and its institutions accountable. The pluralist nature of the South African state with its emphasis on transparency, accountability and participation has led to a 'bottom-up' approach to housing policy. Under such a policy, it can be argued that subsidy applications should be initiated by the community. However, historically disempowered communities may not have sufficient information to undertake a subsidy application. Where a developer submits the application on their behalf, they may not have the capacity to hold the developer accountable for its actions. At Masiphumelele residents have heard of the subsidy but have expressed frustration at not having sufficient information about the extent of the benefits and how the subsidy is administered. At Victoria Mxenge, the community has applied for the subsidy directly without going through a developer and they show a thorough understanding of the subsidy system. In terms of state policy to reduce inequalities in access to a healthier living environment, the administration of the subsidy is not ensuring an equal level of information dissemination regarding its benefits. This is having an impact on the sustainability of services being provided.

The policy of a People's Housing Process (PHP) requires information dissemination by the institutions that control the subsidy and technical support to the various partners for their roles in the sanitation provision process. The PHP assumes that people will supplement the subsidy with their own resources such as savings schemes and their own labour. However, this assumes that people have the time to build; they have the capacity to build (which the elderly or disabled do not have); and they are able to form homogeneous groups with an interest in building their own homes. While members of the Victoria Mxenge CBO described the benefits of savings schemes, the case of Masiphumelele showed the limits of these forms of networks. The social capital[1] envisaged as being promoted by the PHP may not emerge in cases where there are insufficient technical resources to supplement the housing subsidy or where the basis for forming an interest group is not identifiable.

HOW DO CBOS INTERACT WITH NGOS?

The roles of NGOs in South Africa in the future are most likely to be twofold. First, as providers of technical and institutional capacity building to the government and to CBOs. Second, as facilitators of local government and CBO interactions. Where the technical and institutional dimensions of the ability of CBOs have been weak historically, they will not have the capacity to access the subsidy which would provide them with an improved living environment. While the political will of the state is for NGOs to adopt a capacity-building role in terms of the technical skills and institutional knowledge of the housing provision process, not all NGOs have this as their goal.

Interaction between the community and the NGOs varied. At Masiphumelele the dominant NGO has taken the decision not to take an active role in promoting skills and disseminating information regarding the housing development process. At Victoria Mxenge there is evidence of a shared responsibility for establishing savings schemes that has grown out of a common interest in the provision of housing. It cannot be said that the aim of one NGO is 'correct' and another 'incorrect'. What is significant, is the need to recognize that the type of NGO a CBO or community interacts with, will influence the extent to which the CBOs form partnerships and become involved in housing and sanitation provision.

The fundamental difference between NGOs is the nature of the skills being transferred. People's Dialogue, the dominant NGO at Victoria Mxenge, aims to empower and build the capacity of the homeless by transferring the skills necessary to build their homes. This is not only fulfilling an expressed need of improved housing, but is involving historically disempowered people in the inherently political process of housing and sanitation provision. In contrast, the skills being imparted at Masiphumelele are aimed at sewing, pottery, cooking and computing. Such skills do not assist the community in challenging the social-political status quo which is a determining factor in environmental health. By relying on NGOs to be the facilitators of interaction between the government and CBOs, governance becomes dependent on the NGO. A potential result of such a policy will be the emergence of CBOs skilled in sanitation provision and health promotion only where there has been access to NGO support. This may lead to new inequalities in access to a health-promoting living environment.

How do CBOs Interact with Local Government?

One of the legacies of apartheid has been that local government institutional structures are unable to respond to the demands of a housing and sanitation provision process that involves community partnerships in decision making. At the same time, people working in the local government sector lack the technical skills to embark on a partnership approach with CBOs. The Government of National Unity (GNU) is looking towards local governments as the implementers of a governance approach to reconstruction and development. However, evidence suggests that local governments at the front-line of governance may lack the capacity to form effective and equal partnerships with communities.

Local governments have an important role to play in the sanitation provision process in that they are traditionally the level of government at which sanitation provision takes place. In South Africa, as well as being responsible for implementing the changes heralded by the GNU, local governments have themselves been restructured. With new forms of sanitation provision being described as a partnership between local government and civil society, this tier of government will be an important factor in the extent to which CBOs become involved in the sanitation process.

Partnerships that do exist between local government and CBOs are fragmented. Reasons for this fragmentation include, first, the deterioration of the previous means of information exchange, frustration with the existing means of communication, and the failure to find a new means of communication. Second, partly due to the failure of information exchange, an unclear view exists of who is responsible for what aspects of sanitation provision. Third, newly elected local government officials may lack the political will, the technical ability or institutional support to embark on the governance approach of partnerships formation.

The breakdown in communication structure is evidence of a weakness within the institutional dimension of governance. The political and institutional structures are the two most closely linked within the four-dimensional framework of governance. If the political will of the local government to establish the mechanisms for governance does not exist, then the institutional structures will not be formed. If the mechanisms by which the interactions between local government and CBOs take place have been eroded or have failed to find the means of responding to change, partnerships around sanitation will be affected and gaps in the framework of governance appear. However, the failure of the mechanisms of communication between CBOs and the local government may not necessarily have negative consequences. It may lead to the strengthening or formation of other partnerships. For example, at Masiphumelele, one group of participants explained how they had recently established a Housing Saving Scheme and this CBO was part of the partnership of CBOs forming the South African Homeless People's Federation (SAHPF).

The political transformation taking place at a national level and exemplified by the governance speak of the white papers was not reflected in the institutional structures of local government. At the same time, however, evidence provided by the community leaders in Masiphumelele indicated that there is no shared understanding of how leadership should be exercised. It was found that the political will to establish and maintain mechanisms of communication between CBOs and local government, and CBOs and outsiders, needs to come as much from the community as it does from the local authority.

What Social Networks Exist in Communities and Between CBOs?

For CBOs to become involved in the sanitation provision process there needs to be a means of overcoming the legacy of fragmented communities in order to identify common interests and form equitable partnerships. In Masiphumelele the fragmentation of social networks has been a feature of community organization since its formation. There have been no attempts to form partnerships to address environmental health. Cleavages and fragmentation have hindered attempts to form equitable partnerships and have undermined the current GNU policy towards sanitation provision.

In contrast to Masiphumelele, the development of external partnerships has been vital to the Victoria Mxenge HSS achieving its stated aims. The CBO at Victoria Mxenge was formed out of a common interest to build formal houses and to improve the living environment. With the assistance of the NGO People's Dialogue, contact has been established with other CBOs who have a similar interest at international level. At a national level, the SAHPF is now a self-sustaining organization of CBOs. While the residents of Victoria Mxenge have not had to confront internal conflict, they have managed to resolve disputes with external groups. At Masiphumelele, contrary to the principles of social capital, networks were not seen to complement each other. However, at Victoria Mxenge, membership of outsider organizations was accepted and even encouraged as sources of new skills or information.

IS THERE AN IDENTIFICATION OF COMMON INTERESTS?

It was found that the link between sanitation and health is well known and the desire to improve the living environment is based on this know-ledge. At Victoria Mxenge residents reported success in achieving their goal of housing. At Masiphumelele residents had not yet achieved formal housing and there was no consensus among the community as to how they hoped to achieve this goal.

There are numerous examples at Victoria Mxenge of cooperation – from how the development was planned to the way the saving scheme operates. The identification of a common interest to improve the environment and a shared understanding of how this is to be achieved relates to the cultural dimension of governance. Through this shared interest, members of the saving scheme have accessed training collectively through national and international partnerships in order for them to gain the technical skills required to take responsibility for the development project.

Residents of Masiphumelele had been mobilized in the past around resisting eviction from the Cape Peninsula and obtaining security of tenure (Development Action Group, 1996). Subsequent to addressing this interest which had brought them together, residents aimed to improve their living environment through improved housing. However, at the time of the research, this had not yet been achieved. A possible explanation is identified from exploring the interests at Victoria Mxenge. At Victoria Mxenge residents, with the NGO acting as the 'triggering' agent, have engaged in the housing and sanitation provision process. This process is inherently political by nature and challenges the social-political determinants of environmental health. In contrast, residents of Masiphumelele have not had access to the resources or outside organizations to enable the engagement of the political and institutional dimensions of sanitation provision. For the residents of Victoria Mxenge the shared interest in environmental, along with the other factors, led to an engagement with sanitation provision. This is related to the extent to which sanitation is seen as a shared responsibility within equal partnerships.

Is there an Identification of a Shared Responsibility for Sanitation?

Whereas interactions refer to a variety of forms of mutually beneficial actions, partnerships imply a shared responsibility in decision making. It is the intention that the rights of South Africans embodied in the Constitution (RSA, 1996) will be matched by 'civic responsibilities' (Department of Constitutional Development, c1998, pp15–6). Government respondents emphasized the need to adopt a shared responsibility with the private sector and civil society. Informants from the private sector revealed their desire to see the state play a greater role in leading the PHP. At Victoria Mxenge, residents were keen to take responsibility for their development, believing they knew their needs better than anyone else. At Masiphumelele, residents expressed their displeasure at not having the opportunity to be more involved in decision making and were reluctant to take on responsibility for sanitation. These findings are evidence of the balance between a community's right to a healthy living environment and the responsibilities of the community, local government and public sector in realizing that right.

In the process of balancing rights and responsibilities, government structures have the responsibility to enable communities to make informed decisions and communities have the right to choose their sanitation system. The extent to which the government disseminates information will be dependent on institutional and technical capacity and political will. Despite the national political will for local government structures to fit the 'governance speak' description of transparency, accountability, accessibility, efficiency, appropriateness and empowerment, the evidence illustrates that there are political and racial cleavages hampering the formation of partnerships required for governance. In a study of community organization in Jordan, Raed (1998) identified similar limitations to participation in low income housing production. 'Successful' groups were found to be those that had previous experience or access to groups with such experience; could identify the gatekeepers and resource providers in the official system and pressure them; learned empowerment by doing, and found that state-induced participation was different from autonomous participation (Raed, 1998).

The case study findings are summarized in Table 6.1 and the implications for a governance approach towards sanitation provision are highlighted. The dimensions of governance are characterized in column two with sustainability in mind, although not all relate to sustainability. Also, the findings in column three are not mutually exclusive across the dimensions.

Conclusion

The research showed first, how the manner in which CBOs access finance and the nature of the partnerships between the private sector, NGOs and local government will influence the nature of sanitation projects and may give rise to new inequalities. Second, the research found that an envisaged

Table 6.1 *Summary of Case Study Exploring Environmental Health and Governance*

Dimensions of Governance	Characteristics of Dimensions	Case Study Findings
Technical	• Refers to constraints imposed by natural resources, education, skills and industrial capacity • The type of economic growth that takes place influences environmental sustainability • Sustainability requires a balance in development processes to encompass the needs of all groups in society	• The partnerships of governance require civil society to supplement public initiatives with its own resources • Influenced by the role of NGOs – may or may not lead to the ability to challenge social-political context • Local government may lack the technical skills to form partnerships • CBO skills are needed that will challenge the social-political context of environmental health
Political	• Refers to the establishment of objectives and the exercise of leadership • Recognizes the need to incorporate economic and social policy into decision making and emphasizes the participation of all groups in society • The social milieu is seen to provide the setting for civil society to engage with the state	• The state needs to ensure equal access to technical resources such as funding opportunities • NGOs may not wish to follow government policy • Institutional structures of government are dependent on the political willingness of government to set up such mechanisms
Institutional	• Refers to the ability to manage and implement projects • The need for mechanisms of service provision to perform their functions equitably • Requires a legal framework to ensure inequalities are overcome	• The administration of funding opportunities aimed at overcoming inequalities, such as subsidies, requires dissemination of information about benefits • Influenced by the role of NGOs • CBOs found to lack knowledge of government institutions rather than technical skills
Cultural	• Refers to people's shared beliefs and values and ideas of how power should be exercised • Based on the recognition that the state does not exist in a vacuum • Will influence how societies agree to reach the objective of environmental health	• Four-dimensional framework fails to take account of conflicting objectives and historical fragmentation • Governance requires the identification of a common interest and shared understanding of responsibility between partners • Networks are not only useful for skills transfer, but also for achieving a common understanding of environmental health • An identification of a common interest leads to collective action in terms of, for example, skills acquisition

Source: Stuttaford, 1998

role of NGOs in a governance approach is to facilitate the interaction between CBOs and local government. However, not all NGOs will adopt this role and some may control rather than facilitate interaction. Third, local governments were found to lack the technical and institutional capacity to form equal partnerships with CBOs. Fourth, it was shown that CBOs do not necessarily lack the technical skills to engage in the sanitation provision process but rather the knowledge of the institutional system of sanitation. Fifth, while in certain instances social networks within and between CBOs will result in a sharing of skills and resources, in other instances the historical fragmentation and diversity of a community may prevent social networks from forming. Sixth, it was found that although environmental health may be identified as a common interest, this may be insufficient for reaching a common belief on how to address this interest. While at Victoria Mxenge residents were engaging the inherently political process of sanitation and housing provision, residents of Masiphumelele did not have access to the resources or interaction with outsider organizations to 'trigger' a similar engagement with the social-political determinants of environmental health. Finally, there is a need to balance the rights and responsibilities of various partners in the provision of environmental health services.

Once the decision to begin reform in South Africa was taken in 1990, political transformation was relatively swift with the establishment of the GNU in 1994. The new Constitution embodies people's right to a safe and healthy living environment. Institutional reforms, even if slow and chaotic, have progressed with this aim in mind. However, the interactions between government and civil society are more complex than having only a political and institutional level. Measures to improve environmental health also need to pay attention to the cultural and technical dimensions of governance. Moreover, while transformation at a national level has been swift, the institutions of local government – in other words, that level of government responsible for implementing new policies – has been slow to adopt a governance approach to environmental health.

Research on urban health in developing countries quickly identified the quality of urban governance as a key facilitator to improved policy and practice. While the general trend of health sector reform has decentralized some decision making from the central ministry to the local or district level, such reforms have largely addressed health services only. With regard to environmental health, one looks to governments in transition, like South Africa, for new models of governance. The case study presented here demonstrates the use of examining governance in terms of its different dimensions and highlights the gaps between the vision of how new relationships can be forged between the state and civil society in order to improve environmental health and the reality among low income, urban populations. Sustainable urban health development requires new forms of governance. Further, multi-disciplinary research, which combines political, social and health sciences, will continue to identify and analyse best practice which, hopefully, will inform future policy.

ACKNOWLEDGEMENTS

The case study formed part of the PhD research undertaken by Maria Allison with assistance from a South Bank University Research Scholarship awarded by the School of Urban Development and Policy, and the School of Construction. The National Urbanization and Health Research Programme of the Medical Research Council of South Africa provided financial assistance for the recruitment of a focus group facilitator, and provided logistical and moral support during the fieldwork. The study would not have been possible without the cooperation of the many informants who agreed to participate. They gave of their time and of themselves to speak of their experiences and to teach about their lives.

NOTES

1   The establishment of partnerships – in other words, the recognition of a shared responsibility – is similar to the concept of social capital used by Putnam (1993) and Wilkinson (1996). Putnam (1993, pp664–5) defines social capital as 'features of social life – networks, norms and trust – that enable participants to act together more effectively to pursue shared objectives'. A number of limitations of social capital have since been identified (see, for example, Budlender and Dube, 1997; and Harriss and de Renzio, 1997).

REFERENCES

Amselle, J (1990) *Mixed Logic: Anthropological Identities of Africa and Others*, Payot, Paris
Banuri, T and Holmberg, J (1992) *Governance for Sustainable Development: A Southern Perspective*, Earthscan, London
Boeninger, E (1991) 'Governance and development', in *Proceedings of the World Bank Annual Conference on Development Economics*, World Bank, Washington, DC
Boshielo, F, Seager, J, Craffert, L and Mills, G (1996) *Community Perceptions of the Relationship Between Informal Housing and Environmental Health: An Exploratory Study*, Human Sciences Research Council, Pretoria
Budlender, D and Dube, N (1997) *Starting with What We Have – Basing Development Activities on Local Realities: A Critical Review of Recent Experience*, Working Paper, Policy Business Unit, Development Bank of South Africa, Pretoria
Chetty, K S (1992) 'Urbanisation and health: evidence from Cape Town', in Smith, D M (ed) *The Apartheid City and Beyond: Urbanisation and Social Change in South Africa*, Routledge, London, pp216–27
Clark, J (1991) *Democratizing Development*, Earthscan, London
Department of Constitutional Development (c1998) *Integrated Development Planning for Local Authorities: A User-friendly Guide*, Department of Constitutional Development, Pretoria
Department of Housing (1995) *South African National Report Habitat II: The City Summit*, draft report compiled by Division of Building Technology, CSIR, under

the auspices of the South African National Preparatory Committee chaired by the Department of Housing, Pretoria

Department of Housing (1997) *Urban Development Framework*, Department of Housing, Pretoria

Development Action Group (1996) *Masiphumelele: A Case Study of the Role of the Development Action Group in the Informal Community of Noordhoek*, Development Action Group, Observatory

Eberhard, R and Quick, A J R (1995) 'Water supply and sanitation in urban South Africa: getting it right during the transition and beyond', *Development Southern Africa*, vol 12, no 6, pp883–905

Espinosa, L and Rivera, O A L (1994) 'UNICEF's urban basic services programme in illegal settlements in Guatemala City', *Environment and Urbanisation*, vol 6, no 2, pp9–29

Franceys, R, Pickford, J and Reed, R (1992) *A Guide to the Development of On-site Sanitation*, WHO, Geneva

Giddens, A (1998) *The Third Way: The Renewal of Social Democracy*, Polity, London

Gilbert, A and Gugler, J (1982) *Cities, Poverty and Development: Urbanisation in the Third World*, Oxford University Press, Oxford

Hamza, A (1989) 'An appraisal of environmental consequences of urban development in Alexandria, Egypt', *Environment and Urbanisation*, vol 1, no 1, 22–30

Hardoy, J E and Satterthwaite, D (1986) 'Shelter, infrastructure and services in third world cities', *Habitat International*, vol 10, no 3, pp245–84

Hardoy, J E, Mitlin, D and Satterthwaite, D (1992) *Environmental Problems in Third World Cities*, Earthscan, London

Harpham, T and Boateng, K (1997) 'Urban governance in relation to the operation of urban services in developing countries', *Habitat International*, vol 21, no 1, pp65–77

Harpham, T and Tanner, M (1995) *Urban Health in Developing Countries: Progress and Prospects*, Earthscan, London

Harpham, T and Werna, E (1996) 'The idea of healthy cities and its application', in Pugh, C (ed) *Sustainability, the Environment and Urbanization*, Earthscan, London

Harriss, J and De Renzio, P (1997) '"Missing link" or analytically missing?: the concept of social capital an introductory bibliographic essay', *Journal of International Development*, vol 9, no 7, pp919–37

Head, J (1996) 'Health and development: some concerns about South Africa's health policy', *Urbanisation and Health Newsletter*, vol 30, pp33–48

Hirst, P (1993) *Associative Democracy: New Forms of Economic and Social Governance*, Policy Press, Bristol

Holmberg, J, Thomson, K and Timberlake, L (1993) *Facing the Future: Beyond the Earth Summit*, Earthscan, London

Kooiman, J (ed) (1993) *Modern Governance*, Sage, London

Leiris, M (1969) *Cinq Etudes d' Ethnologie*, Gontheir, Paris

Martin, D (1991) 'The cultural dimension of governance', in *Proceedings of the World Bank Annual Conference on Development Economics*, World Bank, Washington, DC

McAuslan, P (1993) 'The role of law in urban planning', in N Devas and C Rakodi (eds) *Managing Fast Growing Cities*, Longman, London

Messkoub, M (1992) 'Deprivation and structural adjustment', in T Hewitt, M Mackintosh and M Wuyts (eds) *Development Policy and Public Action*, Oxford University Press, Oxford

Midgley, J (1986) *Community Participation, Social Development and the State*, Methuen, London

Nutbeam, D (1986) 'Health promotion glossary', *Health Promotion*, vol 1, no 1, pp113–27

Putnam, R D (1993) *Making Democracy Work: Civic Traditions in Modern Italy*, Princeton University Press, Princeton

Raed, H (1998) *Public Participation and Community Organisation in the Low Income Housing Production: the Jordanian Experience*, unpublished PhD thesis, Development Planning Unit, University College, London

Robinson, J (1996) *The Power of Apartheid: State, Power and Space in South African Cities*, Butterworth Heinemann, Oxford

Republic of South Africa (RSA) (1996) *Constitution of the Republic of South Africa 1996*, Constitutional Assembly

Republic of South Africa (RSA) (1997) *White Paper for the Transformation of the Health System in South Africa*, Government Gazette No 17910, Government Printer, Pretoria

Schteingart, M and de Mexico, E C (1989) 'The environmental problems associated with urban development in Mexico City', *Environment and Urbanisation*, vol 1, no 1, pp40–50

Seager, J (1992) 'Urbanisation and public health: the challenge, the effects and the need for intersectoral collaboration', *The Civil Engineer in South Africa*, September, pp295–98

Stuttaford M C (1998) *Health and Housing in Cape Town: Sanitation Provision Explored through a Framework of Governance*, unpublished PhD thesis, School of Urban Development and Policy, South Bank University, London

Swilling, M (ed) (1997) *Governing African Cities*, Witwatersrand University Press, Johannesburg

United Nations (UN) (1996) *Habitat Agenda and Istanbul Declaration*, United Nations Department of Public Information, New York

United Nations Centre for Human Settlements (UNCHS) (Habitat)) (1995) *Guidelines for Assessing Effecting Demand of Communities for Environmental Infrastructure*, CEMIS Module No 4, UNCHS, Nairobi

United Nations Development Programme (UNDP) (1992) *Human Development Report*, Oxford University Press, New York

Werna, E, Harpham, T, Blue, I and Goldstein, G (1998) *Healthy City Projects in Developing Countries*, Earthscan, London

Wilkinson, R G (1996) *Unhealthy Societies: The Afflictions of Inequality*, Routledge, London

World Health Organization (WHO) (1948) Official Records of the World Health Organization, 10, in WHO (1961) *The Public Health Aspects of Housing*, Technical Report No 225, WHO, Geneva

World Health Organization (WHO) (1995) *A Review of the Operation and Future Development of the WHO Healthy Cities Programme*, WHO/EOS/95.11, WHO, Geneva

World Bank (1994) *Governance – The World Bank's Experience*, World Bank, Washington, DC

World Bank (1997) 'World Development Report 1997, The State in a Changing World', Summary [WWW], http/www.worldbank.org, 7 February 1998

Yach, D (1998) 'The role of collaborating centres in the 21st century', paper presented at *The First Meeting of WHO Collaborating Centres in the Americas*, PAHO, Washington DC, 9 October

Yacoob, M and Whiteford, L M (1995) 'An untapped resource: community based epidemiologists for environmental health', *Environment and Urbanisation*, vol 7, no 1, pp219–30

Zwi, A B and Mills, A (1995) 'Health policy in less developed countries: past trends and future directions', *Journal of International Development*, vol 7, no 3, pp299–328

7 SUSTAINABILITY IN SQUATTER SETTLEMENTS

Cedric Pugh

In terms of wide-scaled human welfare and sustainability, the conditions of life in urban squatter settlements have enormous significance. They comprise some 30–70 per cent of the housing stock in many cities and towns in developing countries. Their scale is attributed to the inadequacies of housing finance systems and land development, along with the pressing realities of demographic growth and mass poverty. A major aim of international aid agencies and sometimes of governments is to improve the sanitary services and the legitimacy of property and occupancy rights in some squatter settlements. This raises dilemmas in institutional and organizational approaches, and it changes relationships between residents and their associations to urban politics and economics. More than this, households and communities will sometimes change their attitudes and approaches towards their housing and the environment. The discussions in this chapter explore these themes, some adding new dimensions to the literature.

INTRODUCTION

Many cities and towns in developing countries have self-help and self-build components of their total housing stock which range from some 30 to 70 per cent. In general terms, as household incomes increase, self-build recedes and self-help with its relational contracting with builders increases (Peattie, 1987). Furthermore under conditions of medium-term increases in income, households will tend to improve their houses by replacing inferior with superior materials, adding rooms and workshops, and sometimes personalizing their outside space. Accordingly, what is to be envisaged is a makeshift structure of meagre quality being transformed into something more sub-stantial and homely through 'progressive' improvement. Improvement is frequently enhanced and accelerated when in situ programmes of environ-mental upgrading install access roads, potable water, sewerage systems and the regularization of tenure (ie, providing occupancy and/or property ownership rights). In one sense, all of this is a large process of conservation in terms of economics, urban building and sometimes in environmental, health-related and other social improvements. In other words, squatter settlements beckon for sustainable improvement and state-assisted regener-ation, if well done, expresses sustainability in social, economic, financial and environmental terms. It can be argued that in aggregate terms those sorts of 'progressive' improvements add more economic and social value than high-profiled heritage projects. They have significance for the everyday living conditions and social opportunities for hundreds of millions of people. Of course, in principle it is also possible to add in some forms of aesthetic qualities to squatter settlements.

The opening paragraph does not convey all the social, economic and aesthetic realities of mass land invasion and squatter settlement. Unim-proved settlements are often insanitary. Some 1 billion people do not have access to safe water supplies and 60 per cent of the world's population lacks effective sanitation services. In its world health report for 1998, the WHO says:

> *Poor environmental quality is estimated to be directly responsible for 25 per cent of all preventable ill-health in the world today, with diarrhoeal diseases and acute respiratory infections heading the list (WHO 1998, p123).*

Some 66 per cent of preventable ill-health owing to environmental cond-itions occurs among children, being especially significant in developing countries. Malnutrition continues to be a problem in terms of health, capacity to work and vulnerability for reduced social opportunities: various studies indicate that stunting and low body mass occur among sections of the population in poverty (ie, below US$370 per annum). Residential densities in the poorer parts of Calcutta range between 800 and 1000 people per hectare, compared with some 70 in most North American cities (World Resources Institute et al, 1996). In some cities, especially where housing markets are tight, squatter settlements house moderate- and middle-income groups, as well as the poor and the poorest of the poor. This partly indicates the inadequate supplies from the formal housing sector, reflecting mass poverty, underdeveloped housing finance systems and inadequacies in land policy and land delivery systems. Housing sector development represents only some 3–5 per cent of GDP in developing countries, although this is an underestimate because it omits large amounts of unaccounted self-help housing.

Squatter settlements are varied in their characteristics, and this influ-ences their potential for conservation and regeneration. Some are massive, with populations over 100,000, and others are small, occupying infill sites.

In some cases, the populations have expectations of imminent redevelopment, whereas in others de facto occupancy rights seem secure. Sometimes a settlement generates its own leadership and organizational structures which can be used for negotiating with politicians and bureaucracies for installing infrastructure. Other settlements have either apathy or powerlessness. Housing and environmental improvement can be spontaneous, and this is more likely in those settlements which are well established and where there is an expectation of medium- or long-term security. Also, some settlements may be selected for environmental improvement and the regularization of tenure rights. This will lead to some positive expectations, but also open the possibilities for using political skills and pressures to influence the selection of improvements, and the distribution of costs and benefits among households. State-assisted regeneration will sometimes raise the question of redesigning lay-outs and realignments, with implications for reducing housing densities and for rehousing schemes. In fact, in prescriptive principle – but not always in practice – the improvement of squatter settlements should be co-ordinated with new housing development and the macro-spatial planning of urban areas. Regeneration also increases land and property prices, and this may or may not lead to 'gentrification', depending on the dynamics of submarkets in urban housing.

THE THEORY

As might be expected, post-1960 self-help housing in squatter settlements has some theoretical justifications. Although advocacy for self-help has had various housing authors (see Pugh, 1980; Harms, 1982; Harris, 1998), in terms of timely impacts upon policy and widespread influence the best known theorists have been Abrams (1964) and John F C Turner (1967; 1972; 1976). Abrams, who led UN missions to developing countries in the 1950s and 1960s, wrote about gross housing shortages in rapidly growing cities and the appalling insanitary conditions in widespread squatter settlements. He favoured in situ slum improvement and 'instalment construction'. In comparative terms, Turner injected more social idealism into his advocacy of state-assisted sites and services, and related slum improvement schemes. He based his advocacy upon humans' self-fulfilment and their commitment to housing for expressing things of value in their lives. Turner's phraseology was in terms of 'freedom to build' and 'housing as a verb', a process of popular, participatory activity. His theoretical values were much influenced by the pioneering town planner Patrick Geddes (1854–1932) who had first-hand experience in India and other developing countries in the 1920s. Turner had on-location experience in Peru in the 1950s and 1960s where he noticed that households improved their housing incrementally, and within affordability from earnings and savings. For Turner, this was a better option for low- and moderate-income people than high-cost, subsidized public housing which was often transferred to higher income groups. His advocacies secured a US$25 million loan from the Inter-American

Development Bank in 1958 for rehousing following a devastating earthquake. And, more significantly, his ideas were accepted and adapted by the World Bank in the early 1970s when it entered loan assistance for urban projects in developing countries (see the discussions below).

In the 1980s and 1990s, low-income housing theory and practice has moved on from a focus upon self-help to whole sector housing development (World Bank, 1993; Kessides, 1997). Nonetheless, Turner's theories have remained relevant within this broader housing context, and they have been extended into the 'brown agenda' environmentalism of the 1990s. 'Brown agenda' environmentalism was raised in significance at the UN Conference on the Environment and Development (UNCED), Rio de Janeiro, 1992. In Chapter 7 of Agenda 21 a wide-ranging set of guidelines for sustainable urban development was set out. Essentially, the UNCED meeting called upon local governments to mobilize their communities for broad-based, participatory environmental improvement in urban areas. In effect, and by consolidation through the UN Centre for Human Settlements (UNCHS), Habitat Agenda from the Istanbul, 1996, Habitat II meeting, a new approach to 'environmental planning and management' (EPM) was being proposed. The new EPM envisaged meetings of stakeholders (for example, government agencies, business, professionals and representatives of communities), to identify feasible priorities and transform them into action plans. In fact, EPM aimed to create new institutions and capacities for urban environmental improvement. In developing countries, squatter settlement upgrading would normally be included in the EPM priorities. Although the progress with the localization of Agenda 21 has been slow, and with varied understanding of the idea of sustainability, the principles can be associated with Turner's ideas. The main difference is that sustainability is conceived as bringing together economic, social and environmental with overall development policies (Barbier, 1998). As with the case of advocacies for state-assisted self-help in the 1960s, theory, practice and policy were moving forward together and with widespread impact. More than this, in some circumstances, as in Goiania, Brazil, squatter residents organized themselves to achieve self-help homeownership rather than the less preferred rental tenure they normally experienced.

INTERNATIONAL HOUSING POLICY

Although international housing policy has been conceived and formulated by various international aid agencies, the World Bank has been the most influential. This is largely because it provides large loans for urban and housing programmes, usually with conditionalities to influence strategic directions in policy. For example, in the 1983–92 period, the Bank made some 87 programme allocations, amounting to US$8.8 billion. The World Bank has periodically reformed and redirected its low-income housing policies (World Bank, 1983; 1993). For reasons of logic and convenience, the Bank's policy development can be divided into the 1972–82, the 1983–93 and the post–1993 periods. These will be presented in summary form, with some emphasis on the issues in the upgrading of squatter settlements.

In the 1972–82 period, the World Bank adapted Turner's theories. It advocated sites and services and in situ slum upgrading projects. The underlying principles were based upon affordability, cost recovery and replicability. Affordability meant that land and service costs were to be budget-led rather than from the norms of town planning and engineering design standards. This recognized that the poor spent some 65–85 per cent of their household budgets on food, leaving housing as a residual, lesser priority. Cost recovery fitted the precepts of orthodox economics, applying the user pays principle and reasoned as a way of curbing the growth of rural-to-urban migration. Taken together, affordability and cost recovery also fitted the Bank's financial imperatives – that is, in securing loan repayment so that it could repay its borrowed funds in international capital markets and use its grant money from the leading industrial countries in economically and socially responsible ways. Replicability was a prescriptive principle: it meant that in some hypothetical and practical sense, projects could continue and eventually substantially reduce the growth in squatter settlement. In terms of actual experience, cost recovery was achieved only occasionally, especially in the slum upgrading projects; sites for self-help building were sometimes remote from employment opportunities; institutional capability was often weak, with some indications of corruption; and the projects scarcely led to citywide housing reform (Pugh, 1990a; Nientied and van der Linden, 1985; Skinner et al, 1987; Turner, 1980).

By 1983 the World Bank was ready to redirect its housing policies. First, it was acknowledged that institutional reform and support had to be widened from project management to general urban policy and to full ranges of programmes (World Bank, 1983; 1993). Second, and related to the foregoing point, it was recognized that the geographically delineated projects were self-limiting. They lacked any probability of scaling up and deep impact on the economic and social development of the city or town as a whole. Third, the Bank had suitable, alternative means of advancing its housing programmes. One alternative was to channel funds through the conduits of housing finance systems. The funds would be disbursed more rapidly, but this approach could be applied only in those countries where housing finance systems had been developed, and these were mainly high- and middle-income developing countries. However, the Bank did demonstrate success in India, a poor country: its 1988 allocation of a US$250 million loan was innovative, using the well-managed Housing Development Finance Corporation (HDFC). The HDFC extended its credit lower down the distribution of household income and stimulated the regionalization of new housing finance institutions. By the late 1980s the World Bank gradually reduced its direct sites and services projects, but these continued indirectly where countries allocated funds into social housing programmes that had some self-help components in new development. For example, Chile used Bank loans for housing vouchers in their low-income social housing (sites and services) schemes. The upgrading of squatter settlements continued, but under a revised approach.

The new approach was accomplished in Brazil's Parana Market Towns Improvement Project, 1983–88 (World Bank 1994). A set of towns, encouraged by the state-level government, agreed to create a revolving municipal fund. World Bank loan conditionalities required 'sustainable finance', represented in cost recovery, and in the skilled management of receipts and expenditures. The local governments and their communities could select their type of sub-projects, place price tags on them and rationalize community participation in the selection of priorities. Some of the in situ slum upgrading programmes were implemented on the basis that over 85 per cent of the self-help housing units would be retained in the rationalization of lay-outs and realignments. The Bank's roles were satisfied more readily because the projects were pro-poor and a demonstration of financial sustainability. Meanwhile the programme was 'owned' by the local governments which had decentralized responsibility for maintenance, cost recovery and social effectiveness. Compared to the superseded 1972–82 ways, the new 1983–93 approach was more 'programmatic', with broader and deeper institutional reform and development. The use of municipal development funds was appropriate in developing country contexts where bond and financial securities markets are often undeveloped.

In 1993 the World Bank again redirected its strategic housing policy, extending its 'programmatic' approach from the 1980s (World Bank, 1993). The 'programmatic' approach represented a partial rather than a fully comprehensive conceptualization of housing. It did not set housing in a broader context of its contribution to economic and social development. The question of subsidies and poverty was not included, and the contributing elements of land policy were undeveloped. Also, experience had shown that some town planning and building regulations were inhibiting the expansion of the housing sector. Accordingly, the World Bank's strategic policy reform set out a seven-point programme:

- housing finance systems were to be further developed;
- the backlogs and inadequacies in infrastructure had to be given greater significance;
- land management and land policy often required reform, especially when they slowed down development substantially,
- regulatory audits were recommended as a means of accelerating supplies, especially in low income housing;
- the competitive efficiency of the construction industry was to be monitored;
- targeted subsidies were viewed as appropriate for the poor; and
- further attention was to be given to institutionally loaded reform.

The strategic review had an underlying political economy. Housing was to be understood as economically productive, especially in its capacity to generate income and employment multipliers. In general terms, for any one peso or rupee spent on housing construction or rehabilitation, national income expands by a factor of 1.5–2.0. Housing multipliers tend to be larger than most other sectors because in housing the leakages to spending on import content are lower. Hitherto, many policy makers had regarded housing simply as a necessary item of social expenditure. Of even more significance was the elaboration of the idea of 'enablement'. Enablement was about the state creating the legal, institutional, economic, financial and social frameworks to enhance economic efficiency and social effectiveness in the development of the housing sector.

By the mid-1990s 'enablement' had broadened and deepened in significance. It encompassed not only institutionally loaded reform, but also governance. Governance entered into central positions in virtually all development agendas, with a focus upon state–market–society relations. Its scope covered economic, education, health, environment, housing, urban and other policies. In housing it consolidated the community-based, participatory elements in the upgrading of squatter settlements. An ideal enablement set of principles would bring together technical know-how, a broad participatory approach among residents with wide social inclusion, capability in urban development authorities and a set of rules whereby each partner would know its responsibilities. An underlying socio-economic rationale would be present in order to guide the roles of each stakeholder or partner in the multi-institutional and multi-organizational setting. Firms would contribute efficiency and entrepreneurship; community-based organizations would mediate between households and government authorities; government agencies would provide urban management expertise; and households would variously provide finance, self-help resources and localized relevance in the environmental improvements. Clearly, this represents a complex process with some risks of failure, including institutional incapacity, the political capturing of the process to serve narrow rather than general public interests and market manipulation by firms. More is said about the prospects for relative success and failure in subsequent discussions.

Enablement frameworks also have relevance to new building in whole housing sector development. Again, a facilitative framework to enhance housing supplies would have multi-institutional and multi-organizational characteristics. Builders would be within competitive market conditions, with access to development finance. Land policies would ensure adequate supplies of serviced land, well coordinated with the agencies that installed and maintained infrastructure. The legal-administrative system within government would secure property rights to plots of land. Housing finance institutions would be experienced at managing flows of funds, scrutinizing loan applications and managing various risks, including liquidity, credit and interest rate risks. Beyond functional efficiency, for relevance in social development, the overall policy and enablement framework would have some pro-poor and egalitarian elements. Such has been the case in Chennai, India, in sites and services schemes, in the mass small loans programme in Sri Lanka, in Hong Kong (China), in Singapore and in Chile (Pugh, 1997a). In the period 1973–95, under various militaristic and democratic regimes, Chile has expanded its housing supply at a rate of increase above that of demographic growth and ensured that subsidized social housing has been tilted in favour of low income groups. Of course, most developing countries do not have either the effectiveness or the comprehensiveness of Chile or Singapore in whole housing sector development. The more typical pattern is one of gaps, inadequacies and institutional incapacities in housing, with the consequence that squatter settlement continues to grow at some 30–70 per cent of the stock in many cities.

ECONOMIC PERSPECTIVES AND TECHNICAL-PROFESSIONAL REQUIREMENTS IN SQUATTER SETTLEMENTS

The economic and technical-professional requirements of good practice in upgrading squatter settlements are several and varied. First, it should be appreciated that self-help housing produces individual and social assets of collectively large value in the housing stock. Various authors, including Jimenez (1982a; 1982b) and Frankenhoff (1966), have shown the dynamics of the economics in self-help housing. Unpaid self-help labour increases or decreases as wage rates in the formal sector decrease or increase respectively, reflecting competitive forces and the more highly valued uses of time. Jimenez's case studies also indicate that self-help is valuable and valued at some 190 per cent of low income household income in the Philippines. Even when the house is constructed, it has an ongoing rental value. In fact, rooms may be rented and/or a workshop for informal sector production added to the dwelling. For a more general perspective it should be recognized that low income settlements provide a pool of labour for urban economic development. Second, an appropriately upgraded squatter settlement adds various economic, health and social benefits. Abelson (1996) has used good methods to reveal the benefits for upgrading in Visakhapatnam, India. The scope of his analysis included technical-economic and social surveys and investment appraisals. The individual and social returns were evident in increased land values, raised incomes, better health, and skills upgrading in training and gender programmes. Some of the increased land values were allocated to households from the regularization of tenure rights. Average incomes rose 50 per cent in the 1988–91 period, and the value of housing and land rose 82 per cent, reflecting their increased economic efficiency and social effectiveness.

The literature on the economics of redevelopment and rehabilitation (ie, housing improvement) suggests the widespread merits of rehabilitation. Originally, the investment appraisal criterion charged the value of a demolished property as a cost of an urban renewal project (Needlemen, 1965; Mao, 1966). However, subsequently further sophistication was incorporated into the criterion for comparing the costs and benefits. For example, Needleman adapted the appraisal formula to take account of the variable needs of public policy, including area rather than single property analysis, variable densities and different forms of redevelopment. It was Schaaf (1969) who developed the basic criterion to its most useful form, specifying it as:

Rehabilitate if:

$$C > R + M \left(\frac{1 - (1 + i)^{-n}}{i} \right) + \frac{C(1 + nr)}{(1 + i)^{n}} + D \left(\frac{1 - (1 - i)^{-n}}{i} \right)$$

where:

C is the cost of constructing a new dwelling;
R is the cost of rehabilitation of the old house;
M is the annual savings in maintenance costs with a new dwelling rather than a rehabilitated one;
n is the life of existing dwelling following rehabilitation;
i is the (interest) discount rate;
D is the difference in the annual rental value of a new dwelling and the rehabilitated dwelling;
r is the annual rate of obsolescence of the new dwelling.

Of course, in general terms the investment appraisal would have to be adapted to the particular situational circumstances of the squatter settlement and its comparative redevelopment and rehabilitation possibilities. The econometric simulations indicate that the logic of the criterion establishes the following principles. Rehabilitation is preferred when its standards provide for an extended life – say, over 20 years – where the existing structure has real value, when the differences between rentals on old and new buildings are narrow, where the rate of interest is comparatively high and when the cost of redevelopment is high. In computer simulations applied to a project in an inner suburb of Adelaide, Australia, Pugh (1976) found that rehabilitation was the preferred alternative, especially when rehabilitation offers a substantial improvement. This is exactly what happens under many cases of 'progressive' (incremental) improvement over a period of 10 to 20 years in developing countries.

During the 1990s McGranahan and his co-authors (1997) have expanded the scope and depth of socio-economic appraisals in squatter settlements. They have developed a mixed set of technical-professional evaluations to assess the possibilities for regeneration in squatter settlements. First, a 'broad spectrum survey' is undertaken to establish basic socio-economic and demographic information among households, along with statements about neighbourhood health and environmental problems. Second, a 'participatory rapid assessment' establishes residents and stakeholders' perceptions of how the targets for improvement should be selected and planned. This will often involve a partnership approach among government authorities, experts and organized residents' groups. Finally, contingent valuation analyses can be used to reveal the separated values the residents place upon such improvements as piped water, drainage, sewerage systems, access roads, upgraded pathways and social facilities. The contingent valuations attempt to simulate resident's economic demands (ie, their willingness to pay). They are more or less reliable, depending on the skills of the analyst and the levels of informed perception of the residents (Whittingdon et al, 1990). Other techniques such as hedonic indices also 'unbundle' residents' values on the characteristics of housing and its environment: this technique was used by Struyk and his co-authors (1990) in the massive Kampung Improvement Programme in Indonesia. Residents, as might be expected, will value various elements in environmental improvement differently, according to social group, age, gender and sometimes self-interest. The sophistication of all of the foregoing techniques can be mapped in geographical information systems. As reasoned in the next section, the residents' valuations can go beyond the socio-economic to the aesthetic and personal.

SUSTAINABILITY AND IMPROVING AMENITIES AND AESTHETICS IN SQUATTER SETTLEMENTS

Although much has been written in the literature on the resourcing and organization of improving infrastructure and adding investments to housing in squatter settlements (Choguill and Choguill, 1996), little has been discussed on aesthetics and cultural amenities. What follows relies on my own on-location experience in India, Kenya, South Africa and Mexico, along with some selected interviews and discussions in February 1999. Discussions were held with John F C Turner, Prateep Ungsongtham Hata, Secretary of the Duang Prateep Foundation in Bangkok, Thailand, Sandy Halliday of Gaia, Edinburgh, and Neil Pritchard, a landscape architect and colleague. It is appropriate to place improvements in aesthetics and amenities in a wider context of residents' feelings for their home and its location, sometimes perceiving the improvements as a part of wider resident activities in localized sustainability. Marcus (1995) has written elaborately on the personal meaning of home. Being dissatisfied with the functional dominance of the subject of housing studies, she conducted two-hour discussions with residents, exploring the 'meaning' of home, including the unconscious. It was the 'meaning' that residents attached to their feelings that led them to improve their home design, make plantings and express these expressions in the interior and external areas. More is said about the sustainability roles of home and households in the concluding section.

John F C Turner suggests that such activities as the outside decoration of housing, plantings and pot flowers, and various aesthetic features signify important things about the state of mind of the residents. It represents a commitment to place and home, and such activities tend to occur more frequently where occupancy rights and/or tenure are secure or there are expectations that regularization of tenure will occur in the near future. Some squatter settlements in Latin America, including Colombia, Venezuela, and Brazil, have colourful external decorations on walls of houses. In general, squatter settlements will vary widely in terms of the amount of aesthetic and expressive art activity. A further perspective on aesthetic and design activities emerges when the focus is given to the progressive improvement of a self-help property over a period of some 30 years, 1960–90. Carmen Gomez lives in the San Rafael, *colonias populares*, district of San Miguel in the Spanish colonial heartland of Mexico. In the early 1960s her parents purchased a 30-metre plot and built a kitchen and two rooms. Subsequently, in 1969, a neighbourhood group negotiated with local authorities to provide electricity, water and sewerage system connections. Carmen Gomez saved from her small earnings, contracting with builders who, over a period of some 25 years, added an upper storey, designed and constructed a courtyard with terrazzo and arches. The home now has four rooms, a reconstructed kitchen and an apartment annexe for her mother. The ground floor walls are attractive local stone and the upper storey is in brick. The house has the hand of aesthetic design, plantings of bougainvillaea and other shrubs, and a sense of security and home. In terms of a 'living architecture', local builders are more than functional in their qualities: they have absorbed a sense of historically and locally based merit in design and operations, inventively creating long-term contexts for people to live their choices of value in life. As John F C Turner suggests, the personal expressiveness is deeply human and associated with long-term commitments.

Prateep Ungsongtham Hata grew up in the massive Klong Toey squatter settlement which has had a varying population ranging from 40,000 to 70,000 families in Bangkok's Port Authority land, during the period 1960–2000. As a young girl Prateep scoured rust from ships and used the savings from her intermittent income to finance her secondary school and teacher training education. She then set up a school in Klong Toey and emerged as the leader of the community, being called upon by other residents to negotiate with infrastructure and other authorities. The Klong Toey slum originated as clusters of shacks built on dirty, flood-prone land, without services and with precarious wooden slats as walkways. Over time, housing and infrastructure improvements have occurred and, more significantly, Prateep's social development work expanded to kindergartens, children's art classes, aged persons' centres, self-help credit unions, garbage recycling, job creation and drug counselling. By the 1990s all this activity was set within principles of sustainable community and economic development. Residents personalize their outside areas with plantings and organize themselves to improve cleanliness and amenities in the 'streets' and the children's play areas. Klong Toey extended self-help from individualized efforts in family housing to collective community self-help in environmental improvements. Alongside this, residents have become more expressive in plantings, adding environmental amenities for aesthetic and functional relevance.

It is possible to make some general statements giving an overall perspective on the foregoing. One way of doing this is to draw on elemental principles in architecture and design. Unwin (1997) provides the sorts of principles and attitudes that are useful for a discourse on squatter settlements. For Unwin, architecture is about human drive, vision and interest, and it is mostly about the identification of place. A makeshift hutment is just as much 'architectural' as a professionally designed civic building. The hutment, and especially the improved one, can be viewed as the organization of parts into wholes. Identification relates to use, occupancy and the means of living: in other words, the building and its environment 'incorporates life'. Architecture is also political, revealing beliefs, aspirations and a view of the world. From the foregoing discussions, it is clear that some individual houses, such as Carmen Gomez's in San Rafael, San Miguel, expresses the identification of texture, colour, ventilation (for example, the courtyard) and subtle ongoing modification. In the wider whole settlement scale, Klong Toey in Bangkok has been community led and improved within the precepts of sustainable development, including care and commitment to things and services that are essentially human. Cultural heritages and sustainability have expression in the living cond-itions of the world's poor, sometimes even amid squalor, disease and mass poverty.

CONCLUDING PERSPECTIVES AND EVALUATION

Assisted self-help housing is an important part of overall housing policy in developing countries, but most self-help housing is spontaneous and not assisted by the state. As argued in this chapter, self-help housing has many characteristics, including the theoretical, the economic, the professional-technical and the roles in overall housing, urban and environmental policy. Although it had to win its recognition for policy relevance in developing countries it has a long and interesting history. This includes self-help construction in Roman towns, in medieval towns in Europe and towns of earlier periods in the developed countries (Lawrence, 1997; Ling, 1997; Salmon, 1963; Dyer, 1994; Herlihy, 1980). In some contexts, self-help housing has become part of the folklore of housing history – for example, in the mural wall decorations in Pompeii (Wallace-Hadrill, 1994) and in the Swedish 'magic houses' in Bromma and other suburbs in Stockholm in the 1920s (Pugh, 1980). The 'magic houses' were built by households at weekends and in the evenings, on land supplied by local government which also provided materials and technical advice. For developing countries, although there had been earlier assisted self-help in the rehousing pro-grammes in Chennai in the 1950s and in Kenyan towns in the 1960s, it was the timeliness of the advocacies from Turner and Abrams that were crucial. The advocacies were adapted by the World Bank and converted into international loan-supported programmes. In the context of 'learning by doing', the Bank changed its method of provision from geographically delineated projects to programmatic approaches mediated through housing finance systems and municipal funds.

The progress with upgrading squatter settlements has been variable, but with some influential 'good practice' examples. In the 1970s and 1980s in Chennai, India, internal project cross-subsidization in land pricing and plot allocation enabled sites and services and squatter improvement programmes to reach down the income distribution to the poor households.

Housing investment and housing wealth increased for all income groups, and the relational contracting between the World Bank, the Tamil Nadu government and the implementing urban authorities blended state, market and household self-help roles (Pugh 1990a; 1997a). In the Kampung Improvement Programme (KIP), Indonesia, the World Bank provided four phased project loans amounting to US$439 million. The KIP contributed towards improved living conditions, spontaneous housing investment (ie, improvement), increased incomes and improved health. Some of the 'learning by doing' in the KIP led to wider community participation and deeper institutional reforms (World Bank 1995). Beyond all of this, as reasoned earlier in settled squatter areas, economic value is added to urban assets, and residents add aesthetic and personal expression to their houses and neighbourhoods.

The roles of individuals and households can be elaborated further in the context of thinking about self-help, household economics and a sense of home. Housing theory in this has been developed by Stretton (1976) and Pugh (1990b; 1997b). The theory proceeds from the basis that economists have largely and very restrictively confined their studies in housing economics to market exchange value, to the design and impact of subsidies, and to social questions of poverty and inequality. In a different approach, housing is viewed as the central social and economic asset in the 'domestic sector', which is defined as the part of the economy in which capital, resources, time and energy are used for such things as housework, cooking, recreation, childrearing and housing and environmental improvement. This perspective raises the significance of household economics – that is, the generation of income, domestic sector work, human capital formation in children and other members of the household, and use of time in personal and community activities. The value of the product and human capital formation in the domestic sector can be measured in more or less satis-factory ways. These include the value of time, the value of equivalent market products and the attribution of childrearing in human capital formation. All of this, of course, has gender and child significance in domestic work and in the intra-household distributions of income.

The foregoing is not all that merits attention. A theory of the domestic sector is closely bound up with sustainable development. The domestic sector draws resources from the commercial sector for producing home-based goods and services. Also, the educational and personal development of individuals depends on access to state services and the security of a safe and healthy environment. In effect, the domestic, commercial (private) and public sectors are interdependent and coordinate in economic and social development. This makes household economics basic in sustainable development, both in general terms and in housing and environmental improvement. In one perspective, the domestic sector subsidizes the other sectors in its roles in the formation of human capital and labour potential. (The childrearing time and cost is not fully paid and compensated by the private sector.) Clearly, sustainability is not fully accounted for and understood unless it includes domestic sector roles. Self-help means more than the construction and management of housing and the local environment.

The upgrading of squatter settlements is not always a straightforward and highly cooperative social process. In essence, the neighbourhood improvements can be viewed as 'community rights', but consensus is not always possible in the professional and participatory processes. For example, in reviewing programmes in Jordan in the 1985–98 period, Raed (1998) found that in some cases social groups strongly contended priorities and access to political and economic power. Unified purposes are more likely to occur where there is social homogeneity, good leadership in the community and some prior experience of social cooperation. Socio-political contexts vary: in São Paulo in Brazil some settlements are subject to the power of Mafia-like gangs. All of this is a reminder that social, ethical and aesthetic expressions run the full range of human living and human response.

Finally, it is appropriate to take an overall view of squatter settlement in terms of the theory and practice of sustainable development for low-income households, given here as seven operational guidelines.

1   Sustainable development should be seen simultaneously as environmental, social, economic and political, and for encouraging people to choose lives that they value.
2   Environmental and housing improvement is more probable when various policies together achieve: broadspread stable growth of incomes; acceptance of occupancy rights and expansion of in situ improvement; the development of social capital among the poor, this being reflected in leadership, organization, networking and civic association which leads to mutual trust and political experience.
3   Policies for regenerating and conserving squatter settlements are likely to have greater general urban success when they are set within whole housing sector development and related to the macro-spatial development of cities and towns. Land policy and the development of housing finance systems are especially significant, including extending access down the distribution of household income.
4   It should be understood that environmental improvement has socio-political risks of fragmentation and contest: collective purposes are more likely where there are provisions for conflict resolution, some experience in social cooperation and the development of positive social capital, and relational contracting which sets out responsibilities among partners in a formal or informal scheme of neighbourhood improvement.
5   Following the Parana Market Towns Improvement Project, environmental improvement projects are expanded and achieve some success when they are set in a context of intergovernmental decentralization of resources and organization, along with financial sustainability and choices of costed options.
6   The process of improvement requires some technical know-how. This ranges from social development, relational contracting among partners, and the use of socio-economic surveys, contingent valuations, cost-benefit appraisals and hedonic indices. All of these improve the prospects for informed socio-political choice on the form and substance of selection

among alternatives. Techniques can be adjusted to incorporate various aspects of gender, age and minority group preferences.

7 Both spontaneous and formally organized improvement can be enhanced in social, personal and aesthetic dimensions by encouraging the expressiveness of life, art and design, and such humanly expressive commitments around the house and in the neighbourhood.

All the foregoing is, of course, adaptable to localized contexts. It relates to contexts of varied social characteristics in squatter areas, sometimes within the realities of disease, death, poverty and the full range of human characteristics. The theoretical guidelines are dependent for their effectiveness on good performances in national and local economies, in progressive social development, in conducive state–market–society relationships, and in leadership and institutional capability.

REFERENCES

Abelson, P (1996) 'Evaluation of slum improvements: case study in Visakhapatnam, India', *Cities*, vol 13, no 2, pp97–108

Abrams, C (1964) *Housing in the Modern World*, Faber & Faber, London

Barbier, E (1998) *The Economics of Environment and Development*, Elgar, Cheltenham

Choguill, C and Choguill, M (1996) 'Towards sustainable infrastructure for low-income communities', in C Pugh (ed), *Sustainability, the Environment and Urbanization*, Earthscan, London

Dyer, C (1994) *Everyday Life in Medieval England*, Hambledon Press, London

Frankenhoff, C (1966) *The Economic Role of Housing in a Developing Economy*, Housing Policy Seminar, University of Puerto Rica, Rio Vendras

Harms, H (1982) 'Historical perspectives on the practice and politics of self-help housing', in P Ward (ed), *Self-Help Housing: A Critique*, Mansell, London, pp17–53

Harris, R (1998) 'A crank's fate and the fêting of a visionary: reflections on the history of aided self-help housing', *Third World Planning Review*, vol 29, no 3, ppiii–viii

Herlihy, D (1980) *Cities and Society in Medieval Italy*, Valorium, Reprints, London

Jimenez, E (1982a) 'The economics of self-help housing: theory and some evidence from a developing country', *Journal of Urban Economics*, no 11, pp205–28

Jimenez, E (1982b) 'The value of squatter dwellings in developing countries', *Economic Development and Cultural Change*, no 31, pp739–52

Kessides, C (1997) *World Bank Experience with the Provision of Infrastructure Services for the Urban Poor: Preliminary Identification and Review of Best Practices*, World Bank, TWU-OR8, Washington, DC

Lawrence, R (1997) 'Space and text', in R Lawrence and A Wallace-Hadrill (eds) *Domestic Space in the Roman World: Pompeii and Beyond, Journal of Roman Archaeology, Supplementary Series*, no 22, pp7–14

Ling, R (1997) *The Insula of the Meander at Pompeii, Vol 1, The Structure*, Clarendon, Oxford

Mao, J (1966) 'Efficiency in urban renewal expenditures through cost-benefit analysis', *Journal of the American Institute of Planners*, March 1966, pp95–107

Marcus, S (1995) *House as a Mirror of Self: Explaining the Deeper Meanings of Home*, Conari Press, Berkeley, California

McGranahan, G, Leitmann, J and Sumjadi, C (1997) *Understanding Environmental Problems in Disadvantaged Neighbourhoods: Broad Spectrum Surveys, Participatory Appraisal and Contingent Valuation*, UMP Working Paper 16, World Bank, UNCHS, Stockholm Environment Institute, Washington, DC

Needleman, L (1965) *The Economics of Housing*, Staples, London

Nientied, P and van der Linden, J (1985) 'Approaches to low-income housing in the Third World: some comments', *International Journal of Urban and Regional Research*, no 9, pp311–29

Peattie, L (1987) 'Shelter development and the poor', in L Rodwin (ed), *Shelter, Settlement and Development*, Allen & Unwin, Boston, pp263–80

Pugh C (1976) 'Older residential areas and the development of economic analysis', in J McMaster and G Webb (eds), *Australian Urban Economics*, Australia and New Zealand Book Company, Sydney

Pugh, C (1980) *Housing in Capitalist Societies*, Gower, Farnborough

Pugh, C (1990a) *Housing and Urbanization: A Study of India*, Sage, New Delhi

Pugh, C (1990b) 'A New Approach to Housing Theory: Sex, Gender and the Domestic Economy', *Housing Studies*, vol 5, no 2, pp112–29

Pugh, C (1997a) 'Poverty and progress? Reflections on housing and urban policies in developing countries, 1976–96', *Urban Studies*, vol 34, no 10, pp1547–96

Pugh, C (1997b) 'The household, household economics and housing', *Housing Studies*, vol 12, no 3, pp383–91

Raed, H (1998) *Public Participation and Community Organisation in the Low-Income Housing Production: The Jordanian Experience*, a PhD thesis, University College London, Development Planning Unit

Salmon, H (1963) *Medieval Cities*, Studio Vista, London

Schaaf, A (1969) 'Economic feasibility analysis for urban renewal housing rehabilitation', *Journal of the American Institute of Planners*, November, pp399–404

Skinner, R, Taylor, J and Wegelin, E (eds) (1987) *Shelter Upgrading for the Urban Poor: Evaluation of Third World Experience*, Island Publishing House, Manila

Stretton, H (1976) *Capitalism, Socialism and the Environment*, Cambridge University Press, London

Struyk, R, Hoffman, M and Katsura, H (1990) *The Market for Urban Shelter in Indonesian Cities*, Urban Institute, Washington, DC

Turner, A (1980) *The Cities of the Poor*, Croom Helm, London

Turner, J F C (1967) 'Barriers and channels for housing development in modernising countries', *Journal of the American Institute of Planners*, vol 33, no 3, pp167–81

Turner, J F C (1972) 'The re-education of a professional', pp122–47, and 'Housing as a verb', in J Turner and R Fichter (eds), *Freedom to Build*, Macmillan, New York

Turner, J (1976) *Housing By People: Towards Autonomy in Building Environments*, Marion Byers, London

Unwin, S (1997) *Analysing Architecture*, Routledge, London

Wallace-Hadrill, A (1994) *Houses and Society in Pompeii and Herculaneum*, Princeton University Press, Princeton, New Jersey

Whittingdon, D, Briscoe, J, Mu X and Barron, W (1990) 'Estimating the willingness to pay for water in developing countries: a case study of the use of contingent valuation surveys in southern Haiti', *Economic Development and Social Change*, no 38, pp293–311

World Bank (1983) *Learning By Doing*, World Bank, Washington, DC

World Bank (1993) *Housing: Enabling Markets to Work*, World Bank, Washington, DC

World Bank (1994) *Twenty Years of Lending for Urban Development, 1972–92*, World Bank, Operations Evaluation Department, Report No 13117, Washington, DC

World Bank (1995) *Indonesia Impact Evaluation Report. Enhancing the Quality of Life in Urban Indonesia: The Legacy of the Kampung Improvement Program*, Operations Evaluation Department, Report No 14747–IND, World Bank, Washington, DC

World Health Organization (WHO) (1998) *The World Health Report 1998: Life in the Twenty-First Century: A Vision for All*, WHO, Geneva

World Resources Institute, UNEP, UNDP and World Bank (1996) *World Resources: A Guide to the Global Environment*, Oxford University Press, Oxford

8 THE LOCALIZATION OF AGENDA 21 AND THE SUSTAINABLE CITIES PROGRAMME

Bharat Dahiya and Cedric Pugh

Environmentalism, along with some other supportive socio-political tendencies, has furthered the cause of reform in the planning and management of urban areas. The Earth Summit, Rio de Janeiro, 1992, called on local governments to mobilize their communities for the localization of Agenda 21. This UN Conference on the Environment and Development (UNCED) went further. Its thematic guidance favoured community-led participation in the approach to environmental improvement, introducing an emphasis on bottom-up participation, rather than reliance on top-down ways of doing things in much town planning practice. This new 'environmental planning and management' (EPM) has also been advocated in the Sustainable Cities Programme (SCP), organized as demonstration projects in designated cities by the UN Centre for Human Settlements (UNCHS) and the UN Environment Programme (UNEP). In application, the localization of Agenda 21 and the SCP would clearly have local variation in accordance with the perception of sustainability and the economic, social and political dialectic in community-based environmentalism. This chapter contains an analysis and evaluation of the planning methods, the progress and the dilemmas in the modern localization of environment-alism. Although the chapter has some general evaluations and reflections, as is appropriate at this early phase of EPM, it also has much descriptive detail.

INTRODUCTION

The analytical-conceptual framework for the localization of Agenda 21 (and its companion piece, the Habitat Agenda from the UNCHS Habitat II

Conference, Istanbul, 1996) has its foundations in the idea of sustainability. Sustainability is, of course, the guiding principle for the UNCED Agenda 21 (Chapter 7). In terms of localizing the notion of sustainable urban development, Agenda 21 called on local governments '. . . to undertake a consultative process with their populations and to achieve consensus on Local Agenda 21 for their communities'. However, this in itself set no blueprint or guide on how this should be done. In fact, owing to the variations of localized environmental and developmental circumstances, along with the enormous scope and intricate complexity of sustainability, it is not surprising that some things were left open for further thought and experience. In the broadest sense, the general requirement was quite straightforward: what was needed were some procedural and operational aims and programmes, systemically related to some version of sustainability. Stated in these terms, the application of localized sustainability depended on the elaboration of schema for EPM. In context, this means that local authorities, acting within broad-based community participation, would set a strategic view of legal, institutional, organizational and action-orientated directions for environmental enhancement and protection. Along with other relevant precepts from the 1990s historical context, prescriptively this would be undertaken within social inclusion, social equity, capacity building, and the participation of major stakeholders in government, in the private sector, in non-government organizations (NGOs), in the community and among citizens. Obviously, the various feasibilities in resourcing, financing, administration and technical know-how would shape the selection of activities, along with socio-political dynamics and leadership at the local levels. More than this, prescriptive social idealism would sometimes be compromised by vested interests and political or organizational limitations in achieving full social inclusion. National legislative and policy initiatives, together with growing environmental management and policy networks, would also influence the shape and scope of localized response.

The development of ideas and frameworks for EPM is an evolutionary, historical and experiential course. This occurs in various international organizations, in associations of local governments, in the professions and among independent researchers. Such has been the case in the UNCHS, reflected in various post-1992 publications, in the Habitat Agenda and in the information emanating from the SCP, which it developed in collaboration with UNEP. The historical perspective indicates a rapid and purposeful approach towards the recommended practice of EPM. Following the Rio de Janeiro UNCED meeting in 1992, the UNCHS published its reflections on sustainability in 1998 (UNCHS, 1998). This publication sets out the nature and extent of environmental problems, their causes and, most significantly, points out the necessities of improving urban governance and for a process of continuous reform in urban planning. In the following year UNCHS (1994b) took the rationale for the reform of urban planning a few steps further. UNCHS had also obtained legitimacy for sustainability in urban environments from its Habitat II conference in Istanbul, 1996. Habitat II had an affinity with UNCED, but with greater influence from the developing countries in agenda setting and guiding policy. UNCHS position statements were in terms of developing symbiotic relationships between economic development and the environment, bridging any identified resource gaps, steering policies toward the reduction of environmental poverty and placing some reforms of governance into an enablement framework. Also, appropriate governance was understood to promote cross-sectoral integration in policy development and implementation because the widely prevalent administrative separatism of government agencies sometimes led to inertia in dealing with growing environmental problems in infrastructure services and in reducing pollution.

All the foregoing concepts and principles were widened, deepened and became more coherent for practical applications. First, the Habitat Agenda (UNCHS, 1997) elaborated policy and global programmatic intent, relating this to Agenda 21 and to social learning from research reports and networking with organized associations of local authorities. Consequently, the theory and practice of EPM began to take a consolidated conceptual form, with its own characteristic language and guidance. This was set out in detail in the first two of a set of three EPM source books aimed at disseminating and extending the application of sustainability from Agenda 21 and the Habitat Agenda (UNCHS/UNEP, 1997a; 1997b). In the source books, EPM is explained as a new approach to urban planning, not at all like land use 'master plans' but capable of integration with these if appropriate. EPM is conceived as a mixture of top-down and bottom-up processes, driven by broad-based community participation rather than by technocratic imperative. In the end result, as prescription, EPM would enhance the collective know-how on urban environmental improvement, applying sustainability to social, economic and environmental dimensions. However, as noted earlier, the idealism in the guideline books for EPM would be compromised by localized political realities and by some inherent limitations in implementing a full community-based approach to environmentalism.

For practical guidance, EPM would have various planned phases and processes, commencing with an environmental profile which would set out relevant objects and problems for policy and action. This would be followed by some prioritizing for the short- and long-term, with some assessment of feasibilities and resourcing. Various stakeholders (for example, government agencies, leaders from the private sector, relevant NGOs, community-based organizations (CBOs), resident groups and professionals) would participate in planning and policy. In the best of conditions for social inclusion and wide representation, all of this would consolidate the nexus between the social, the economic and the environmental, enhancing productivity, health and welfare. Implementation would focus on action plans, the monitoring of performance and ongoing adaptation in an operational learning by doing. The overall process would normally require institutional and organizational reforms, set within political and social mobilization. Furthermore, as revealed in the source book on actual city experiences with EPM (UNCHS/UNEP, 1997b), the selection of issues and the way they are dealt with can be more or less comprehensive.

The foregoing has some necessary appearance of EPM as an ideal, without much reference to its limitations and problems. In fact, although implementation is only in its first phases, experience shows that the prescriptive principles are being influenced by local political, economic, social and cultural conditions. Also, the conceptualizations and aims that are locally formulated do not always coincide either with the precepts from UNCED's Agenda 21 or UNCHS' Habitat Agenda. Additionally, Local Agenda 21s are not the only approaches to EPM. The SCP has been adapting its own approaches to environmental planning and management, initially guided by the principles set out in Bartone et al (1994) and Leitmann (1994a; 1994b). These principles placed emphasis on making 'rapid environmental assessments', mobilizing support among stakeholders, selecting policy, reforming institutions and governance, and decentralizing management. Another localized application of the new ways of accomplishing environmental planning is the Metropolitan Environmental Improvement Programme (MEIP). This initiative was launched in 1989 by the World Bank and United Nations Development Programme (UNDP) to assist major Asian cities to tackle their rapidly growing environmental problems. During the implementation of MEIP in five Asian cities (namely, Beijing, Mumbai (erstwhile Bombay), Colombo, Jakarta and Metro Manila), it was realized that air pollution was an important environmental problem. Hence, another programme called Urban Air Quality Management (URBAIR) was started by the World Bank with financial and technical support from the Royal Norwegian Ministry of Finance and the Dutch Ministry of Foreign Affairs. URBAIR pursues objectives in Chapter 7 of Agenda 21 and in the Framework for Climate Change, both from the 1992 UNCED agreements. The World Bank's preliminary reports (Shah et al, 1997a; Shah and Nagpal, 1997) indicate an approach to environmental planning, as would be relevant to air quality improvement, emphasizing appraisal of damage impact, the selection of options for abatement and installing action plans, with monitoring provisions. The programme accordingly depends on the technical-analytical in more fundamental ways than the EPM in Local Agenda 21s or, in a more critical vein, the Local Agenda 21s may not have given the necessary attention to the role of analysis, appraisal and know-how in the participatory approach. In what follows, the discussions will first explore the human settlements agendas and then review the localized variations in Agenda 21 and the SCP, also providing critical evaluation of limitations and some proposals for improving EPM.

THE HUMAN SETTLEMENTS AGENDAS IN ENVIRONMENTALISM

Agenda 21 from the UNCED meeting was at once influential in adapting human settlements agendas and at absorbing influences from international housing, urban and environmental policy. The continuities and adaptations are what might have been reasonably expected in the context that the World

Bank and UNCHS had been refining and revising their international policies since the mid-1980s. Accordingly, in order to obtain useful historical and conceptual interpretations of Local Agenda 21s and the Habitat Agenda, it is necessary to evaluate both the impact of the UNCED meeting, 1992, and the significant elements of earlier reforms in the UNCHS and World Bank policies. The impact of the UNCED meeting can be summarized readily from the existing literature on sustainable development (Grubb et al, 1993; Pugh, 1996a). Agenda 21 had widespread impacts on international thinking and policy. The Rio de Janeiro meeting attracted over 30,000 visitors, including leaders of NGOs who had access and influence. Furthermore, the nature of the central topic, sustainable development, raised important and sensitive issues in North–South relations. The priorities in developing countries were to seek economic growth and to reduce mass poverty, and the political leaders of these countries were opposed to significant restrictions on economic development. They were also sensitive to policy pronouncements on demographic problems, and cognizant of high per capita consumption in the developed countries which had some adverse environmental consequences. Nonetheless, the Rio de Janeiro meeting was more than an opportunity to discuss principles, issues and the idea of sustainable development: it also required negotiations, agreements and post-conference plans for action. The issues would remain relevant in international relations by virtue of the creation of the UN Commission on Sustainable Development in 1993 and the call for local governments to mobilize their communities for planning and implementing Local Agenda 21s. Agenda 21 can be seen as having ideational and behavioural impacts. Its 40 chapters were broad in scope and deep in relevance, addressing poverty, natural resources and socio-economic development. The Declaration on Environment and Development expressed the centrality of human welfare in environmentalism, the right to development, the need to reduce poverty, the inclusion of women and youth in the participatory approach, and the facilitation of economic growth through international trade.

The section of Agenda 21 on human settlements, Chapter 7, incorporated some of the language and principles which had been advocated and rationalized by UNCHS and the World Bank in the 1980s and early 1990s. The flavour of the guidance in Chapter 7 can be seen in such phraseology and favour for 'enablement policies', 'partnerships' among state agencies, the private sector and community organizations, developing 'institutional' capacity and extending 'decentralization'. This language had political, policy and advocacy connotations in its historical setting of the early 1990s. Enablement required a reconfiguration of state roles in creating legal, institutional, economic and political frameworks for housing, urban and environmental development. Partnerships were supposed to have the roles of market efficiency, NGO and CBO mediation between people and government agencies, and community-based participation in EPM. The enhancement of institutional reform and their capacity indicated a variety of things. First, it meant that reforms were necessary in legislation, norms and ways of acting in environmental policy development, and in housing and urban policies. Second, it implied that state–society relations were central in environmental reform and in due course would bring matters of governance into sustainable urban development. Third, it meant that market liberalism, though necessary for development, was insufficient: elements of collective choice and community were required in participation and institutional enablement. This would broaden development from economic growth to the inclusion of the social and environmental.

All the foregoing are formulated in various UNCHS and World Bank documents on strategic policy development, although the 1992 UNCED meeting in itself raised environmentalism up the policy and programmatic agendas in urban and housing policies. The overall aims of the UNCHS and World Bank fundamental policy revisions were to take policy from limited, geographically delineated projects (for example, sites and services schemes) towards a comprehensive approach to urban development and whole housing sector expansion. Some of the major elements of comprehensiveness are 'the new urban agenda', the Global Strategy for Shelter (GSS), and the 'brown agenda' environmentalism which had increased significance from the World Commission on Environment and Development (Brundtland Report), 1987, to the UNCED meeting in 1992. These elements were not formulated and resolved at one specific time in the period 1986–93, but evolved in a context of programmatic reform and a new political economy of urbanization. The official documentation has burgeoned, revealing the evolution from simpler to more sophisticated principles for comprehensiveness in policy. (The major documents are: World Bank, 1988; 1991; 1993; UNCHS/World Bank/UNDP, 1994; UNCHS, 1987; 1989; 1990; UNDP, 1991.) The vision and application of comprehensiveness widens and deepens scope (including 'brown agenda' environmentalism), and provides a rationale for urban policy significance resting on economic productivity, the reduction of poverty and improved urban governance. In content, the joint World Bank, UNCHS and UNDP Urban Management Programme includes urban finance, land management, urban poverty, the environment, decentralized governance, infrastructure and health. Advocacies for participation, capacity building, partnerships and the enablement approach to political economy are conspicuous in the UNCHS documents (for further details, see Pugh, 1997a).

Localization is inherent in urban and environmental programmes. It has been advocated within the principles of decentralization in the 'new urban agenda' which often is based on notions of comparative efficiency and relevance to centralization. However, it should be borne in mind that decentralization has relevance beyond local government and intergovernmental relations: it also includes privatization, partnerships and the mobilization of local communities, as in EPM. For application to government roles, Bernstein (1993) argues for coherent jurisdictional authorities among different levels of government. Dillinger (1994) also emphasizes the clear assignment of responsibilities among levels of government, and the primary importance of decentralization in service delivery in such aspects as neighbourhood infrastructure, solid waste collection and disposal, and in other basic urban services. Advocacy and principle are, of course, one thing, and economic and political reality are another. This can be seen in a case study evaluation of circumstances in India (Mathur, 1997). Under the 74th Constitutional Amendment Act, 1992, local governments were given constitutional recognition, alongside the Government of India and the states' governments. Local governments in India obtain their functions from states' governments. They have wide variations in size and significance, accounting for only some 4.6 per cent of the total public sector revenue. As noted by Mathur, functions in utilities, infrastructure and public health have been downloaded to local governments, but not adequacy in the transfers of financial resources. Financial limitations are not confined to inter-governmental inertia, but also include the property tax base which is derived from assessments which often fall below market values. Here and there local governments have taken innovatory initiatives in finance. In Ahmedabad, the municipality has raised some Rs1,000 million on the bond market for infrastructure and health, having first reformed revenue collections so that investors had confidence in the security of their invest-ments. Tirupur in Tamil Nadu created a joint venture between local government and the New Tirupur Area Development Corporation to improve the infrastructure for enhancing exports and the necessary improvements to the port. The Corporation will construct and operate the infrastructure and transfer it to the local government.

The foregoing reveals some of the limitations of decentralization, but also some creative innovations. Localization in urban development and the maintenance of infrastructure is frequently more complicated than it would appear superficially. Spatial functions and jurisdictions often involve a variety of agencies and stakeholders from several levels of government. Functions can overlap among housing, utilities and environ-mental authorities, raising the question of coordination. Coordination can be weak or strong, depending on the relationships that were secured either informally or within the political-administrative authority. For Ostrom and her co-authors (1993) effectiveness is often a matter of how well institutions are embedded and representative of general public interest, rather than the separated, narrow interests of any single authority which has an urban development function. Also, in discussions of decentralization it should be recognized that central authority can have a comparative advantage in the social redistributions of benefits in housing, land and environmental improvements. For example, the redistributive land policies in Taiwan, the socially expressive allocations of housing resources in Singapore and the egalitarian small loans housing schemes in Sri Lanka, all depended on a balance between centralized allocation and decentralized operation (Pugh, 1997a). The centralized components dominated the redistributive functions.

Since the United Nations Conference on the Human Environment held at Stockholm in 1972 and Habitat I at Vancouver in 1976, various UN agencies and the World Bank have been making efforts to incorporate environmental considerations in their development activities. One of the major outcomes of such efforts is the publication of *Environmental Guidelines for Settlement Planning and Management* in three volumes (UNEP/UNCHS 1987a; 1987b; 1987c),[1] 'a major joint UNEP/UNCHS (Habitat) project designed to distil then available knowledge about the relationship between the natural environment and the built environment, and to provide guidelines to planners and decision makers that would help them use that knowledge in settlements planning and management' (Ramachandran and Tolba, 1987, piii). The guidelines became necessary as administrators, planners, managers and policy makers responsible for human settlements in developing countries were 'coming to understand' that safeguarding the natural environment was not an obstacle to settlements development. Further, environmental management was perceived as a means of ensuring sustainable development (Ramachandran and Tolba, 1987). These volumes offered guidelines for institutionalizing EPM and integrating other disciplines, these being metropolitan planning and management, and regional planning and management. It is important to note that these EPM guidelines called for the involvement of 'potentially concerned groups' for decision making as following:[2]

> *Potentially concerned groups fall into three categories. There are those for whom environment is a subject of direct concern, such as agriculture, water supply and natural resources agencies. There are those who may initially see EPM as an obstacle or constraint to the fulfilment of their mission, such as transport, infrastructure and housing agencies. And there are those whose responsibilities relate to the co-ordination of development activities across metropolitan sectors, space and time, such as general city planning agencies. Participation in the decision-making process should also include the public interest groups, economic enterprises and affected populations who influence the interactions at issue or are likely to be affected by any policy. (UNEP/UNCHS, 1987b, p38).*

In August 1990, UNCHS launched the SCP formally which 'puts into practice the concepts and approaches developed in these *Guidelines*' (UNCHS, 1994b, emphasis original) as mentioned above. In the official document the SCP is seen as: '. . . the principal activity of the international community for promoting and supporting sustainable development in the cities and towns of the world. The SCP does this by helping municipal authorities, and their public, private and community sector partners, to improve their capacities for urban environmental planning and management' (UNCHS, 1994b, p6). It has also been mandated by the United Nations to implement Agenda 21. Moreover, serving as the operational arm of the Urban Environment Component of the joint UNCHS and UNEP Urban Management Programme (UMP/E), the SCP has developed the practical framework for an urban EPM process, has mobilized the required resources and has initiated city-level demonstrations of the process with a series of cities around the world (UNCHS, 1994c).

The SCP focuses on the sustainable development issues in the cities around the world. These issues relate to 'dirty' production techniques, soil and water contamination, resource depletion, and so on, in industrialized countries, and to the overwhelming urban growth, rapid industrialization, resultant inadequate infrastructure, limited managerial, technical and institutional capacities, and weak financial capabilities in developing countries. The SCP holds that environmental degradation is a common but not inevitable outcome of urban growth. Rather, it is caused primarily by inappropriate urban development policies, ineffective planning and management, and by the inadequate consideration of the constraints and opportunities of the natural environment. To address these problems, the SCP is guided by a number of 'principles and viewpoints' (UNCHS, 1994b):

- the environment is a resource to be managed in a sustainable manner;
- there is a two-way relationship between development and environment where development depends on the natural resources available and, in turn, it has an impact on these resources;
- the natural environment represents both development resources and development hazards;
- urban development has negative but also (potentially) positive impacts on the natural environment, both short-term and long-term;
- environmental problems cut across traditional administrative and organizational boundaries and must be addressed with new types of political and managerial action;
- a successful response to urban environmental problems requires the active participation of all sectors of the community; and
- the SCP approaches should be applied by cities to address local concerns and priorities with the help of local partners.

In establishing an effective and appropriate EPM capacity, the SCP helps the cities to:

- identify and understand local environment issues; establish priorities among such issues;
- work out procedures and mechanisms for building consensus and developing cooperation; apply modern planning and management approaches and techniques;
- develop up-to-date strategies and action plans that command wide-spread support;
- implement strategies and convert action plans into projects and pro-grammes; and
- monitor and follow up the actions taken (UNCHS, 1994b).

This becomes necessary because cities have to deal with a variety of existing and potential conflicts such as current demands for the use of a resource and the requirements for its sustained availability, the vulnerability of environmental systems from the impact of development activities and competition for resources (for example, water) between organizations and groups in different development sectors and in different locations. In addition to these conflicts, the limitations of traditional urban admin-istration and management systems need to be overcome.[3]

In tackling the conflicts, limitations and environmental issues of a different nature in a local context, the SCP follows a 'bottom-up approach', focusing on local solutions. To fulfil its aim of providing an improved EPM capacity to a city, the SCP follows a request from cities in need of assistance. A city is selected as a demonstration project only in response to a clear demand by the concerned city authorities. Then the SCP helps to formulate and develop a demonstration project which becomes that city's sustainable city project (for example, the Sustainable Ibadan Project). The SCP believes that such a 'bottom-up' approach leads to a strong sense of 'ownership' of the project among the local partners in turn, resulting in a strong sense of commitment by them to see the project through to a successful conclusion. This is followed by the implementation of an EPM process through its designated phases which begins with the preparation of the city's environmental profile, as indicated in the introductory discussions.

An SCP project helps its local partners to gain a better understanding of the range, complexity and interrelationships of the problems which their city faces. What it does not tell them is what those problems are and how they could be tackled. More particularly,

> ... the SCP does **not** come in with a 'pre-cooked' agenda or with a roster of 'experts' to tell local people what the city's problems are. Every city's situation is different – and every city must identify and explore and prioritise its own problems, in its own way ... Thus, a specification of local priorities is not an input or starting point in an SCP project, but instead is one of the outputs – one of the concrete results of the early stages of project activity (UNCHS, 1994b, p39, emphasis original).

Once the problems are prioritized, key environmental issues are identified and then assessed by their degree of seriousness, their relationship to existing city initiatives, their political visibility and/or popular demand, their resource requirements, the timescale for action, relevant national policy priorities, and so on. The key environmental issues undergo discussions and deliberations in the action planning phase through the working group mechanism that leads to the formulation of some viable projects. Thus, the 'local' is ensured in the SCP through those viable projects that grow out of local environmental concerns and priorities, and are developed in collaboration with local partners.

As discussed earlier, localization as advocated within the principles of decentralization has its own limitations, and in this sense the SCP is no exception. The *EPM Source Book* (UNCHS/UNEP, 1997a) itself acknowledges that external aid and technical know-how play a valuable supporting role, albeit that the vast majority of technical and financial resources for EPM come from local sources. It further states that it is important for cities to work out appropriate roles for external assistance, to limit most effectively the city's EPM needs with the relevant external capabilities and support. All action plans and viable projects prepared in the aforesaid local context could be shelved owing to the non-availability of funds. Hence, seeking external support is a logical step given the weak financial condition of urban governments in developing countries. But the local also has administrative, political and policy-related limitations that could delay or hamper the progress of an SCP in a city. For instance, the Sustainable Chennai Project (the erstwhile Sustainable Madras Project) took more than three years to be accepted and cleared by the government of India and the state government of Tamil Nadu in 1995.

In recent years, local government reforms have been undertaken in countries around the world. Although a milestone for the better management of cities and towns, it has also significantly shifted the locus of power in urban government and their political dynamics. Localization has gained a much wider meaning: it proposes new ways of doing things, including coordination among various government departments, between different levels of government, among different urban and regional development agencies, promoting privatization and partnerships, and the mobilization of local communities. In effect, the SCP emphasizes these new ways of acting and helps cities to institutionalize them, but thereby opens up challenges and dilemmas in political decision making and urban governance.

PROGRESS WITH LOCAL AGENDA 21S AND RELATED PROGRAMMES

Local Agenda 21s have been formulated and sometimes implemented in developing countries, in countries in transition from state socialism to mixed market-state modes and in developed countries. In order to obtain a useful comparative perspective and a fuller appreciation of how developmental context influences the socio-political choices taken in localized environmentalism, the discussions will cover the three types of countries.

Case Studies from Developing Countries

In its published listings of case studies, UNCHS reviews the city experiences of some 24 countries from developing countries in a total of 32 cases (UNCHS/UNEP, 1997b). Although this apparently reveals useful first-phase progress with response to Local Agenda 21s, other testimony from expert review committees puts a circumspect view, suggesting that in both developing and developed countries, the coverage and depth of initiatives is small in relation to the full global task (UNCHS, 1998). However, it should be acknowledged that some nations, states and cities have been progressive and successful in the implementation of housing, urban and environmental policies since Habitat I in Vancouver, 1976. For example, Singapore has created long-term land, social housing, environmental improvement, health and education policies to spread urban assets and social opportunities on a broad scale. Sri Lanka has used a mass small loans programme and innovation in housing finance to create a mass low-income housing programme, also supported with pro-poor community development (partnership) programmes since the mid-1970s. Taiwan has used land acquisition and land tax policies to make land affordable for moderate- and low-income groups. And in Chennai, India, the World Bank-Tamil Nadu government sites and services, and slum upgrading projects have demonstrated the potential of these approaches to simultaneously improve wealth distribution, access to social and infrastructure services, and to reduce the risks of environmentally related diseases. Chile has decentralized its pro-poor social programmes and reformed housing policies to widen low-income access to subsidized housing and expand supplies of housing for all social groups. From one perspective, and with regard to the needs and lesser progress elsewhere, these examples indicate the potential value of developing the Local Agenda 21s in developing countries (for further detail of the cases, see Pugh, 1997b). But performance, of course, depends on the localized conditions of leadership, policy reform, and institutional and cultural settings.

The case examples in the UNCHS/UNEP review (1997b) are varied in the localized context, local response, the scope and ambition of initiatives, and the way in which sustainable urban development has been conceived. A selection can be summarized for illustrative purposes. Accra, Ghana, approached participation and community development by using the principles of group dynamics for structuring and grouping people, set in a context of deep environmental problems in substandard housing, waste collection, insanitary conditions in neighbourhoods, lagoon pollution and land degradation. Calcutta adopted pilot projects for addressing air and water pollution, waste collection and inadequate housing. The city authorities also relied on analytical and evaluative studies of EPM in solid waste management, respectively by the Government of West Bengal and the Institute of Hygiene and Public Health. Concepción, Chile, developed a wide scope in EPM, having joined the UNCHS/UNEP SCP. Consequently, it built on the catalytic effect of earlier participatory experiences with sectoral meetings of relevant stakeholders, then proceeded to action plans which variously addressed urban improvement projects, urban poverty, city-rural relationships and degradation from the port area industry.

Hanoi, Vietnam, adapted the inherited state socialism model and partially integrated EPM into city plans in such problems as land subsidence, groundwater pollution, flooding and water pollution. All of this required institutional reform in adapting socialist to mixed market-state economic development. A Kenyan 'Small Towns Project' was mediated through the Kenyan Ministry of Local Government with financial support from the Netherlands government agencies. The issues addressed included land degradation, backlogs in infrastructure and informal business sector wastes. Ougadougou, Burkina Faso, had only the capacity to adopt a small-scale version of EPM. Considerations of feasibility made centralization necessary in the broad issues of inadequate water supply, surface pollution and contaminated soils.

The variability in approach emphasizes the relevance of localized differences' and effectiveness depends on the capabilities for technical, governmental and participatory work. Additionally, the aforementioned successes in Singapore, Taiwan, Sri Lanka, Chennai and Chile point to the importance of sustained political commitment, social learning and embedding institutional reform into economic and social development in legislation, resourcing, finance and the political goodwill in the community.

Case Studies from Countries in Transition

For the transitional economies the change from centralized economic planning to mixed market-state societies has many challenges. First, the introduction of the market is more than a change in economic policy: it also implies a change in law, in property rights (including in urban land) and in the roles of the state. The changes in property rights and in the roles of the state associated with the market takes time, and it can have transitional problems in market development, production and trade. Second, the command mode or organization alters to a new emphasis on macro-economic control, sometimes accompanied by first-phase inflation as consumers begin to spend their accumulated savings and, sometimes, their increased earnings. Third, the transition always brings fundamental structural-spatial changes, giving new enhanced local economies to some urban areas and unemployment to others. This is accompanied by new forms of poverty, accentuated by altering the employment-based welfare for social security and housing in state economic enterprises to reformed provisions in state roles and public finance. Finally, state socialism often leaves legacies of substantial environmental degradation from manufacturing, including air, water and other forms of pollution, including contaminated land. The examples are extensive in the oil industry in the Caspian Sea region, in steel and other heavy industry, and more generally as a reflection of earlier problems with environmental regulation.

Poland represents an example of purposeful and rapid activity in economic, political, social and environmental transitions. The environmental transitions included local authority initiatives in support of Agenda 21 (Ministry of Environmental Protection, 1996). The progress in implementing localized environmental protection occurred in planned stages. In 1989 the 2500 local authorities were given decentralized rights for decision making, though their financial resources were limited and restricted the implementation of environmental and other reforms. But in 1993 the local authorities were given guidelines and information for sustainable development. This was followed up in 1995 when the Ministry of Environmental Protection issued statements on the methodology for preparing environmental plans and the programmes selected for implementation. All of these initiatives were encouraged by a competition for the most progressive localized policies, organized by the Office of the President of the Republic of Poland. Some 139 urban authorities responded. In the wider perspective, the legislative and administrative reforms have led to the development of sustainable development plans in Upper Silesia, in the Pomeranian region, in Lower Silesia, in Random, in Elle, in Warsaw, and in other cities. Programme development has been assisted internationally from the European Union Regional Development Programme and from other programmes.

Further appreciation of Polish initiatives in the localization of Agenda 21 can be ascertained from a brief review of EPM activities in Katowice, Silesia, a city of 2 million people. Katowice is a centre of heavy industry and electricity generation. Many of the economic enterprises, with characteristics of inefficiency and high pollution, are still state owned. This has detrimental effects on the quality of life, but income levels exceed the household averages for Poland. Industrial and residential areas are intermingled and suffer the environmental problems associated with waste, untreated sewage, land degradation from mining and manufacturing, subsidence, damaged buildings and health risks (UNCHS/UNEP, 1997b). In response, the EPM activities are expressed in the 1993 Sustainable Katowice Agglomeration Project. This has proceeded with stakeholder conferences, seminars, action in environmental management and institutional reforms to consolidate cooperation among municipalities in the agglomeration. Katowice has taken a systematic and comprehensive approach, with new methods of management and the introduction of new technologies. This provides elements for a wider 'good practice' in heavy industry regions in transitional economies.

Case Studies from Developed Countries

Although developed countries have often commenced environmental reform at national and local levels preceding the UNCED meeting in 1992, the Local Agenda 21s from UNCED aimed at setting a new path towards sustainability. This has meant that most developed countries have not completed their Local Agenda 21s programmes and also that local progress varies from the strong and innovative to the slow and uncertain. As might be expected, the idea of sustainability sometimes elicits confusion and often the 'new' is more or less incorporated within the existing norms of public administration. The environmental literature and some official reports provide useful indications of initiatives and activities (see UNCHS/UNEP, 1997b; ICLEI et al, 1996; President's Council on Sustainable Development, 1996; Lafferty and Eckerberg, 1998).

The US federal government has provided some national leadership, including some top-down steering for Local Agenda 21s. The President's Council on Sustainable Development reported in 1996, writing in terms of 'A New Consensus for Prosperity, Opportunity and a Healthy Environment for the Future'. The urban problems that were noted included congestion, pollution and crime. Those advocacies from the UNCED meeting in 1992, such as decentralization, community participation, partnerships, action planning, and so forth, were endorsed. The President's Council was also interested in examples of good practice in American cities. Chattanooga in Tennessee has become something of a 'laboratory of ideas', with environmental innovation beginning in 1984 and in responding to some of the worst problems of urban sprawl, a declining central city area and pollution in the 1970s. It instituted public-private sector partnerships to set out new visions of economic, social and environmental aspiration. The consequent planning projects had a broad scope in improving affordable housing opportunities, education, water supply, the abatement of air pollution and city centre regeneration. Another notable long-term environmental improvement programme is associated with a 40-year period of reform in Los Angeles. In the 1940s smog, ozone and health problems attracted public concern. The improvement programme centred on air quality, with an extensive package of necessary reforms. These included legislation for the regulation of technical standards in vehicles and oil refineries, research and development in the applied science of pollution, and care in avoiding recession in the vehicle and oil industries in the region. Political support was nurtured and a process of publicity, negotiation and review assisted the effectiveness of the reforms (for more details, see Pugh, 1996a).

A wide-ranging review of the 1990s application of Local Agenda 21s in some European countries by Lafferty and Eckerberg (1998) gives information on the first-phase progress of new initiatives. The countries included in the review are Sweden, Norway, Finland, Denmark, The Netherlands, Germany, Italy, Spain, Britain and Ireland. The general findings indicate a gradual top-down steering by relevant ministries, commencement of activities in municipalities ranging from 100 per cent in Sweden to much lower ratios in other countries, and with a tendency to insert 'sustainability' into existing patterns of environmental programming. Local authorities which have made most progress are beginning to install performance indicators and monitoring into their periodic evaluations. Some notable innovations have been made in Sweden, especially in the proactive approaches taken in schools, aimed at introducing environmental studies and empowering students in public policy issues. Accordingly, youth networks have been influencing local and wider policies. At this stage nothing in the way of detailed evaluations of comparative policy performance is available.

Evaluation, Commentary and Emergent Issues

The foregoing case study examples range from using community-based EPM in elements of macro-spatial planning to the removal of neighbourhood nuisances. However, it is not only significant that EPM has a range of levels and scale, but also that localization leads to diverse understandings and feasibilities in sustainability. This obviously has implications for the progress of sustainable urban development. It also suggests that research agendas could usefully focus on comparative evaluation, with emphasis on identifying the underlying reasons for better and worse performance. At this stage, a few useful things are known about progress. It is dependent on creating and developing institutional and social capital. When institutions are fitted to enhance developmental patterns which are balancing pro-environmentalism and pro-growth, the prospects of success in some important aspects are enhanced. Social capital is about using networks, mutual trust and associational experience to achieve the socio-political common and useful purpose in development. As noted earlier, sometimes participation leads to conflict and sectional interests. Productive cohesion is more likely when the rules or norms include contracts or agreements setting out responsibilities, assignment of costs, monitoring, enforcement of the rules and incentives for social cooperation. This is especially relevant in environmentalism which sometimes has the economic-organizational dilemmas associated with the tragedy of the commons. It can also add cohesion to partnership arrangements, bringing together state agencies, markets, NGOs and organized households or other stakeholders. However, as revealed in the review of law and its enforcement in this volume (Perry, 2000), the localization of environmental political-legal conditions can be subject to various problems, including corruption, apathy, the power of vested interests and administrative incapacity.

PROGRESS WITH THE SUSTAINABLE CITIES PROGRAMME AND ITS APPLICATION IN CHENNAI, INDIA

The Origins and Development of the SCP in Chennai

Soon after the UNCHS launched the SCP in 1990, Chennai Metropolitan Development Authority (CMDA) volunteered to implement the SCP demonstration project which came to be known as the Sustainable Chennai Project (SChP). Although it was initiated in the year 1991, the SChP formally commenced in October 1995, just after the project agreement was signed (September 1995) and associated funding was secured. The SChP has been supported by what is called the Sustainable Chennai Support Project (SChSP). Prior to the formal commencement of SChP, the time lag between 1991 and 1995 was used to build up the interest and involvement of NGOs and various interest groups, including business and industry (SMSP-SMP, 1996), along with the preparation of Chennai's first environmental profile.

The EPM process involves three broad phases that form the general structure of a typical SCP demonstration project. These are now set out below in their context for implementation in Chennai:

Phase 1: The Envisaged Procedures, Phases and Application of the SCP in Chennai

In the first phase – Assessment and Start-up – three EPM functions are initiated and then continued throughout the process.[4] These functions are: clarifying the environmental issues to be addressed; involving those whose cooperation is required; and setting priorities. Phase I has three outputs to achieve: a project agreement (which was signed in 1995 in Chennai); a purposefully organized *City Environmental Profile*; and a carefully prepared and structured *City Consultation* which was a high-profile, large-scale public meeting lasting for four or five days. According to UNCHS (1994b, p49) a *City Consultation* should be designed to:

- raise the level of awareness and understanding, locally and nationally, of the key urban environmental issues;
- confirm the identity of 'stakeholders' and consolidate their interest and role in the SCP process;
- achieve a consensus on the priority issues to be tackled;
- obtain a commitment to the SCP process and to a general work programme, as well as a commitment of participation in that process; and
- begin the process of establishing working groups and other working procedures and mechanisms in the overall SCP process.

Phase I of the SChP began its consultative process in October 1995. The Vice-Chairperson of the CMDA held six meetings with representatives from public, private and popular sectors in which 21 environmental issues were identified. Based on these issues, five consultative groups (CGs) were formed on the subjects of: economy and urban poverty; urban infrastructure (excluding water and sanitation); environmental management and pollution control; water and sanitation; and land use planning and development. The CGs involved various 'stakeholders' from diverse professional backgrounds, including business, academia, administration, NGOs, planning, etc. They deliberated on these subject areas, following a pre-set agenda[5] to identify the problems facing Chennai City and Chennai Metropolitan Area (CMA), and to give recommendations. The CGs submitted their reports in August 1996, identifying five main environmental issues which were: the cleaning of waterways; the reduction of road congestion; improving sanitation in the city's poor and peri-urban areas; the conservation of natural resources and the built heritage; and improving incomes and poverty alleviation. Of these, the first three issues were prioritized for 'immediate further action' under the SChP (CMDA, 1997c). Accordingly, priority was given to upgrading squatter and slum living areas, water pollution and improved efficiency in urban transport.

As stated above, the introduction of the SCP often disturbs pre-existing urban policy agendas and introduces new ways of doing things. Some of the new 'requirements' have greater significance in urban management and governance than others. Two matters of particular significance are coordination and intervention. Coordination is often a routine problem in urban management. It arises from 'administrative separatism' in which various utilities, local government authorities, town-planning commissions, and so on, have their own (conflicting) mandates, powers, budget capacities and sense of their own missions. Power is unevenly distributed among them, and each has different emphases towards negotiation and cooperation with other urban authorities. Some coordination will have been built up informally, but large areas of 'administrative separatism' will often prevail. Intervention is, of course, a disturbance in ongoing processes and activities of urban government. The character of the intervention is variably understood, misunderstood, welcomed, ignored and incorporated with more or less effectiveness into some prevailing codes, conventions and norms. Significantly in the SCP-type of interventions, some accommodation is required in the participatory and community elements of EPM. The new interventions have the high-minded ambitions of full social inclusion, coproduction between authorities and communities (for example, in infrastructure in residential areas), and much else besides in using 'governance' as a device and process to steer reform in urban planning and management. Taken together, coordination and intervention simultaneously have the potential for strong cooperation at one extreme and contested authority at the other extreme.

Coordination and some of its requirements are now elaborated on further. People from all walks of life are affected by the decisions and activities which relate to the urban environment. It was mentioned in earlier discussions that the 1987 EPM guidelines specified which 'potentially concerned groups' were to be involved. The situation changed significantly by the late 1990s: EPM practised through the SCP now calls for the involvement of all those who have a 'stake' in the process. These fall in to three groups – that is, those whose interests are affected, those who possess relevant information and expertise, and those who control relevant implementation instruments. Moreover, these 'stakeholders' include persons and organizations from the public sector (especially at the local level), the private sector (especially the business community), and the popular sector (especially communities and NGOs) (UNCHS, 1994b). Coordination requirements are thereby made more fully inclusive and more complex in terms of governance.

Coordination is the fundamental concern of EPM and is dependent upon the willing involvement of stakeholders. This means that in management perspectives the SCP is focused on different dimensions of coordination (UNCHS, 1994b, pp32–3):

- coordination between public, private and community sectors;
- coordination between levels of government;
- coordination across public sector departments;
- coordination across urban space; and
- coordination over time.

Before holding the *City Consultation*, it was necessary for the SChP to ensure channels of coordination among the aforementioned stakeholders. This could not be done without Tamil Nadu government's (GTN) consent for the institutionalization of coordination and consultative processes owing to the varied interests of different government departments, various municipal governments, and statal and parastatal agencies that have their jurisdiction in the CMA. Such consent came forth when the Chief Secretary of the GTN issued an order (GTN, 1997) for the constitution of action committees and working groups for the three priority issues of the SChP.[6] This government order (GO) also set the common tasks for all the working groups which were to:

- review study reports;
- prioritize public sector actions;
- agree action plans and coordinate implementation;
- decide community, private and public partnerships;
- review legal instruments;
- redefine rules and responsibilities;
- enhance institutional capabilities;
- evolve institutional mechanisms;
- optimize financial and human resources;
- develop monitoring indicators; and
- establish a community information system.

In terms of whether the reforms would tend towards cooperation or contest, the government had acted perceptively in issuing its GO. The discussion now turns to consider the aspect of intervention. Since effective environmental management requires the coordination of multifaceted actors, the SCP operates at three levels of intervention: first, at the technical/operational level where coordination becomes necessary to avoid the dangers of compartmentalization of effort in order to ensure that the people working at this level have broadened perspectives, and that they become more aware of the environmental dimensions and the consequences of their actions outside of their own narrow scope of work. Second, at the institutional/ managerial level, it becomes important to have shared strategic views and a common commitment to the new approach of EPM in order to avoid conflicts of interest. For this purpose, broader mechanisms of coordination and collaboration can be established, with formal and informal procedures for ensuring a shared strategic view. This was implemented by the institutionalization of the aforementioned 'working group' mechanism.

Finally, at the political level, the SCP ideals assume that the basic support for sustainable urban development must be generated and maintained both from the formal political institutions and within the population. A high-visibility commitment to the SCP is crucial not only to mobilize the political 'will' necessary to resolve conflicts and make hard decisions, but also to maintain momentum. Furthermore, to give environmental management the long-term support it requires, a high political profile becomes necessary (UNCHS, 1994b). For this purpose, SChP managers sought the support of the highest executive, the Chief Minister of Tamil Nadu State, which they finally attained.

As the second main output of Phase I, the city's environmental profile had been completed (Appasamy, 1997a; 1997b; 1997c; 1997d). By September 1997, when *City Consultation* took place, the SChP was running 11 months late. In Chennai's case, although environmental issues were finally prioritized in August 1996, the *City Consultation* could not be organized by the end of the first year – that is, in September 1996. The *City Consultation* was delayed because its date had to be finalized with political consent at the Government of Tamil Nadu level; this took time. The SChP prepared 'proposition papers' for the three prioritized environmental issues, which were housing conditions in low-income living areas, water pollution and transport efficiency that had to be presented at the time of *City Consultation*. Although the SCP has set the purpose of a *City Consultation* as mentioned at the beginning of this subsection, the SChP determined its own objectives for this event, which were (CMDA, 1997c, p53):

- to prioritize the key environmental issues for Chennai (which had been done in the meantime);
- to mobilize political and administrative support (this had already been secured);
- to develop a new mechanism based on participation (this had been done through the GO (GTN, 1997)); and
- to agree on a general institutional framework for follow-up action. This was important and took time to achieve agreement because stakeholders initially had varied perspectives.

During a three-day event (4–6 September 1997), all the objectives of *City Consultation* were met and it attracted high-level publicity. Thus, all three outputs of Phase I were achieved, as follows: a formal project agreement; the city environmental profile; and a carefully prepared and structured *City Consultation*.

Phase 2: Strategy and Action Planning

Strategy and Action Planning is the longest of the three phases, mainly because it is concerned with detailed planning, specification, and the preparation for implementation (UNCHS, 1994a, p50). Its requirements are to:

- provide detailed information to clarify environmental problems and options for their resolution, organized into an on-going **information system**;
- publish specific **strategies** agreed among all those whose cooperation for their implementation is required, coordinated into a rolling overall urban environmental management strategy;
- coordinating actor-specific **action plans** involving mutually supportive interventions at operational, institutional and political levels; and
- outline the technical cooperation and capital investment **projects** for presentation to potential national and external support agencies during a consultation at the beginning of the third phase [emphases in the original].

To achieve these outputs, Phase 2 involves additional EPM functions which are to: negotiate issue-specific strategies; coordinate overall environmental management strategies; and agree on environmental action plans. These functions are performed with the help of intersectoral issue-specific working groups, which, as stated earlier, were established through the GO (GTN, 1997). Further, the EPM process aims at a long-term institutionalization of working group mechanisms.

Phase 3: Follow-up and Consolidation

The Follow-up and Consolidation is an open-ended phase in which agreed programmes and projects are initiated, policy reforms and institutional improvements are consolidated, the overall process is made routine, and procedures for monitoring and evaluating the effectiveness of this routine are put in place. According to the EPM process, it is useful to begin the third phase with another *City Consultation*, the focus of which is on 'presentation and discussion of the Environmental Management Strategies and the Environmental Action Plans'. Particular emphasis is laid on presenting the investment projects to the representatives of bilateral and multilateral agencies along with other public and private organizations which have the potential for funding assistance. This phase, according to SChP, is 'an open-ended follow-up and implementation phase which begins during the final months of the project and carries on after the project itself has terminated' (CMDA, 1997c, p17).

THE CHENNAI EXPERIENCE AND PRINCIPLES

The discussion proceeds by an exposition and evaluation of the three selected priorities in the SChP.

Improving Sanitation in Poor Class City Areas and Peri-urban Areas

Soon after the issue of the GO (GTN, 1997), work began for the constitution of action committees and working groups. The cross-cutting issue of sanitation had to have an action committee and four working groups on the issues of: improving the primary level collection of liquid and solid waste; improving the secondary level collection of solid waste; strengthening solid waste disposal systems; and encouraging the formation of a recycling network. During the first meeting of the action committee, it was decided that the action committee and working groups would concentrate only on solid waste management for the time being. The decision to deliberate on primary level liquid waste collection was deferred for a date in the future (CMDA, 1997b). Moreover, it was decided that the action committee would meet once a month and the working groups as frequently as possible. The geographical scope of the solid waste management (SWM) was also broadened to include all areas of the city and not just the poorer areas.

   The work was carried forward in three working groups, the first with scope on SWM in Chennai city, the second on SWM in peri-urban areas, the third on recycling and hazardous waste management. However, the three working groups encountered various internal and external problems. The first working group – that is, on SWM in Chennai City – found that the Chennai Municipal Corporation (CMC) did not take the SChP seriously, instead adopting its own efforts to upgrade SWM in the city. The CMC proceeded to involve the private sector in SWM in May 1998, but the working group failed to achieve any action plan from its discussions with the various stakeholders. Following a paper presented by one of the authors (Dahiya, 1998c) to the CMC, the Deputy Commissioner in charge of Health and SWM at CMC agreed in principle to involve NGOs/CBOs for local environmental planning and management, with the focus on SWM; but nothing practical could be done in terms of any project/programme formulation because it needed political consent at the mayoral and council level.

The working group on SWM in peri-urban areas held discussions with stakeholders from the popular sector, research organizations and different government departments, and certain actions were initiated. First, the fact that 2 out of 8 municipalities and 6 out of the 28 town panchayats had solid waste dumping yards led to the decision that all these urban local bodies (ULBs) were asked to designate land for solid waste dumping yards. Some of the municipalities and town panchayats (ie, former village governments) have identified lands for solid waste disposal. Second, eight residential communities were selected in eight municipalities as 'model projects' for community-based SWM, including the source segregation of organic and inorganic solid waste and the composting of organic solid waste. And finally, following a paper presented by one of the authors (Dahiya, 1998d) in one of the working group discussions, it was decided that the ULBs should prepare lists of CBOs and NGOs working in their areas and involve them in SWM for creating a cleaner local environment (GTN, 1998). At the time of writing, efforts were being made by the municipal governments to implement 'model projects' and to involve CBOs/NGOs in SWM.

The working group on Recycling and Hazardous Waste Management divided into three subgroups responsible for organic waste management (OWM), hospital waste management (HWM) and hazardous waste management (HzWM). These three working subgroups organized discussions and a variety of ideas were put forward, including two issue base papers prepared by one of the present authors (Dahiya, 1998a; 1998b). But the working subgroups could not reach a collective decision on the basis of which a waste management strategy could be formulated. On many occasions, the representatives of one of the key organizations were either absent from the discussion or they did not commit themselves to the collective viewpoints achieved. At times, many of the representatives did not agree to the views of the other stakeholders and repeatedly postponed points for discussion for future working group sessions. This finally led to sheer frustration among the participant stakeholders and the recruitment by the SChP of a consultant to prepare a HWM strategy for the project. Since no 'lead projects' could be formulated through the working group discussions, proposals for a number of independent projects from four CBOs/NGOs were accepted as the 'demonstration projects' for implementation. The SChP, through its working groups, has yet to finalize the Strategic Environmental Management Framework (SEMF), as well as the

Strategy Implementation Profile (SIP) for SWM in order to implement the third phase of the SCP.

The Reduction of Road Congestion

An Action Committee was set up in mid-1997 to address the issue of road congestion. The Committee met in July 1997 and constituted three working groups on the following tasks: maximizing the existing infrastructure investments; improving the modal share of transit systems; and the improvement of air and noise quality. The working groups have met on several occasions with their stakeholders to formulate a strategy and to prepare 'lead projects'. Their efforts have been successful by and large as they have been able to formulate a strategy that was discussed in the *Workshop* on the issue in July 1998 (CMDA, 1998). The strategy focuses on various aspects: reducing fuel subsidies and increasing fuel taxes; promoting the bus-way system; improving interchange facilities between bus and rail systems; reducing sulphur and lead content in gasoline; and switching from two-stroke to four-stroke engines, etc. In addition, a Traffic Action Plan has been formulated with short-term schemes, including the improvement of road geometrics, traffic signals, a close-circuit television system, pedestrian grade separator, etc. For the medium-term, plans include mini-flyovers; the long-term projects indicate additional flyovers, ramps, and grade separations. At the time of writing, it was felt that insufficient progress had been made by the working groups in implementing the 'lead projects' owing to the insecurity of the SChP's future.[7] Since many 'lead projects' have been formulated, an independent consultant has been asked to evaluate and recommend those that appear suitable for implementation as demonstration projects for later scaling up.

Cleaning the Waterways

The main waterways in Chennai include the Adyar and Cooum rivers, and Buckingham Canal, all of which are highly polluted. The *Proposition Paper* (CMDA, 1997a) quotes a study that reveals that as many as 727 outlets of untreated liquid waste that drain into the waterways have been identified, with Cooum (323) and Adyar (222) being the worst affected. What makes this one of the most complex environmental issues in Chennai can be seen from the following (CMDA, 1997a, p4):

> While the PWD [Public Works Department] 'owns' the waterways, it has no powers to prevent entry of wastes. CMWSSB [Chennai Metro Water Supply and Sewerage Board] has the powers to plan and implement water supply [and] sewerage systems but is compelled by necessity to give priority for water supply systems. The TNPCB [Tamil Nadu Pollution Control Board] has the powers to monitor environmental conditions but finds it difficult to enforce where public institutions like CMWSSB or PWD are involved. The CMC maintains

the public toilets but the evacuation of the sewerage has to be ultimately handled by the CMWSSB. The storm water drains are also maintained by CMC but cross connection between surface flows of storm water drains and human wastes [flowing out] of sewers are well evident but not controllable by either CMC or CMWSSB. Internal sewer system in tenements constructed by TNSCB [Tamil Nadu Slum Clearance Board] suffers from want of maintenance due to lack of technical skill and/or non recognition as a priority issue by TNSCB.

The Proposition Paper suggested different strategies to address the problem but cautioned that it was a capital intensive exercise. It was also realized during the first consultative phase that the solution to the waterways problem requires heavy investment and a long-drawn plan for implementation, and effective operation and maintenance (CMDA, 1996). At the time of writing, the World Bank and other international agencies were involved through global tender for international consultancy firms to prepare bids. The global tender process is a significant deviation from the SChP/EPM approach where all environmental issues are handled through some 'lead projects' which are then scaled up and form a demonstration for the future.

EVALUATION, COMMENTARY AND EMERGENT ISSUES IN CHENNAI[8]

Broad-based Public Participation

Broad-based participation is one of the distinctive achievements of the SChP. There is no precedent in Chennai for the representation of such a wide cross-section of citizens in a programme that addresses urgent civic problems. The public participation process started 18 months before the official starting date of 1 October 1995 and involved leading businessmen and industrialists, eminent scientists, consultants, training outfits, professional institutions, Chambers of Commerce and Industry, CBOs and NGOs of various kinds, along with local government bodies, public agencies and departments of government.

Environmental Issues Addressed with Stakeholder Involvement

The SChP has successfully clarified the environmental issues faced by the CMA through the prescribed first phase – *Assessment and Start-up*. This was achieved through broad stakeholder involvement (as described above), followed by prioritization of the environmental issues. Stakeholder involvement has been characterized by sharing information and ideas, participating in discussions, consultations and working groups at different levels, and being fully involved in the process.

Selection of Implementing Agency

Generally it is the city/municipal government that is selected as the implementing agency for a SCP demonstration. In Chennai's case, the CMDA was selected as the implementing agency mainly for two reasons: first, there was no elected government in Chennai for 23 years until 1996; second, the CMDA has the legal authority to regulate urban and physical development in the CMA. Further, it had some experience of working in a multi-institutional context, with various agencies, during the late 1970s and early 1980s while overseeing World Bank assisted projects for the CMA. Since the late 1980s, the CMDA has concentrated more on its own projects and its regulatory work. It has limited the scope of the CMDA's operations. Moreover, in 1996 a council with a mayor was elected in Chennai after a gap of 23 years. On the one hand, the newly elected council wanted to establish itself as an efficient service providing agency. On the other hand, it did not want the credit of its works to go to other agencies; this obviously had political connotations. As a result, the SChP received little attention from the elected council.

Large City Size

It has been realized that a large city like Chennai, having a population of almost 6 million, has a very complex management structure with as many as ten independent statal and parastatal agencies (which are not answerable to an elected municipal council). In such a context, it takes a longer time than is prescribed in the SCP manuals for the merits of such a consultative approach like the EPM to percolate down to the crucial decision making and operating levels. A comparatively smaller city with a population of less than a million, and with some tradition of elected government and a strong municipality, could be a better candidate for the SCP.

Problems in Stakeholder Coordination

The stakeholder coordination in the pre-project and consultative phases was highly successful, and generated great enthusiasm among citizens and the operating staff of the various service agencies. But when the Action Committee and working group phase started, the whole movement slowed down. The SChP and CMDA (the implementation agency), contrary to their expectations, did not receive the coordination they expected from the different departments because at the Action Committee level, the traditional bureaucratic style of administration of the powerful and autonomous government agencies and departments became active. This led to principal-agent problems, as explained below.

Problems of Commitment

Since the higher officials were not dedicated to the new concept of 'coord-ination', the officials who attended the working group discussions/meetings could not commit themselves to the collective decisions which were taken. In the SWM working group discussions, it was often seen (since one of the authors [Dahiya] attended many of the discussions) that either the CMC officials did not come to attend the discussions or they said that they would convey the decisions of the working groups to their seniors in the department. When this was repeated many times, the other stakeholders saw no point in wasting their time in attending such discussions.

Unilateral Action by Various Departments/Agencies

Various government departments and parastatals have their own agenda and plans of action which need not coincide even with the city's prioritized environmental issues. Such plans prepared by the CMWSSB, the CMC and the PWD are launched by these agencies whenever the funding is available. The SChP could do little to bring such unilateral action on the part of some of these agencies under its umbrella. This re-emphasizes the fact that all the ongoing efforts 'need' to be made use of by the EPM process. But how this could be done still needs to be answered.

Role of the Higher Echelons of Government

During the SChP period, there were a number of changes in the higher echelons of government – for example, a change in the state government (the Government of Tamil Nadu), a change in Chief Secretaries, several changes in Secretary, Housing and Urban Development, and the election of Chennai Municipal Council in October 1996. The newly installed government failed to see the merits of the SChP which focuses more on (consultative) process as it was more intent on attracting major funding to the state. This was a major impediment and a diversion of urban policy priorities.

Private Sector Involvement

The private sector's involvement as a stakeholder and contributor of funds is very important for the success of an SCP. In Chennai, it was present during the consultation phase of the EPM process. But the private sector's active involvement faded during the action-planning phase, unlike the case of CBOs and NGOs. It has been argued that if the private sector is provided with a share in the decision-making process as a stakeholder (which ought to be the case under the EPM process), it could offer (much needed financial) support to the SCP activities.

Impact on the CMDA

The SChP has given a breath of fresh air to the CMDA which had become quite insular for almost a decade. The opportunities for closer interaction with various governmental and non-governmental entities on specific environmental issues and being exposed to different facets of the urban environmental planning and management of Chennai and its metropolitan area have given the CMDA a sustained exposure and put the same in the current developmental context of the CMA. It has further helped the CMDA to start recovering its lost mandate of being a planner, coordinator and monitor of spatio-economic development in the CMA.

Long-term institutionalization of the EPM Process

The third phase of the SChP according to the CMDA (1997c) would start in the final months of the project. At the time of writing, it was not clear whether the CMDA has embarked on this process or not.

EVALUATION AND CONCLUSIONS

The foregoing discussion of Local Agenda 21s and the SCP has necessarily been largely descriptive and by way of recent historical narrative. It is important, of course, in the first phases of new urban ideas and programmes to set out the historical circumstances. However, for the final concluding sections the discussions can broaden, with some reflections on the evaluative and the theoretical. In terms of urban management and policy, the localization of environmentalism during the 1990s was thoroughly reformist and challenging in both ambition and content. It was not confined to the narrow programmatic technicalities of urban environmental improvement, and it was not meant to be a simple adjunct to the prevailing urban management and planning activities. Instead, the new environmentalism carried with it strong advocacies for change in governance, in institutional–organizational approaches, and for turning professional practice closely towards community participation. Those advocacies were understood to be central components of a new approach to urban management and are seen virtually as a requirement for fulfilling environmental reform and sustainability. Moreover, these advocacies could not be readily cast aside because they were contained within the authority of the major UN conferences at Rio de Janeiro in 1992 and Istanbul in 1996. Their authority and legitimacy was even greater than their association to the UN and the persuasive power of its urban and environmental agencies. The broader agendas for development and urban policy contained theories and reformist persuasions for socio-political partnerships, for community-based initiatives, and for bringing urban planning closer to the realities of the lives of the poor and other groups.

It is relatively easy to find good reasons for the new advocacies in urban management and environmentalism. A summarized perspective will convey this for our present purposes. A change in state–market–society relations (ie, in governance) has developmental advantages. In developing countries, the state has often done both too much and too little. It has often encroached on market production, but neglected socio-economic development roles proceeding from environmental improvement, from social and institutional capital, and from broadly spread human capital development. Social and institutional capital in this context refers to those civic associational elements and practices which enhance development. Partnerships can have various advantages. These include a cooperative division of labour among markets, states, voluntary organizations and households to achieve useful combinations of economic efficiency, environmental relevance and socio-political representation. Also, partnerships can lead to interactions that improve work practices – for example, guiding government agencies regarding the reduction of poverty and environmental squalor. All the foregoing then appears to have greater legitimacy and reason because the older ways of urban management have their shortcomings. The examples of the shortcomings are several and varied: the administrative agencies of government can fail to coordinate and will act narrowly rather than for comprehensive environmental development; the poor and other groups have been isolated and excluded from decision making; and residents in many squatter settlements have not developed community organization and political experience to raise their qualities of life.

It is from the foregoing that the new approaches to urban management and environmentalism become intellectually and programmatically accepted in broad principles. But in practice the useful persuasions are not sufficient for reform. They have to be accommodated to the realities of administrative separatism. Vested interests in city-regional politics can counter the advocacies for social idealism and the redistribution of resources. Not everything in the older ways of doing things has been bad for development. In some jurisdictions useful professional and administrative capacity has been built up, and this could be developed further for enhancing 'bottom-up' aspects of the new planning. Apart from this positive possibility, the reality of pre-existing institutions and organizations in urban planning has to be countenanced. In some ways this may mean that outcomes often result in incomplete assimilation, in adopting only fragments of the new ways, or in using the language of the new, but practising the old, along with its limitations. Also, as shown in other chapters in this book, the new sometimes has to be contested politically, legally and economically. Furthermore, the new is inherently complex, without blueprints for practical application. The principles of execution differ from those of advocacy and both are necessary for reform. Once the issue is put in this way, various centrally relevant questions are raised. Are the new ideas adequate in principle? Even if the ideas are adequate in principle, can they be implemented? What are the conditions and requirements for implementation and good practice?

The questions raise the matter of future research agendas. One aspect of this is to go beyond the stage of thick historical description and detail.

This can be done in various ways, including sharply focused case studies and comparative studies. Focused case studies can track the prescriptive ideas, the selection and discarding processes, and the ways they are opposed or accommodated. Comparative studies can be designed to establish the socio-economic and political conditions under which the new urban management and governance can have some success. This adds understanding to lessons from experience and social learning. It does not mean that good conditions can be applied to all administrative and political systems. Future research agendas also include the adaptation of various technical and statistical analyses to extend data systems and concepts to serve the needs of the new approaches, and to display their limitations. Finally, the localization of environmentalism has to be set in the context of urban change. The urban change is fundamental, covering demographic transitions, global economic and financial integration, institutional reform, and the tensions between the causes from private sector growth and improved socio-environmental development. Institutional reform is sometimes slow and uncertain, but its intensities increase when trade, agglomeration economies and demographic imperatives run in favour of required reform. The localization of environmental agendas includes much more than has been conceived in the UNCED meeting in Rio de Janeiro, 1992, and at the Habitat II meeting in Istanbul, 1996.

Much of the foregoing evaluative commentary can itself be 'localized', which is essential for environmental agendas which are prescriptively for community-based urban application. In local contexts, the new environmental planning and management occurs where inequality of power among government agencies, community groups and other stakeholders is the norm. This places limitations on social inclusion and, sometimes, on effective environmental improvement. Often gaps will occur in know-how, but the use of consultants can reduce local ownership. This dilemma is heightened because local governments often have gaps in professional and resource capacity. These realities mean that perspectives on social learning should be long term and realistic. This similarly applies to the inclusion of the poor and the process of embedding new institutions in socio-political contexts. The poor will often have different perceptions of environmental and developmental priorities from other stakeholders. Their livelihoods often depend on the allocation of some 65–85 per cent of their budgets on food. Also, their needs are several, including income generation, access to health services, and trade-offs between child labour and education. In many instances the NGOs will be somewhat adrift from the idea of total social inclusion and of balancing the environmental and the developmental. Also, in other instances, of which the Chennai experience with the SCP is a good example, political changes in regimes and in the framework of urban government, can influence the course of events, for better or worse, in programmatic environmentalism. All of this suggests that in developing countries the new environmental planning and management will be slow, distorted, and more often than not, incomplete. It may, nonetheless, with adaptation and realistic expectations, be a worthwhile project.

NOTES

1   These three volumes included guidelines for *Institutionalizing Environmental Planning and Management for Settlements Development*, Volume I (UNEP-UNCHS, 1987a), *Environmental Considerations in Metropolitan Planning and Management*, Volume II (UNEP-UNCHS, 1987b), and *Environmental Considerations in Regional Planning and Management*, Volume III (UNEP-UNCHS, 1987c).

2   These 'potentially concerned groups' are replaced by 'stakeholders' from a variety of backgrounds, as will be discussed later in the same section, as the EPM goes through a 'learning by doing' phase.

3   The limitations of traditional administration and management systems include: 'chronic failures in inter-departmental, cross-sectoral, and inter-governmental co-operation and collaboration; lack of effective strategic planning capabilities; out-dated and ineffectual urban planning; inadequate mechanisms and practices for meaningful public participation; lack of modalities for public-private collaboration; weaknesses in municipal public finance; shortage of appropriate skills and experience; and inadequate information availability' (UNCHS, 1994b, p28).

4   'Ultimately, when the EPM process is firmly established, urban environmental issues will be systematically and routinely identified and assessed through a continuous over-all environmental monitoring and analysis function' (UNCHS, 1994b, p45).

5   Identification of the principal issues in each group's sector; prioritization of the issues identified for necessary action; suggested action, in broad terms, that is considered feasible and viable for improving the present status of the prioritized issues; identification of the cross-sectoral linkages possible with the prioritized; assessment of the extent of involvement of the stakeholders in the implementation process and how their involvement could be achieved; consideration of whether, and how, existing programmes of the government and private sectors could be integrated to provide solutions to the issues listed (*Towards Singara Chennai*, 1997, p4).

6   'Each Working Group has a Convenor or Moderator, a widely respected expert in the topic, as well as a Co-ordinator who usually comes from the full-time staff of the Project Team. The members of the Working Groups are the stakeholders relevant to that particular environmental issue: representatives from the public, private and community sectors, those with technical know-how, those whose substantive concerns may be directly affected and those who have decision making powers' (UNCHS, 1994b, p50).

7   It needs to be mentioned that the SChP temporarily stopped functioning in October 1998 as the funding for the project agreement was for three years starting in October 1995. The SChP was extended by one year until September 1999.

8   Information on the following points has been collected by one of the authors (Dahiya) through a series of semi-structured interviews with various team leaders of the SChP and SChSP.

REFERENCES

Appasamy, Paul P (1997a) *Sustainable Chennai Environmental Profile Volume I: Executive Summary*, MIDS (Madras Institute of Development Studies), Chennai

Appasamy, Paul P (1997b) *Sustainable Chennai Environmental Profile, Volume II: Institutional Framework*, MIDS, Chennai

Appasamy, Paul P (1997c) *Sustainable Chennai Environmental Profile, Volume III: Urban Environmental Indicators*, MIDS, Chennai

Appasamy, Paul P (1997d) *Sustainable Chennai Environmental Profile, Volume IV: Data Book*, MIDS, Chennai

Bartone, C, Bernstein, J, Leitmann, J and Eigen, J (1994) *Towards Environmental Strategies for Cities: Policy Considerations for Urban Environmental Management in Developing Countries*, Urban Management Programme, Paper 18, World Bank, Washington, DC

Bernstein, J (1993) *Alternative Approaches to Pollution and Waste Management: Regulatory and Economic Instruments*, Urban Management Programme, Paper 3, World Bank, Washington, DC

Chennai Metropolitan District Authority (CMDA) (1996) *Sustainable Madras Project: Executive Summary of Reports of Consultative Groups*, CMDA, Chennai

Chennai Metropolitan District Authority (CMDA) (1997a) *Environmental Issues – City's Waterways: Proposition Paper*, CMDA, Chennai

Chennai Metropolitan District Authority (CMDA) (1997b) *Minutes of the Meeting of the Action Committee on Solid Waste Management*, Government of Tamil Nadu, Chennai, 4 July

Chennai Metropolitan District Authority (CMDA) (1997c) *Sustainable Chennai Project City Consultation: Participants Manual*, CMDA, Chennai

Chennai Metropolitan District Authority (CMDA) (1998) *Sustainable Chennai Project Workshop: Reduction of Traffic Congestion and Improving Air Quality*, CMDA, Chennai

Dahiya, Bharat (1998a) *Sustainable Chennai Project: Discussion Paper on Organic Solid Waste Management*, presented in UNCHS' Sustainable Cities Programme Working Sub-Group Discussion, Chennai, 24 May

Dahiya, Bharat (1998b) *Sustainable Chennai Project: Discussion Paper on Hospital Waste Management*, presented in UNCHS' Sustainable Cities Programme Working Sub-Group Discussion, Chennai, 25 May

Dahiya, Bharat (1998c) *Urban Governance for Sustainable Urban Development: A Framework for Institutionalising Relationships between NGOs/CBOs and Chennai Municipal Corporation*, presented to CMC in a Focus Group discussion, Chennai, 17 June

Dahiya, Bharat (1998d) *Urban Governance for Sustainable Urban Development: A Framework for Institutionalising Relationships between NGOs/CBOs and Urban Local Bodies in Chennai Metropolitan Area*, presented in UNCHS' Sustainable Cities Programme Working Group Discussion, Chennai, 25 June

Dillinger W (1994) *Decentralization and its Implications for Urban Service Delivery*, Urban Management Programme, Paper 16, World Bank, Washington, DC

Government of Tamil Nadu (GTN) (1997) *Government Order for the Constitution of Action Committee and Working Groups*, Chennai, 15 May

Government of Tamil Nadu (GTN) (1998) *Minutes of the Meeting of Working Group II on Solid Waste Management in Peri Urban Areas of Chennai*, Chennai, 25 June

Grubb, M, Koch, M, Munson, K, Sullivan, F and Thomson K (1993) *The Earth Summit Agreements: A Guide and Assessments*, Earthscan, London

International Council for Local Environmental Initiatives, International Development Research Centre and UN Environment Programme (1996) *The Local Agenda 21 Planning Guide: An Introduction to Sustainable Development Planning*, ICLEI, Toronto

Lafferty, W and Eckerberg, K (1998) *From the Earth Summit to Local Agenda 21: Working Towards Local Agenda 21*, Earthscan, London

Leitmann, J (1994a) *Rapid Environmental Assessment: Lessons from Countries in the Developing World, Volume 1, Methodology and Findings*, Urban Management Programme, Paper 14, World Bank, Washington, DC

Leitmann, J (1994b) *Rapid Environmental Assessment: Lessons from the Developing World, Volume 2, Tools and Outputs*, Urban Management Programme, Paper 15, World Bank, Washington, DC

Mathur, O P (1997) *Fiscal Innovation and Urban Governance*, National Institute of Public Finance and Policy, Delhi

Ministry of Environmental Protection (1996) *Progress Report 1992–96*, Government of Poland, Warsaw

Ostrom, E, Shroeder, L and Wynne, S (1993) *Institutional Incentives and Sustainable Development: Infrastructure Policies in Perspective*, Westview Press, Boulder, Colorado

Perry, A (1999) 'Sustainable Legal Mechanisms for the Protection of the Local Environment', in C Pugh (ed) *Sustainability in Cities in Developing Countries: Theory and Practice at the Millennium*, Earthscan, London

President's Council on Sustainable Development (1996) *Sustainable America: A New Consensus for Prosperity, Opportunity and a Healthy Environment for the Future*, Council on Sustainable Development, Washington, DC

Pugh, C (1996a) 'Introduction', in C Pugh (ed) *Sustainability, the Environment and Urbanization*, Earthscan, London, pp1–22

Pugh, C (1996b) 'Sustainability and Sustainable Cities', in C Pugh (ed) *Sustainability, the Environment and Urbanization*, Earthscan, London, pp135–77

Pugh, C (1997a) 'International Urban and Housing Policy: A Review of the Cambridge Studies, 1989–1995', *Environment and Planning A*, no 29, pp149–67

Pugh, C (1997b) 'Poverty and Progress? Reflections on Housing and Urban Policies in Developing Countries, 1976–96', *Urban Studies*, no 34, pp1547–96

Ramachandran, Arcot and Tolba, Mostafa (1987) 'Preface', in UNEP-UNCHS (1987a) *Environmental Guidelines for Settlements Planning Management, Vol I: Institutionalizing Environmental Planning and Management for Settlements Development*, UNCHS-UNEP, Nairobi, piii

Sustainable Madras Support Project/Sustainable Madras Project (SMSP/SMP) (1996) *Sustainable Madras Project, India*, SMSP/SMP, Chennai

Shah, J and Nagpal, T (1997) *Urban Air Quality Management Strategy in Asia, Jakarta Report*, World Bank Technical Paper No 379, World Bank, Washington, DC

Shah, J, Nagpal, T and Brandon, C (1997a) *Urban Air Quality Management Strategy in Asia, Guidebook*, World Bank, Washington, DC

Towards Singara Chennai (1997) 'First Steps to a Better City', *Towards Singara Chennai* (Official Newsletter of the Sustainable Chennai Project), vol 1, no 1, p4

United Nations Council for Human Settlements (UNCHS) (1987) *Global Report on Human Settlements*, Oxford University Press, Oxford

United Nations Council for Human Settlements (UNCHS) (1989) *A New Agenda for Human Settlements*, UNCHS, Nairobi

United Nations Council for Human Settlements (UNCHS) (1990) *The Global Strategy for Shelter to the Year 2000*, UNCHS, Nairobi

United Nations Council for Human Settlements (UNCHS) (1992) *Improving the Living Environment for a Sustainable Future*, UNCHS, Nairobi

United Nations Council for Human Settlements (UNCHS) (1994) *Sustainable Human Settlements Development: Implementing Agenda 21*, UNCHS, Nairobi

United Nations Council for Human Settlements (UNCHS)/World Bank/United Nations Development Programme (1994a) *Urban Management Programme: Annual Report 1994*, UNCHS, Nairobi

United Nations Council for Human Settlements (UNCHS) (1994b) *Sustainable Cities Programme: Concepts and Applications of United Nations Programme*, UNCHS, Nairobi

United Nations Council for Human Settlements (UNCHS) (1994c) *Environment Component of the Urban Management Programme (UMP/E): Project Brief*, UNCHS, Nairobi

United Nations Council for Human Settlements (UNCHS) (1997) *Istanbul Declaration on Human Settlements*, UNCHS, Nairobi

United Nations Council for Human Settlements (UNCHS) (1998) *Implementation of Habitat Agenda at the Local Level*, United Nations, New York

United Nations Council for Human Settlements/United Nations Environment Programme (UNCHS/UNEP) (1997a) *Implementing the Urban Environmental Agenda*, Vol 1, UNCHS/UNEP, Nairobi

United Nations Council for Human Settlements/United Nations Environment Programme (UNCHS/UNEP) (1997b) *City Experience and International Support*, Vol 2, UNCHS/UNEP, Nairobi

United Nations Development Programme (UNDP) (1991) *Cities, People and Poverty*, UNDP, New York

United Nations Environment Programme/United Nations Council for Human Settlements (UNEP/UNCHS) (1987a) *Environmental Guidelines for Settlements Planning Management, Vol. I: Institutionalizing Environmental Planning and Management for Settlements Development*, UNCHS/UNEP, Nairobi

United Nations Environment Programme/United Nations Council for Human Settlements (UNEP/UNCHS) (1987b) *Environmental Guidelines for Settlements Planning Management, Vol. II: Environmental Considerations in Metropolitan Planning and Management (MPM)*, UNCHS/UNEP, Nairobi

United Nations Environment Programme/United Nations Council for Human Settlements (UNEP/UNCHS) (1987c) *Environmental Guidelines for Settlements Planning Management, Vol II: Environmental Considerations in Regional Planning and Management (RPM)*, UNCHS/UNEP, Nairobi

World Bank (1988) *Addressing the Urban Challenge*, Policy Planning and Research Staff, Urban Development Division Report, INU 33, World Bank, Washington, DC

World Bank (1991) *Urban Policy and Economic Development: An Agenda for the 1990s*, World Bank, Washington, DC

World Bank (1993) *Housing: Enabling Markets to Work*, World Bank, Washington, DC

World Commission on Environment and Development (1987) *Our Common Future* [The Brundtland Report], Oxford University Press, Oxford

9 ECONOMIC AND ENVIRONMENTAL SUSTAINABILITY IN SHANGHAI

Peter Abelson

We want to make Shanghai one of the international economic, financial and trade centres [of the world] as soon as possible, and bring about a new leaf in the economic development of the Yangtze River Delta and the whole Yangzte River Valley.

Chinese Government (1992) 14th Session of the National Congress of the Communist Party of China

INTRODUCTION

Over much of the past 150 years, Shanghai has been an economically dynamic and politically turbulent city. In 1842, Shanghai was one of the first Chinese cities to be formally opened to trade with Western countries. By the 1930s, it was China's leading industrial and trading city. Shanghai was also, in 1921, the birthplace of the Communist Party. In the 1960s, the city was in the vanguard of the Cultural Revolution and the local economy stagnated. However, following the political and economic reforms of the 1980s, by the late 1990s, Shanghai was both politically stable and China's most productive city.

As shown in Figure 9.1, Shanghai is located midway along China's highly populated and generally prosperous Eastern seaboard. The city itself sits on mainly flat land at the confluence of the Yangtze and Huangpu rivers, on the south-east edge of the Yangtze delta.

Shanghai is one of four special municipalities in China with a status equivalent to a province. This means that the Shanghai Municipal Government (SMG) reports directly to the central government in Beijing. The SMG administers a total area of 6340 square km of land. This area includes the central city, with its ten urban districts, which covers only 280 square km;

★   Economic and Technology Development Zone
---- County boundary
—·— Provincial boundary
Central city
City proper (Shiqu)

Source: Yusuf and Wu, 1997

Figure 9.1 *Shanghai Location and its Environs*

five suburban districts – namely, Baoshan, Minhang, Jiadang, Jinshan and Pudong New Area (the latter is actually a new central business district) – and five suburban counties – namely, Nanhui, Fengzian, Sonjian, Qingpu and the island of Chongming.

By most counts, Shanghai is China's largest city, although some estimates put Chongqing in first place. Currently, the total population of Shanghai Municipality is about 16 million. This comprises some 11 million residents in the urban areas and 5 million in the suburban counties. These numbers include about 3 million unregistered mobile city dwellers. However, there are no accurate data on these unregistered city inhabitants.

Shanghai is also China's largest economic centre, with a gross domestic product of $30 billion. By Chinese standards, the average household income of $5500 is high and many households are affluent.

Shanghai is evidently not a typical city in China. Nor, indeed, is it typical of cities in other developing countries. Shanghai is an economic powerhouse that is already one of the world's major business cities. In the words of Yusuf and Wu (1997, p49):

> *None of the other crowded cities in the developing world, such as Calcutta, Dhaka or São Paolo, conveys the extraordinary sense of teeming humanity as does downtown Shanghai during peak hours. Industry has been and remains the lifeblood of the municipality.*

In terms of economic power, Shanghai will almost certainly become one of the world's leading cities.

But Shanghai is not, and cannot be, isolated from the rest of China. Its future is integrally related to the conditions of life elsewhere in China. If these remain poor, or even modest, people will flock in increasing numbers to Shanghai. There will be increasing overcrowding, slums, traffic congestion, air pollution, waste disposal and other environmental problems that especially afflict most large cities. In a free and mobile society, the welfare of the marginal resident in Shanghai can be little different from the welfare of the marginal resident in any other Chinese town or village.

Shanghai's economic success is almost assured. But herein lies the seeds of its ongoing environmental problems. Like Bangkok and Bombay, it is a honeypot for the rural poor. Shanghai's problem is how to manage economic growth with environmental sustainability in the face of an ever-increasing population – this is the main theme of this chapter.

The chapter contains two main parts. The first part focuses on economic development. It describes the history of economic development in Shanghai, recent market reforms, and Shanghai's economic strengths as well as some weaknesses. The second and longer part discusses the main environmental problems confronting Shanghai and how it is responding to them. There is a short concluding section.

THE ECONOMIC DEVELOPMENT OF SHANGHAI

Descriptions of Shanghai in the mid-19th century vary. Yeung (1996) describes it as a 'third-class local town'. Yusuf and Wu (1997) describe it as a significant commercial centre for regional commerce and a 'gateway for exports from the lower Yangtze valley to other parts of the country and overseas'. Whatever the truth is, there is no doubt that the growth of Shanghai took off rapidly after its designation as a Treaty Port and the opening up of the country with the 'unequal' Treaty of Nanking in 1842. Within ten years, it had overtaken Canton (now Guangzhou) as China's premier trading city.

By the turn of the century, Shanghai was, along with Canton, Tianjin and Wuhan, one of China's main centres of population and industry. In 1928, Shanghai benefited further, materially at least, from the move of the capital from Peking to Nanking. By 1936, Shanghai had a population of 3.8 million. It was the seventh largest city in the world and easily the largest in China. These were vintage years when Shanghai was 'as crowded as Calcutta, as decadent as Berlin, as snooty as Paris, as jazzy as New York' (Yeung, 1996).

Although many Western companies fled Shanghai during the war with Japan, Shanghai's overall economic configuration and its role in the regional economy in the late 1940s remained broadly as before the war (Howe, 1981). Shanghai was still China's largest port. It had a large industrial sector, especially strong in light manufacturing such as textiles and food processing, as well as in small-scale engineering and metalworking subsectors. But service sectors provided the most employment, with many employed in banking, trading and retailing.

This economic structure was to change radically after the Communist takeover in 1949. The new government had three main policies that would particularly affect Shanghai. First, the central government in Beijing, not market forces, would determine the allocation of capital and industrial structure. Second, the government viewed manufacturing as more productive than services and considered heavy manufacturing industry, such as petrochemicals, metallurgy and machinery, to be the most important ingredient to economic development. Third, the government strongly favoured national and provincial autonomy. This meant that Shanghai developed an even more diversified economy than before, but it lost both international and domestic trade.

Government controls over labour flows complemented its controls over capital. Moreover, the new government viewed urbanization as neither necessary nor desirable, especially in cities tainted by foreign influences. Household registration (the *hukou*), which was introduced formally in 1958, controlled access to food, housing and other urban services and checked the flow of people to cities (Ma and Fan, 1994). Moreover, between 1950 and 1964, over 800,000 young educated residents of Shanghai were sent to work in the rural areas of China. These labour controls contained the overall urbanization of China to about 19 per cent from 1950 to 1980 (Zhou, 1991), but they did not stop the population growth of Shanghai. Shanghai's population rose from an estimated 6.2 million in 1953 to 10.0 million in 1970 to 11.8 million in 1985, and throughout this period it remained China's largest city (Yusuf and Wu, 1997).

The economic reform process, which began in 1978, unleashed another set of dynamic forces. These reforms had three main features. First, over the next 20 years, market forces would increasingly determine capital and labour flows and prices within China. Second, the reforms transferred significant responsibilities from the centre to the provinces and major cities. Third, they encouraged international trade and investment flows. In due course, all of these factors would favour Shanghai's development.

Initially, in the 1980s, reform and development were slower in Shanghai than in many other cities, especially those in the south of China. Between 1978 and 1991, Shanghai's GDP rose by an average rate of 7.4 per cent per annum, compared with 12.6 per cent in Guangzhou and 8.7 per cent for the whole of China. This slower growth reflected political and economic factors. The government in Beijing still viewed Shanghai with suspicion as a foreign-tainted city. But economically Beijing depended on Shanghai's strategic industries and finances. Cheung (1996) estimates that between 1949 and 1983, a full 87 per cent of Shanghai's total public revenues of RMB350 billion were remitted to Beijing, leaving only 13 per cent for its own uses. According to Yeung (1996), in the reform period as much as one-sixth of the revenue of the central government was derived from Shanghai. Also, the heavily state-owned businesses in Shanghai were slow to reform.

The 1990s have been dramatically different. Change in Shanghai has been extraordinary, based on an average rate of growth of GDP of 14 per cent per annum. A local environmental consultant told the author in 1996 that one-fifth of all the cranes in the world were currently employed in Shanghai. Whatever the basis for this statistic, it certainly seemed credible as one walked around the streets of the city, watching buildings being demolished ceaselessly and replaced at remarkable speed with vast new structures.

According to Cheung (1996), it was the Tiananmen incident and its international impacts that led to the central government's choice of Shanghai as a launching pad for economic reform and openness in the 1990s. In 1992, at the 14th session of the National Congress of the Communist Party of China, the government declared that Shanghai should be developed into a world economic, financial and trade centre. Today, with both China's president (Jiang Zemin) and vice-premier (Zhu Ronji) former mayors of Shanghai, the city's political rehabilitation is complete.

In 1990, China's first stock exchange was opened in Shanghai, and Pudong (a major new business district) was established on the eastern side of the Huangpu River as an open area for international investment. In 1992, foreign direct investments into Shanghai amounted to US$3.4 billion. This exceeded the total of the whole previous 12 years. In 1994, the figure rose to US$10 billion. In 1997, there were some 2000 approved projects supported by nearly 50 countries. Areas of investment included all forms of real estate (including hotels), transportation (cars and aircraft), and large industrial projects (including computers, electronics, telecommunications, building materials, and so on).

During the 1990s, under the national policy of the 'socialist market economy', central and provincial governments placed increasing emphasis on markets. Prices were freed gradually from political controls and the prices of most commodities, including energy, increasingly reflected market forces. This encouraged investment and the efficient allocation of capital.

In 1994, China adopted a 'tax sharing system' whereby a uniform formula across the nation replaced the previous system of bilateral bargaining between provinces (and major cities) and the central government. Between 1990 and 1995, investment in the urban infrastructure in Shanghai amounted to US$7.1 billion, which was three times the amount in the ten years from 1980 to 1989. The change in the national tax system frees even more resources for Shanghai.

One must question whether the 'Asian Crisis' which developed in the second half of 1997 has affected, or will affect, Shanghai? From 1979 to 1993, one-half of all foreign investment came officially from Hong Kong and one-fifth from Japan and the US combined (Yusuf and Wu, 1997). But the Hong Kong capital includes Taiwanese and doubtless other foreign-sourced capital. Also, there has been an increase in American and European investment in the last five years. Informal information gleaned from media reports and discussions with Shanghaiese suggest, at this stage, that vacancies are high in commercial buildings but not a serious problem in residential buildings. Investment is being postponed rather than cancelled permanently. On this reading, the Shanghai economy is undergoing a downturn in a business cycle rather than a structural change in the economy. As discussed below, the city's underlying strengths far outweigh its weaknesses.

Finally, it should be observed that economic growth has not only improved material conditions, but also greatly improved health. As a result of family planning, childhood immunization, accessible primary health care, improved nutrition, and improvements in housing and sanitation, China's achievements in health and life expectancy over the last four decades have been remarkable. In Shanghai, life expectancy has almost doubled from 42 years in 1950 to 76 years in 1996. Infant mortality has fallen from an appalling 120 per 1000 to 9.5 per 1000 over the same period. The mortality of mothers has dropped from 320 out of 100,000 births to 22. The city has basically eradicated the diseases of diptheria, smallpox, snail fever, filariasis and leprosy.

Shanghai's Economic Strengths and Weaknesses

Many of Shanghai's economic strengths are evident from its history. These strengths include its outstanding domestic and international location, its huge store of human capital and skills, and the breadth and depth of its industrial base. Shanghai is a major producer of steel and steel products, industrial plant and equipment, transport equipment, textiles, chemicals, electronics, food, synthetic fibre and clothing. 'In sheer scale of manufacturing capability, Shanghai has no rival in the developing world' (Yusuf and Wu, 1997, p77). Shanghai is China's largest port and services centre. The handling capacity of the port is some 200 million tonnes, about one-quarter of China's total handling capacity.

Shanghai is located at the centre of an arc of large and prosperous Asian cities, which include Guanzhou, Hong Kong, Manila, Taipei, Tokyo, Seoul, Tianjin and Beijing. All of these are less than two hours' flight time from Shanghai. Such a location is highly attractive to international capital. Nearly one-half of the world's top 100 multinational corporations are represented in Shanghai. In addition, Shanghai is integrated with the most prosperous hinterland in China. Eighty million people inhabit the rich Yangtze River delta. Another 300 million live in the upstream Yangtze River basin.

Moreover, the workforce in Shanghai is well educated and resourceful. Over 80 per cent of the workforce have graduated at least from junior high school. There are nearly 50 universities and colleges, and at least 266 independent research institutes (Yusuf and Wu, 1997). Industries are undergoing drastic change as they face competition in newly opened markets at a time when they are losing state support. In the last few years, 400,000 jobs (one-half of the total) have been lost from Shanghai's once dominant textile industry. But unemployment is low as the workforce adapts to new jobs.

There are other economic advantages. A temperate climate is attractive to workers and conducive to work around the year. There is a reasonable supply of flat and usable land on the urban fringe. And there is a strong, stable and capable municipal government.

What, then, are Shanghai's economic weaknesses? Five main weaknesses, or potential weaknesses, are noted below. The first three of these are all related in some way to its successful economic development.

First, Shanghai's very economic success attracts large numbers of workers into the city. Sample data suggest that immigrant workers in Shanghai rose dramatically from 1.06 million in 1988 to 2.51 million in 1993 (Daben, 1998). These workers provide cheap labour, especially to the construction and sanitation industries, often doing work that local residents are unwilling to do. At the margin, their real wage (inclusive of living conditions) is only a little better than that in the area from where they have come. Many of these immigrants to Shanghai live in extremely poor, insanitary and crowded housing (with less than four square metres per person), often in illegal squatter settlements, and have little access to the city's health, education and social services.

Second, the increasing city population places ongoing stress on the environment – on housing, transportation systems, air and water quality, solid waste disposal, land uses and so on. For example, there is only 1.17 square metres of green (recreational) area per person in Shanghai, compared with over 20 square metres per person in London and New York and most other major developed cities (Anxin et al, 1998). These various environmental stresses are discussed further below. Suffice to note here that the responses often require large expenditures of public funds. Such defensive expenditures to manage the environment may actually increase GDP but, when the expenditures are in response to new problems, they do not reflect an increase in living standards.

Third, Shanghai's economic performance is sensitive to international conditions and to foreign investment. Foreign investment, averaging over US$8 billion per annum in the 1990s, is double the annual revenue of the Shanghai government. There is also a high reliance on Hong Kong capital, although the exact amount from Hong Kong itself is difficult to estimate.

Fourth, notwithstanding its pre-eminence in China, much of Shanghai's industry in not internationally competitive. As reported by Bei and Haojie (1998), Shanghai has not developed a stable international market for many of its products. The city is not competitive in high technology areas. Many of its enterprises are inward looking and relatively small scale.

Fifth, the Shanghai economy is still highly reliant on the public sector. In the mid-1990s, the public sector employed 3.5 million people. In 1995, it reduced employment by 200,000 people, mainly in textiles, and it planned to reduce the employment of state-sector workers by another 400,000, mainly in light industry, chemicals and building materials. This presents considerable adjustment pressures. Although there are some internationally competitive state-owned enterprises (SOEs), many are inefficient and starved of capital funds for improvements. In the mid-1990s, one-third of SOEs were losing money. These inefficiencies and losses reflect systemic disabilities: soft budget constraints, poor incentive structures, overstaffing and a confusion of economic and social welfare roles (as most SOEs provide an array of social welfare supports).

Given these weaknesses, is economic growth sustainable in Shanghai? The answer appears to be that growth is sustainable in the sense that total and average real incomes will continue to rise in Shanghai. Given inherited and present natural advantages, private and public industry are likely to be increasingly efficient under the pressure of market and international competition. And, as discussed below, there are adequate solutions to Shanghai's environmental problems. International investor interest in Shanghai is global, not just East Asian. This diversity of support will generally, although not always, reduce the volatility of capital inflows.

However, increased reliance on markets tends to increase inequality of income. This is particularly the case when, as in Shanghai, the welfare role of SOEs is being eroded. Moreover, Shanghai will always attract a high proportion of poor immigrants. The greater the growth of most incomes in Shanghai, the higher the number of poor immigrants is likely to be.

ENVIRONMENTAL ISSUES AND REPONSES

In this review of environmental issues, we start with a brief discussion of housing conditions, which are critical to individual welfare. We then discuss the specific issues of water and air quality and solid waste management. Lastly, we discuss the more general issues of transportation and land-use planning.

Housing

Housing has been, and still is, a major problem in Shanghai. In 1985, the average population density in downtown Shanghai was 40,000 persons per square kilometre. In some densely populated areas, the density rose to 160,000 persons per square kilometre. Average per capita living space in the city was only 5.4 square metres. An official survey found that 1.8 million households were living in overcrowded conditions, including over 200,000 households in dwelling units with less than 2 square metres per person (Xiangming, 1996).

Moreover, much of the housing was delapidated and lacked basic sanitary services. In the early 1990s, 16 million square metres of stone-framed-gate housing lacked toilet amenities. Four million square metres, housing three-quarters of a million people, were considered dangerous substandard housing.

During the 1990s, an average of 50,000 households have been rehoused each year. This means creating housing space at an average rate of 1.2 million square metres a year. In ten years, 1.5 million people have been rehoused. By 1995, average per capita living space had increased to 8 square metres. Over one-half the dwelling units now have private kitchens and toilets. The government's aim is to increase average living space to 10 square metres per person by the year 2000.

Two reforms have underpinned the housing programme. One has been the gradual upward adjustment of rents from 3 to 5 per cent of household income to 15 per cent. This has increased the resources available to the government. It has also facilitated the second reform – the privatization of the housing sector. Since 1994, older state-owned residential units with independent kitchens and toilets have been sold to individuals. Also, new housing has been supplied increasingly by the private sector, with considerable foreign capital input. Yeung (1996) states that there are over 4000 foreign companies supplying housing in Shanghai. There is now an active market in second-hand housing.

Water Quality

The Huangpu is Shanghai's mother river, as the Thames is to London and the Seine to Paris. The Huangpu River is the source of most of the city's water supplies, feeding 14 waterworks in the municipal supply system. It is also a huge port, a water transportation system and a sink for many of the city's industrial discharges. Eighty per cent of the delta landform on which the municipality is located is drained by the Huangpu River catchment. This catchment is a complex interlocking network of canals, drains, minor watercourses and rivers. Groundwater is generally only about a metre below the surface. There are seven urban tributaries of the Huangpu, including Suzhou Creek which is another major watercourse running through Shanghai.

With the exception of the Changiang (Yantzse) estuary, where water quality is quite high, most waterbodies in Shanghai are moderately to very severely polluted (Guoyuan and Chun, 1998). In the Water Source Protection Zones of the Huangpu River, only parts meet the Chinese Class 3 standard, which is required for potable water. Many parts of the Protection Zones are Class 4 and 5. The main pollutant in these water bodies is ammonia-nitrogen. Kinhill et al (1994) monitored 622 kilometres of Shanghai waterways for ammonia-nitrogen, dissolved oxygen, COD, biological oxygen demand (BOD), volatile phenols and mineral oil and found that all the waterways were significantly polluted. Most fell into the lowest categories, Chinese Classes 4 and 5 (the latter is not suitable even for industrial use). Sixty per cent of the whole Huangpu basin was found to be seriously contaminated by toxic substances (phenol, cyanide, mercury, arsenic and chromium). In 1996, Kin-che and Shu described the Huangpu River as 'a chemical cocktail composed of raw sewage, toxic urban wastes and huge amounts of industrial discharges'. Pollution in the Huangpu's tributaries and in the urban canals is generally worse, falling in places to Class 6 – the lowest of all classes.

There are three main sources of wastewater discharges and polluted effluents: industrial discharges, domestic sewage and non-point sources. In the mid-1990s, industries discharged about 50 per cent of their waste-water into the Huangpu River and Suzhou Creek, 10 per cent into the Yangtze Estuary, Hangzhou Bay and the East China Sea, and 40 per cent into sewerage pipelines. The pipelines in turn discharged two-thirds of their wastewater into the rivers. Thus, only a small amount of wastewater went, directly or via pipelines, into the capacious Yangtze River or the sea, where it could be assimilated more readily. Moreover, although about two-thirds of industrial wastewater is treated, a high proportion does not meet discharge standards. Kinhill et al (1994) reported that in some industries, such as leathers, pulp and paper, pharmaceuticals, less than one-quarter of discharges complied with standards. In others, including foodstuffs, beverages and tobacco, textiles, gas and coking, building materials and metal products, one-half or less of discharges complied with standards.

The amount of domestic sewage discharged in Shanghai is about 100 million tons annually. In 1993, only one-quarter of this was treated, due to insufficient treatment capacity. The rest was discharged untreated into the waterways.

Non-point sources of pollution for the Huangpu River are distributed throughout a 5000 square kilometre catchment (80 per cent of the munic-ipality) which drains into the river. Twelve thousand rural industrial sites discharge 10 tonnes of BOD per day into the Huangpu catchment, which far exceeds its natural assimilative capacity. Agricultural runoff in the Huangpu basin is around 1.5 billion cubic metres per year. This carries with it 4600 tonnes of nitrogen and 900 tonnes of phosphorus into surface waters. In 1992, livestock wastes from pigs, poultry and cattle were 72 million tonnes. The 84 million livestock in the municipality generated 630 tonnes of BOD per day, two-thirds of the total BOD for the Huangpu basin (Kinhill et al, 1994).

What policies have been, or are being, used to deal with water pollution? The Shanghai Environmental Protection Bureau (SEPB) has adopted a zoning system, which sets objectives for each part of the waterway system. The most important zoning is the Class 3 that applies to the upper part of the Huangpu River, which is designed to provide a potable water source.

The principal potable water intake for Shanghai is at Linjiang on the Huangpu. There, ammonia-nitrogen, total nitrogen, total phosphorus, phenols and oil far exceed their respective Class 3 standards. Toxic materials, such as mercury, reach almost the Class 4 maximum – that is, 0.001 mg/l. To obtain Class 3 water, the SMG is spending several hundred millions of dollars to relocate the major urban intake upstream close to DiQiao, 65 kilometres upstream of the outlet of the Huangpu River. This diversion will have a capacity of 5.4 million cubic metres per day. In order to manage water demand and to fund water quality investments, the SMG has recently increased tap water prices by 25–40 per cent.

The SMG is also carrying out some very large sewerage projects. In the mid-1990s, it completed a major (US$145 million) sewerage project to collect industrial and domestic wastewater along the Suzhou Creek, serving 2.6 million people, and to discharge the sewage after treatment into the Yangtze estuary. Currently, the second and much more expensive phase of the project will establish a large-scale centralized sewerage system for Shanghai, which will collect a large proportion of the industrial and domestic wastes from industry and households discharging into the Huangpu River. This will discharge wastes after primary treatment into the East China Sea.

Third, the SEPB has adopted a large number of discharge regulations. The regulations prevent any new production activities in areas that might pollute the Water Source Protection Zones. The authorities have also reduced the permitted total discharges into the Huangpu River in these zones. Fourth, all enterprises in Shanghai must have discharge permits and excess discharges are subject to an effluent charge. Fifth, under the national Environmental Protection Law, all major new activities depend on approved Environmental Impact Assessments.

However, these regulations have not proved very effective. The regulations are not always enforced, especially for established SOEs. The law is 'softened' in order to spare the companies, and the state banks that support them, from bankruptcy and to shield their workers from unemployment. Nor are the regulations effective for the numerous rural and non-point sources of pollution in the catchment. Much pollution continues to occur via the spread of contaminants through food chains, soil and groundwater, or a complex of minor watercourses. Moreover, the effluent charges are very low and do not provide an incentive to introduce or upgrade treatment of wastewater.

What are the implications of this extensive water pollution for Shanghai people? The principal implications are economic and aesthetic rather than threats to life and sustainability. Adequate treatment and disposal of wastewater will require expensive solutions for both the public and private sectors. Recreational activities, such as fishing and swimming, will continue to be impossible in Shanghai waterways. Many of the waterways will continue to be odorous and unsightly. However, the health impacts appear to be minor and under control. Nearly all urban residents receive treated tap water supply. There is little evidence that this tap water is a source of disease, partly because most households boil the water before use. The relocation of the main water supply upstream in the Huangpu River will improve the quality of the water source, although some supply may still be below the desirable standard. Moreover, one-third of Shanghai residents in the rural areas depend on deteriorating catchment resources. Tighter controls on activities in the catchment will be needed to prevent this deterioration.

Air Quality

At the start of this discussion of air quality, we should note that ambient measures are not very reliable owing to limited monitoring. In 1996, there were only five urban sampling sites and eight rural sites for monitoring sulphur dioxides (SO_2), nitrogen oxides (No_x) and total suspended particulates (TSP) (Mott MacDonald et al, 1996). Industrial emissions of heavy metals and toxics are not measured routinely.

Nevertheless, it is clear that air quality is generally very poor in Shanghai. Concentrations of sulphur dioxides (SO_2), total suspended particulates (TSP) and lead are far above healthy levels in the urban districts. Ambient levels are not so bad in suburban counties. The major cause of air pollution is coal consumption, which rose from 9.1 million tons in 1970 to 30.3 million tons in 1993 (Jingchun, 1998). Much of this coal is poor quality, high in sulphur and ash content.

The estimated annual mean concentration of SO_2 in the urban districts of Shanghai was 68 micrograms per cubic metre ($\mu g/m^3$) in 1998 (SEPB, 1998). This is substantially higher than the WHO's standard of 40–60 $\mu g/m^3$ for health safety. It is also higher than the Chinese Class 2 level of 60 $\mu g/m^3$ that is designed to protect public health, animals and plant life. Given that there are considerable variations around this mean, sulphur dioxide emissions are clearly a very serious risk to health in Shanghai.

The annual mean concentration of large particulates (up to 100μ in diameter) in urban districts was 233 $\mu g/m^3$ in 1998 (SEPB, 1998). These levels of particulate air pollution from energy and industrial processes in Shanghai are among the highest in the world (World Resources Institute et al, 1998). This concentration is far in excess of the WHO standard for healthy living of 70 $\mu g/m^3$ and well above the Chinese Class 2 standards of 150 $\mu g/m^3$. Although health risks depend more on levels of finer particles of less than 10μ, aeroallergens and toxic materials, which have not been measured, it is clear that TSP in the atmosphere are greatly excessive and that health damages are likely to be very high.

Both SO_2 and TSP are products of coal combustion. There are over 10,000 point sources of air emissions in Shanghai, including 7000 coal-burning boilers. Ten major industrial sources (power plants, large iron and steel works, and chemical works) consume large amounts of coal and contribute one-third of all SO_2 emissions, smoke and dust in Shanghai. However, because of their greater stack heights, they contribute about 10 per cent to ambient concentrations in the city. Industrial emissions of heavy metals and toxics are also significant contributors to air pollution in Shanghai.

Overall, the high combinations of SO_2 and TSP create significant levels of respiratory disease and bronchitis (Kinhill et al, 1994). The World Bank (1997) estimates that the health damages from air pollution (in terms of premature deaths, morbidity, restricted activity days, chronic bronchitis, and other health effects) are several times higher than the damages from water pollution in China. This is almost certainly the case in Shanghai.

The transport sector is also now a major contributor to air pollution. The problems stem not just from the growing size of the motor fleet, but also from low emission standards and poor road infrastructure. Vehicle emission standards are equivalent to the standards of the developed world in the 1970s. Chinese vehicles emit 2.5 to 7.5 times more hydrocarbons, 2 to 7 times more nitrous oxides (NO_x) and 6 to 12 times more carbon monoxide (CO) than foreign vehicles (Kebin et al, 1996). In central Shanghai, motor vehicles are responsible for 70 per cent of CO and NO_x emissions (Kinhill et al, 1994).

In recent years, the mean NO_x ambient concentration level in the urban districts has almost doubled from around 60 $\mu g/m^3$ to 105 $\mu g/m^3$. Although this is below the WHO standard of 150 $\mu g/m^3$, it is over the Chinese Class 2 objective of 100 $\mu g/m^3$ and is another serious threat to public health (SEPB, 1998). The risk from CO is unknown because of lack of measurements.

Ambient lead levels have also been a major concern. Until recently, the motor vehicle fleet was fuelled mainly by leaded gasoline. Few cars had catalytic converters. Although data on lead levels in the atmosphere are scanty, Kebin et al (1996) noted that ambient lead levels in Chinese cities often exceeded 10 $\mu g/m^3$ compared with the national standard of 1 $\mu g/m^3$. Blood-lead levels are far above the threshold associated with impaired intelligence, neurobehavioural development and physical growth. Over two-thirds of children in Shanghai have blood-lead levels greater than 10 μg per decilitre (the US standard). In industrial and congested areas, the levels averaged between 21 and 67 μg per decilitre. (WRI et al, 1998). Studies in Shanghai and elsewhere have shown that high blood-lead levels in children are significantly associated with lower mental development (World Bank, 1997).

The central and Shanghai governments are dealing with air pollution in several ways. These include a major industry relocation programme (see below), the development of natural gas in the East China Sea and the conversion of household coal burning to gas. From 1 October 1997, the use of leaded petrol in motor vehicles in Shanghai was banned. These are substantial programmes which should improve air quality. Factories are required to have waste gas treatment facilities. Excess discharge fees are based on the pollution load and type of pollutants. There are also current proposals to increase emission charges greatly. Improving coal quality, by reducing its sulphur and ash contents, could greatly improve air quality. A slowing down of the frenetic construction activity in Shanghai will reduce TSP concentrations.

On the other hand, there are new challenges, especially with the growth of motor traffic and currently with the highly polluting growth of two-stroke motorcycles. Moreover, as with water pollution, the effectiveness of the regulations and discharge fees may be questioned. On balance, the SMG's policies seem likely to produce a net improvement in Shanghai's air quality. But it may be many years before it achieves WHO standards for all parameters of ambient air quality.

Solid Waste Management

Like all mega cities, Shanghai produces a huge amount of solid waste daily. In 1994, the city generated 35,000 tonnes of solid waste per day, equal to 12.5 million tonnes over the year. Two-thirds of these wastes were generated by industry, one-third by households.

Although industry reuses 80 per cent of its wastes, disposal of the rest is a major problem. Three industries (smelting, power and chemical engineering) account for three-quarters of all industrial waste in urban Shanghai. The principal wastes are smelting residue, fine coal ash and slag. The city contains some 1400 industrial stockpile sites covering 4.1 square kilometres. In 1992, industry also generated 600,000 tonnes of hazardous wastes. These were principally heavy metal waste, organic waste, waste acids and alkalis, calcium carbide residue, organic sludge and various organic chemical compounds.

Municipal solid waste amounts to about 12,000 tonnes per day in the Huangpu basin, including 10,000 tons of domestic garbage. Transport is by fully closed transport. However, there is a lack of facilities for proper disposal. In the early 1990s, 40 per cent of the waste was barged along canals and rivers to two poorly designed landfills. The rest was either disposed at 410 unofficial stockpile sites or dumped, often into waterways.

Outside the urban areas, and even in some residential areas around the outskirts of the city, municipal waste was not collected. Around the urban fringe, where no nightsoil collection of sewerage is available, residents dispose of plastic bags of nightsoil into canals, wastecourses and sundry locations where municipal waste is dumped. Most river and canal banks are littered with domestic and other wastes. Leachate from wastes, washed into the catchment, is a further source of polluted water.

Shanghai's capacity to deal with solid waste has improved in recent years. The amount of waste from heavy industry has actually decreased due to energy saving, technical innovation and integrated pollution controls. The second phase of the Laogang landfill plant increased the average disposal capacity from 3000 to 6000 tons per day. Much of the rest of the urban domestic waste was collected and dumped temporarily at two other sites (Jiangzheng and Sanlintang). At the end of 1998, the Jiangzheng landfill site was closed and a new temporary landfill site was established at Bainoggang, close to the East China Sea in New Pudong Area. The Shanghai government has also invested in additional collection and transfer stations, and garbage-transport trucks and barges (Xiangming, 1996). The government plans to treat 80 per cent of domestic waste by the year 2000, including the incineration of 40 per cent.

In summary, Shanghai's waste-disposal practices have lagged far behind its economic development. As with water and air pollution, the city has a long way to go to achieve developed country standards. Dealing with waste disposal is mainly a matter of political will, organization and municipal finance. The SMG is well aware of the problems and, provided the economy continues to grow and to provide the financial resources, there should be continued improvement in solid waste disposal practices.

Transport

Not surprisingly, in an old, densely populated city like Shanghai with a very rapid rate of economic development, traffic is a major problem as a source of congestion, noise and accidents, as well as air pollution. Road space in the city is only a little over 2 metres per person. Road widths in old established areas are often only 9–10 metres, with vehicles restricted to 7 metres. On the other hand, the number of motor vehicles increased at a staggering rate from 212,000 in 1990 to 372,000 in 1994. It is expected to increase to 800,000 by the year 2000 and to 1.4 million in 2010. There has also been a rapid increase in motorcycles in recent years. In addition, there are over 7 million bicycles in the city. Between 1985 and 1995, average traffic speeds fell from 19 to 15 kilometres per hour (Xiangming, 1996).

The Shanghai government spent billions of dollars in major projects to increase transport infrastructure in the 1990s. Major road and bridge projects include two large-span bridges over the Huangpu River and a tunnel underneath, a six-lane north–south highway along Chengdu Road, construction of an elevated 48 kilometre inner ring road and the start of the outer ring road. The Yangpu Bridge over the Huangpu River, which cost nearly US$200 million, is the longest suspension bridge in the world. The government completed the first part of the subway system (17 kilometres of track and 13 stations) in 1994 at a cost of US$680 million. A second segment of 32 kilometres, connecting East Pudong with western Shanghai, is due to be operational in 2000. A second international airport is also being constructed in East Pudong. In all cases the rate of construction has been exceptional.

However, in Shanghai, as in most mega cities, the demand for transport can never be fully satisfied. There has to be demand management. The city has started to do this via traffic management schemes that limit vehicle use of some roads, including Nanking Road in peak hours, one-way systems and the segregation of motor vehicles, bicycles and pedestrians. There are also frequent bus services as well as metro services. However, vehicle ownership is not heavily taxed, vehicle registration costs are low and fuel is cheap. It is difficult to see how the growth in vehicle ownership and use can be managed without making vehicle ownership and use much more expensive.

Land-use Planning

Ever since the production of the first *Metropolitan Plan for Shanghai* in 1927, Shanghai's municipal government has been actively involved in land-use planning (Yuemin, 1998). In the 1950s, under Soviet expert guidance, Shanghai was planned as a metropolitan city with only one centre. Typically, industry and housing were closely located, often in inner city areas, as SOEs provided a complete package of jobs, housing and social services to their employees.

However, the monocentric city became impractical with population growth, and the SMG has sought increasingly to set up alternative commercial and industrial districts and residential towns and suburbs. In the 1980s, major new industrial/residential areas were developed in the Baoshan-Wusong area on the southern bank of the Yangtzse River and in the Jinshanwei-Caojing area on the northern bank of Hangzhou Bay. Satellite towns, such as Minhang, Jiadang, Sonjiang and Anting, with separate industrial districts, were established 30–40 kilometres away from the city centre. Today, the Shanghai urban system consists of 230 centres, including 7 satellite towns, 31 county seats (designated towns), 2 industrial districts, 175 market towns and 15 farm market towns. Each of these centres is required to have a development plan.

A key feature of recent planning has been the break in the nexus between industry and housing. This has been essential for the provision of both environmental amenity and housing space. In the 1990s, large numbers of polluting factories in the inner areas have been closed down or relocated to urban fringe areas. Bei and Haojie (1998) claim that 455 enterprises have been relocated in the last five years, which has freed up 163 square kilometres for redevelopment in central Shanghai. As an example of the benefits, the closing down or relocation of 25 heavy polluting factories in the Xinghua Road area has contributed to Class 2 SO_2 and TSP levels in that area (Xiangming, 1996).

Two other features should be noted. First, the opening of a major new financial and industrial centre in Pudong on the eastern side of the Huangpu has removed some of the critical physical limitations of old Shanghai. In 1996, over one million square metres of office space came on to the market, including 18 major office blocks in Pudong alone. The development of Pudong has been a major catalyst for the development of Shanghai.

Second, however, the planners are also highly conscious of the need for more green space. The current plan calls for public green space to be increased from 1.1 square metre per person in 1992 to 4 square metres in 2000 and to 8 square metres in 2010. The land will be acquired by the demolition of substandard housing. This will require a significant expansion of the city, along with substantial expenditures on expanded urban services and transport systems.

CONCLUSIONS

For most of the past 20 years, Shanghai has experienced high and accel-erating rates of economic growth. Material prosperity has greatly increased. Moreover, the city's economic strengths substantially outweigh its weak-nesses and future economic growth seems assured.

The environmental report is more mixed. Shanghai has had, and still has, a poor environment. Water and air are heavily polluted and solid waste collection practices are inadequate in many parts of the city. On the other hand, housing conditions, air and water quality, and waste collection practices have all improved in the last ten years. Current policies and projects should produce further environmental improvements.

Rather less is published about the social impacts of the economic reforms in Shanghai. Unless market reforms are complemented by adequate publicly financed social services, the reforms may increase inequality and unemployment in the community. Casual information suggests that this may have happened in Shanghai.

More fundamentally, Shanghai is confronted with the issue of how to deal with potential and actual immigrants and the possibility of a popul-ation in excess of 20 million in the near future. Even low incomes in Shanghai are often double or triple those in many other parts of China. Increased government support for low-income households and environ-mental improvements would make Shanghai even more attractive. There is little that the SMG can do about this. In 20 years' time, the real income of poor households in Shanghai, including the environmental standards they experience, will be more closely related to the real income of poor house-holds elsewhere in China than to average real incomes in Shanghai.

ACKNOWLEDGEMENTS

I am grateful to the SEPB for inviting me to work in Shanghai and for their hospitality on several trips to Shanghai. I also thank Windy Zhang (Environmental Resources Management, Shanghai) for her comments on an earlier draft. I am of course responsible for the opinions expressed in this chapter.

REFERENCES

Anxin, M, Jianping, W and Luxi, Z (1998) 'Shanghai's Land Use' in H D Foster, D C Lai and N Zhou (eds) *The Dragon's Head: Shanghai, China's Emerging Megacity*, Western Geographical Press, Victoria

Bei, Y and Haojie, F (1998) 'The Spatial Distribution of Shanghai's Industries', in H D Foster, D C Lai and N Zhou (eds) *The Dragon's Head: Shanghai, China's Emerging Megacity*, Western Geographical Press, Victoria

Cheung, P T Y (1996) 'The Political Context of Shanghai's Economic Development', in Y M Yeung and S Yun-wing (eds) *Shanghai: Transformation and Modernisation Under China's Open Door Policy*, Chinese University Press, Hong Kong

Daben, W (1998) 'Analysis of Labour Resources and Related Supply and Demand', in H D Foster, D C Lai and N Zhou (eds) *The Dragon's Head: Shanghai, China's Emerging Megacity*, Western Geographical Press, Victoria

Guoyuan, W and Chun, S (1998) 'Shanghai's Water Environment', in H D Foster, D C Lai and N Zhou (eds) *The Dragon's Head: Shanghai, China's Emerging Megacity*, Western Geographical Press, Victoria

Howe, C (1981) *Shanghai: Revolution and Development in an Asian Metropolis*, Cambridge University Press, Cambridge

Jingchun, Z (1998) 'Urban Climate and Atmosphere: Environmental Quality', in H D Foster, D C Lai and N Zhou (eds) *The Dragon's Head: Shanghai, China's Emerging Megacity*, Western Geographical Press, Victoria

Kebin et al (1996) 'Status and Developments in China's Vehicle Emissions Pollution', *Environmental Science*, vol 7, no 4, pp15–17

Kin-che, L and Shu, T (1996) 'Environmental Quality and Pollution Control', in Y M Yeung and S Yun-wing (eds) *Shanghai: Transformation and Modernisation Under China's Open Door Policy*, Chinese University Press, Hong Kong

Kinhill-PPK Joint Venture and Shanghai Academy of Environmental Sciences (1994) *Shanghai Environmental Masterplan*, Shanghai Municipal Government, Shanghai

Ma, L J C and Fan, M (1994) 'Urbanisation from below: The growth of towns in Jiangsu, China', *Urban Studies*, vol 31, no 10, pp1625–40

Mott MacDonald, ACER Environmental, AEA Technology, Environmental Resources Management (1996) *Support Programme for the Urban Rehabilitation of Shanghai, Part 2, Monitoring Activities*, Shanghai Environmental Protection Bureau, Shanghai

Shanghai Environmental Protection Bureau (SEPB) (1998) *Shanghai Environmental Bulletin, 1998*, SEPB, Shanghai

World Bank (1997) *Clear Water, Blue Skies*, China 2020 Series, World Bank, Washington, DC

World Resources Institute, UNEP, UNDP and World Bank, 1998, *World Resources 1998–99*, Oxford University Press, New York

Xiangming, W (1996) 'City Case Study of Shanghai', in J Stubbs and G Clarke (eds) *Megacity Management in the Asian and Pacific Region, Volume 2, City and Country Case Studies*, Asian Development Bank, Manila

Yeung, Y M (1996) 'Introduction', in Y M Yeung and S Yun-wing (eds) *Shanghai: Transformation and Modernisation under China's Open Door Policy*, Chinese University Press, Hong Kong

Yuemin, N (1998) 'City Planning and Urban Construction in the Shanghai Metropolitan Area', in H D Foster, D C Lai and N Zhou (eds) *The Dragon's Head: Shanghai, China's Emerging Megacity*, Western Geographical Press, Victoria

Yusuf, S and Wu, W (1997) *The Dynamics of Urban Growth in Three Chinese Cities*, Oxford University Press, New York

Zhou, Y (1991) 'The Metropolitan Interlocking Region in China: A Preliminary Hypothesis', in N Ginberg, B Koppel and T G McGee (eds) *The Extended Metropolis: Settlement Transition in Asia*, University of Hawaii Press, Honolulu

10 A MILLENNIAL PERSPECTIVE AND CONCLUSIONS

Cedric Pugh

This chapter has some new substantive content in its various reflections and it provides a summary of selected findings from the contributory authors in this book. The discussions provide millennial reflections on sustainability, urban development, poverty and welfare, new theory on agglomeration economies and urban change, governance, housing, and the changing roles of major international organizations such as the World Bank and the UN Centre for Human Settlements (UNCHS). Some of this is done under the subheadings of the creation of knowledge and political economy. Sustainable urban development has a rapidly growing literature, but some significant gaps occur. Accordingly, this chapter also discusses research agendas. Some of the general themes provide contrasts, revealing the pessimistic and optimistic realities of sustainable development.

INTRODUCTION

The discussions in the introductory chapter emphasised some of the long-term and fundamental conditions in sustainable urban development. These include continuities of the explosive growth phase of demographic transitions, the ways in which health and nutrition can retard development at low stages of economic development, and the important impacts of trade and hypermobile finance capital which can influence urban economic growth (or recession) and the changing sets of social opportunities. All of these will have varied effects, carrying well into the 21st century. They provide a context which sets the shifting boundaries on abatement policies for improved environments, socio-political trade-offs in development, the extent and nature of poverties, and the varying dynamics or sluggishness of different city-regions. Some changes in this context can be sudden and dramatic. For example, in the first six months of 1997 some US$35 billion of finance capital flowed into Asian countries, but in the last six months of 1997 a precipitous reversal of some US$50 billion occurred. However, by 1999 some foreign investment returned, exports began to rise and GDP started to grow in the afflicted countries. This was caused by non-inflationary growth in the US, thereby opening up imports, and by gradual reflationary economic policies among Asian countries. But the financial crisis led first to an economic austerity crisis, and then to a deepening social crisis of aggravated poverty and decreased incomes in other social groups. This coincided with drought-induced and conflagration effects of the *El Niño* phenomenon, causing urban air pollution. In the following year, Hurricane Mitch literally redrew the contours of Honduras and disrupted national production. Mass disturbance from financial crises, from global-regional environmental disturbances, and from ethnic or religious wars are shaping parts of urban and environmental agendas. At the same time, long-term historical evidence in growth and development indicates probable improved abatement policies and less environmental degradation over periods of 50 years or more. This, of course, leaves the serious problems of health, child labour, and rigidities that impede economic and environmental reform in the meantime.

The contributing authors have largely addressed issues of sustainable urban development in the short- to medium-term perspectives. Three chapters reflect this in their case study approaches. Peter Abelson evaluated the tensions between growth and environmental consequences, set in the context of Shanghai in the 1990s. The governing authorities have much ambition for creating a national and international city-region for finance, industry and exports. They negotiated strong lines of autonomy in essentials from the central government in Beijing, attracting large first-phase foreign direct investment. Vast new areas were developed and planning pursued aims of structural-spatial change. But the lags in infrastructure services and in implementing effective environmental policies meant that raw sewage, toxic wastes and squatter settlement become significant problems in development. This is not unusual, of course, in rapidly growing cities in developing countries. Amanda Perry's review of environmental law and public administration in Bangalore, India, has similar findings. The law and its enforcement are impeded by 'administrative separatism', inequalities in access to remedies, and various elements of bribery in an imperative for development. Both cities require much 'social learning' in their development transitions, along with enlarged capability in public administration. The case studies written by Trudy Harpham and Maria Allison look at the specific detail of participatory low-income housing programmes in South Africa. Residents were induced towards housing and local environmental improvement. The South African government introduced one-off capital grant subsidies of some US$2400 for households with monthly incomes below US$50. However, with variable experience in community participation some schemes experienced a lack of cohesion and fragmentation. In short, in some circumstances the new participatory approaches to environmental planning and management has shortcomings and the need to adjust professional practice.

The findings from the potential reconciliation between 'green' and 'brown' agendas by Gordon McGranahan and David Satterthwaite has longer term frames of reference. They seek a more flexible form of environmental planning and management. This would place reconciliation to the fore, with relevance to the demand management of water and other natural resources. One aspect of this would be greater attention to education in hygiene and health. The chapter by Bharat Dahiya and myself also evaluates environmental planning and management, but related to Local Agenda 21s and the UN Sustainable Cities Programme (SCP). Early phase experience indicates that in many applications, the comprehensive community-based approaches to environmental planning have problems of 'administrative separatism', and limited capacities of non-governmental organizations (NGOs) to achieve effectiveness. This leaves some continuing dilemmas because local governments have often had their responsibilities expanded, but higher levels of government neglected to download resources and skills to them. As will be discussed below, Chile did achieve effective decentralization in its pro-poor programmes. My other chapters reveal the development of new concepts in sustainable urban development, including in economics, governance and environmental health. In other words, concepts and theories are being developed to guide policy and professional practice. One example is in the interactive relations between several types of capital – social, human and environmental. The chapter on the improvement of housing and environmental conditions also has large and long-term significance. Squatter settlements often provide some 30–70 per cent of the housing stock in city-regions. Improvement is dependent on more than physical upgrading. It is influenced by income generation, community organization, security of occupancy and use rights, and the quality of analytical-statistical appraisals to discern the better cost-effectiveness options.

SUSTAINABLE DEVELOPMENT: THEORY AND REALITY

In the earlier literature, including the forerunner book in 1996, *Sustainability, the Environment and Urbanization* (Pugh, 1996), it was familiar to commence discussions on sustainable development with reference to the positional statements in the Brundtland Report (World Commission on Environment and Development, 1987). This set conceptual discussions within the framework of development that meets the needs of present generations without compromising those of future generations. One advantage of such a statement is that it places emphasis on the consequences of present actions on long-term futures. However, it has limitations. The key terms of 'development' and 'needs' admit to no straightforward definitions or consensus in the real world of policies and programmatic actions. Worse than this, given the explosive growth of population from the demographic transitions and the low stages of economic development, the positional statement could reduce the significance given to the welfare of millions in poverty and deprivation in this generation and the next. But once it is recognized that development should continue with its long-term economic growth and social restructuring, then sustainability has greater subtleties and scope than a limitation to environmental conservation. Development is achieved through interactive social, economic, political and environmental processes and policies. Policies make a big difference to the rates of economic growth, to the distribution of income and environmental welfare, and to the environmental conditions and qualities of life in cities and regions. Sustainable development then largely becomes a debate about various macroeconomic and urban policies, along with assessments of poverty, social inclusion, and how to shape and implement policies for the abatement of environmental degradation. This has been the general position adopted by most authors in this book, although they exhibit differences in detailed perception and in applying the principles to particular issues.

From the foregoing it is clear that sustainable development is at once economic, social, political and environmental. It is not limited to what rates of economic growth are environmentally tolerable. Rather, it is more about patterns of development and their environment, social and economic impacts. The question then becomes: what have been the lessons of development during the phases of explosive growth in population in the developing countries. Lindenburg (1993) has been persuasive in addressing this question, combining economic, income distributional, health and education indicators. First, he notes that ranking in development can be vastly changed over periods of some 30 years and more. This is largely attributed to policies and their implementation. Second, institutionally loaded reform is important, but often this is glacially slow. (The circumstances which speed up institutional reform are discussed in the following sections of this chapter.) Third, in summary form the development policies that have achieved growth, poverty alleviation and the progressive restructuring of social opportunities have the following characteristics. They achieve long-term comparative macro-economic and political stability. The economic foundations rest upon export-led growth and the expansion of trade. This occurs within a framework of competition and the creation of the appropriate private and collective property rights. All of this improves incomes and expands the sets of social opportunities, but these can be expanded further by complementary policies which develop and broaden access to human capital. This is achieved in effective and well resourced policies in health and education, and in encouraging progressive improvement in childrearing. However, markets alone do not create the conditions for superior performances in development: it is also necessary to create high-quality public administration, which is set to serve the general public interest rather than for sectional interests or for corruption.

Lindenberg's findings have been widened in the foregoing, particularly with regard to childrearing and tipping the scales in the education of girls and boys rather than readily tolerating the urgency of child labour in bad conditions of life and work. Drèze and Sen (1997) have elaborated the significance of this in their comparative study of state-level variations in

Indian development. The north-western state of Uttar Pradesh has 'The Burden of Inertia' with apathy towards social sector development, gender deprivation, and a militaristic dominated caste culture which tends to condone the allocation of private income in favour of male rather than female children (Drèze and Gazdar, 1997). The end result is a distorted male-to-female ratio of 1000:865. All of this reduces the agency of women in developmental roles, especially in nutrition, childrearing, employment and the use of property rights. By contrast, the south-western state of Kerala has made substantial development achievements (Ramachandran, 1997). In Kerala the male-to-female ratio is 1000:1040, in broad lines of biological tendencies where there has been no gendered deprivation of resources. More than this, Kerala has made broadscaled developmental progress in literacy and health, and in breaking the concentration of ownership in agrarian land rights. Government spending on health and education is 6.9 and 17.3 per cent of budgets, the highest in India. Literacy in 1991 was 94.5 per cent for boys and 87 per cent for girls, and child labour at some 1.5 per cent, compared with 6.15 per cent in India as a whole. In short, policies and the empowerment of women are influential and progressive in the social, political and economic transformations of development.

The foregoing does not say anything specific about environmental, housing and urban policies for sustainable development. Comment can readily be made, drawing on the contributions of authors in this book and adding supplementary relevant material. As shown in Amanda Perry's chapter, environmental law can fail where there is a lack of enforceability, as occurs in Bangalore. Singapore is entirely different: landscaping, the planting of a green mantle, and a spate of legislation in the 1970s regulated air and water pollution. In Singapore the law is enforced and public administration has commitment and capability. Furthermore, the macro-spatial planning has created a ring of new towns, along with tough economic and regulatory controls on motor vehicle use, but with continually improving systems of bus, underground and light rail systems. The Land Acquisition Act (1966) limits speculative profiteering from private land-owners and public ownership is at some 80 per cent, being asserted strongly in social housing programmes. It is a representation of the reconciliation of the brown and green agendas as advocated in the chapter by Gordon McGranahan and David Satterthwaite (for more detail, see Sandhu and Wheatley, 1989). Singapore's urban policy has even larger achievements, especially in the consideration of housing policies.

Singapore has pursued a policy of whole sector housing development, integrating housing finance, the development of capacity in construction, controlled subsidization, and the redistribution of housing wealth in developmental transformations (Phang, forthcoming 2001; Pugh, 1995). The island-state has been transformed from a largely foetid slum in 1961, the date the Housing and Development Board (HDB) was founded, into a city of new towns, massive and residentially mixed housing estates, and continuously improved housing environments. Housing investment has been to a high level of 9 per cent of GDP in the 1976–97 period, with HDB housing accommodating some 86 per cent of the population. Singapore used its housing sector as part of its 'development state' roles. Apart from the significance of housing in GDP, its 'economic multipliers', which generate income in housing-related industries, are in the order of 1.5 to 2.0, these being higher than other sectors because the construction sector is less dependent on imports than other sectors. Also, the HDB has created institutional arrangements with contractors to stimulate improvements in their factor productivities and access to building materials. Cross-subsidization occurs within HDB finances, which especially favour low-income groups in rental housing. Further subsidization is instituted in government grants to HDB and in the terms of which the Central Provident Fund (CPF) loans are made for homeownership in HDB and private sector housing. The CPF is a mandated social security fund, financed from employer and employee contributions into individualized accounts. The distributional characteristics of housing are significant in both the current income of households and in wealth formation. Public housing forms some 48 per cent of housing wealth, with some equalizing redistributive impact upon middle-, moderate- and low-income groups. Housing wealth in Singapore is a higher percentage of GDP than in the US or Britain.

Although the downward redistribution of income and wealth in housing is limited because the rich derive most of their wealth from businesses, insurances and financial (tradable) assets, it is nonetheless important. It provides collateral for home-based economic activities; it enables households to meet their changing life-cycle needs more effectively by the recomposition of their assets; and it facilitates study and other uses of time which increase the lifetime social opportunities of children and adults. In the context of developing countries, this often means that social, economic and political transformation is limited because housing policies are usually ad hoc rather than in the Singaporean model of whole housing sector development. However, although limited, it has some significant partial potential. Some of the arguments and themes can be recalled from my earlier chapter on sustainability and the improvement of housing and environments in squatter settlements. On the one hand, squatter settlements can sometimes be squalid, vulnerable to health risks and devastation from fire and landslips. In statistical terms some 25 per cent of preventable ill-health occurs in bad environmental conditions, with diarrhoeal diseases and acute respiratory infections heading the list. But, on the other hand, state and/or voluntary improvements can achieve large progress towards sustainable urban development. It may regularize tenure rights, occupancy rights and use rights, thereby inducing responses by residents to add physical and aesthetic amenities. Also, the improvements can extend to education, training, gender equality and health services, thereby adding to income and the land-with-housing asset values of households. In policy perspectives, the post-1983 reforms by the World Bank have adopted broad programmatic transformations for economic, social and political development. This includes financial sustainability in local government cost recovery and cross-subsidization.

THE CONTRASTS OF PESSIMISTIC AND OPTIMISTIC REALITIES IN SUSTAINABLE URBAN DEVELOPMENT

It is easy to find horror stories and pessimism in a context of discussions on urban sustainable development. The poor air quality in Mexico City is estimated to be responsible for US$1 billion annually in health damage. Earlier attempts to improve the conditions failed: it was easy to evade the regulated limitations on vehicle use. A new World Bank policy framework is based on a broader package of interventions, including vehicle and industrial emissions standards, the expanded use of liquid petroleum gas, raised investment in public transport, scientific research for designing better policies and introducing monitoring capability. The air remains unhealthy. Also, in Mexico the growth of the *maquila dora* industries on the US–Mexico border regions over the period 1960-2000 has led to extensive environmental degradation and disease. Some 36 municipalities, with a total population of 2.4 million, have grown up in the border areas. Some of the 2000 industrial plants are workshops and some are the creations of transnational corporations. Air and ground water is heavily polluted, and children have consequent deformities. Disability is one significant result of this sort of economic and spatial development, thereby limiting the life-cycle social opportunities of vulnerable children. The vast remedial programmes for environmental improvement was placed in the hands of the Border Environmental Cooperation Commission. The devaluations of the Mexican peso in the 1980s structural adjustment programme and in the 1994–95 financial crisis added to the economic activity in the *maquila dora* industries.

The inadequacies in the practice of urban development are repeated in theory, technique and policy making for subsidizing housing and environmental improvement. Economists have developed principles and techniques for the total economic valuation (TEV) of environmental and related investment. TEV measures both the direct and indirect effects of investment upon environmental, social, and economic assets. This includes non-market valuation of environmental degradation. For example, in the upgrading of squatter settlements this would include income generated from human capital formation and the improved economic production and productivity from reduced disease and absenteeism. But the techniques are seldom used in formulating policies and appraising programmes. Also, problems of implementation occur in programmes to improve urban air quality. These programmes require a synthesis of scientific research, action programmes, monitoring, cross-sector coordination in public services and continual adaptation. The post-1992 World Bank programmes in Asian cities are being retarded by a lack of capacity in implementation. Similarly, the housing subsidy programmes in some Latin American and subSaharan African countries tend to be regressive rather than progressive (Aldrich and Sandhu, 1995) – that is to say, they favour moderate- and middle-income groups because eligibilities are limited to trade union workers in the formal sector or to salaried public servants. When the effects are cumulative and additive – that is, the inadequacies occur in the same city-region – they frustrate the progress which can be made in sustainable urban development. This is because developmental patterns which advance sustainability depend on a simultaneous package of programmes in, for example, environmental investment appraisal, housing finance and the improvement of air quality.

Experience with development and sustainability also has some more optimistic and positive themes. These are seen in the collection of reviews of the work over some 35 years by the Harvard Institute of International Development (HIID) (Grindle, 1997). The reviews include structural economic reform, finance sector development, health and education systems development, and gender and community development. The mission and practice of the HIID is to combine high-quality professional work with on-locational capacity building in developing countries. The central themes of the reviews are improving the quality in human resources, especially within the public sector. This improvement is aimed at enhancing qualities of governance and steering a course towards the developmental state. Grindle sees this as a correction to an overemphasis on markets and the voluntary sector in the 1983–89 period of the political economy of development. As she argues, the major question is not whether the state is too large or too small, but rather whether it is capable of achieving social, economic, political and environmental transformations. Useful transformations ensure that institutional and policy reforms become embedded in the relationships affecting civil society, state-society relations, attitudes, skills and supportive coalitions. Grindle's approach in this is to favour a secular sermon for practical rather than ideological welfare. For the HIID the focus is on training for sustainability rather than on a narrow-based 'work done' to complete one-off projects.

Grindle's collection has great significance for urban governance and pro-welfare development. Two reviews refer to spatially relevant case studies. The first discusses the successful implementation of co-production and joint public sector and organized self-help in developing major sewerage and water systems in Pakistan. The affordable outcomes were satisfactory for poor households and, more than this, they contributed to and received a social learning through meetings, planning, implementing and achieving team work in productive behaviour. These are now the ways of the 1990s international orthodoxy in the World Bank's approach to various urban infrastructure services and environmental improvements. The second review of direct urban relevance is the massive and complex Applied Diarrhoeal Disease Research project, operated in 16 developing countries in 1985–96 under partnership agreements between a consortium of interdisciplinary research centres in the US and medical research centres in developing countries. The project was conceived to develop research skills, to create career structures for researchers and community development personnel in developing countries. In the end result, the project had a rapid impact on governance and institutional reform, and it advanced scientific medicine and medical prescription. The optimistic vein in all of this is that the intellectual and the pragmatic can be bolted together for reducing premature death and promoting economic and social opportunities.

Sustainable urban development can be seen more broadly than just by reference to pessimistic and optimistic characteristics. It has a context in the very nature of city-regions in developing countries, within some basic characteristics of modern economic and political functioning. These basic characteristics can be drawn from the studies of various authors who have written on underlying economic and political issues (see, Blair et al, 1996; Harris, 1997; Haynes, 1997; Mohan, 1994; Pugh, 1997). Cities are the engines of economic growth and innovation, injecting an open-ended adaptation into life and culture. They are places where prosperity and poverty co-exist. In circumstances where the social conditions of life are pressed hard, such as in the first phases of structural economic adjustment or global-regional financial crises, some cities experience socio-political reactions, street demonstrations and signs of the emergence of civic society. On the one hand, the urban is adapting to the globalization of real and financial capital, but on the other hand it inherits structures and industrial path dependence with long-term historical roots. Nonetheless, under extreme competitive conditions, past economic specializations can be broken down. An example of this in the 1990s has been disinvestment of international capital in the motor vehicle industry in São Paulo and relocation to less costly cities in Brazil. Old agglomeration economies can be broken down rapidly. In general economic terms in developing countries, structural-spatial change is occurring within an internationally competitive premium on flexibilities in labour and capital markets. This requires powerful reform, some of it in transport and infrastructure. Economic growth depends not only on 'base' export industries serving other regional and international markets, but also on diverse sources in the service industries. Also, as seen in this book, the economic growth and change can place great pressures on the qualities of air, water and human settlements, as, for example in Shanghai. Various aspects of the foregoing can be given further attention, and the millennial reflections continue with the focus on poverty and agglomeration economies.

POVERTY AND WELFARE

Lipton (1997) writes of a late-1990s consensus on poverty. With some adaptation to account for the work of Ravallion and other authors, the consensus runs along the following lines. The techniques used for measuring poverty have improved substantially, with applications to 'poverty lines', headcounts, incidences, calorific needs and intensities. Also, the evaluations and narratives of the poor have been incorporated into the literature. Economic growth tends to decrease poverty in the long run, but in accordance with the reasoning by Anand and Ravallion (1993) this occurs largely through better patterns of income distribution and increased expenditure on basic health. Although for developed countries, at their earlier stage of development, per capita incomes first revealed increased inequality then subsequently reduced inequality, this is not generally repeated in developing countries. In many countries the growth patterns over time indicate reductions in inequality. However, the pattern is not stable – for example, Taiwan had large reductions in inequality in the 1960–80 period, but increased inequality in the 1990s. What the Taiwan experience of the 1960–80 period shows is that reductions in the inequalities of consumption and land ownership leads to reduced incidences and volumes of poverty. As revealed earlier in this chapter, regional variations in literacy and health risks can be substantial, and in Uttar Pradesh and Kerala, India, these can be attributed to public policies and cultural attitudes which influence private spending in households. This, of course, has an impact upon gender and childhood. The formation and broadspread allocation of human capital can both increase growth and reduce poverty, this being particularly evident in the high-performing countries of Asia.

In a world of macro-economic fluctuations, austerity phases in structural adjustment and financial crises, then the introduction of temporary 'safety nets' has significance. These can be applied variously to employment, public works, nutrition and micro-enterprise credit. However, it is often difficult to achieve effective design and targeting. Policies for economic stabilization, as they reduce incomes in their processes, can add significantly to head-counts of poverty and undernutrition (Ravallion, 1990; Ravallion et al, 1991). In a medium-term perspective of some ten years, structural adjustment programmes had variable effectiveness in the majority of cases they reduced poverty and increased average incomes, but scarcely had any effect upon inequality (Jayarajah et al, 1996; Sahn, 1994). The main reasons for these results were variations in implementation, income growth in rural communities from rising prices of food and the dependence of equalizing on the long-term redistribution of land and human capital. Most poverty is long-term structural: it is not greatly affected by structural adjustment programmes lasting only some five to ten years. Poverty reduction requires longer term and deeper structural adjustment in private and public invest-ments. As Lipton (1997) emphasizes, more needs to be known about the long-term impact of redistribution to the poor, the regulation of child labour and institutional incentives.

Poverty can be understood further by evaluating 'bottom-up' pro-grammes for its alleviation. Rakodi (1999) takes up these themes in her study of urban poverty programmes in Kenya. Her study emphasizes the importance of local community ownership of programmes, rather than those dominated by foreign consultants. Embedding the programmes in local political development also gives them legitimacy and proximity to the survival strategies in the livelihoods of the poor. The institutional embedding of programmes adds to the prospects for sustainability and replicability. Rakodi also indicates the limitation of community-based approaches. They are set within the contexts of the inequalities of power, resources and organizational capability: this influences the extent of effective social inclusion in the outcomes. When the programmes are donor-assisted, differences can emerge between the donor norms and the community wishes. It is better to achieve reconciliation before the funds are disbursed and set into programmatic application. Local governments frequently have limited resources and managerial capacity, and local communities seldom have access to technical 'know-how'. In terms of planning horizons for public sector social development, the local government level is frequently adrift from resourcing and administrative capacity at the higher regional and central government levels. In Chile, such problems were overcome in the 1970s and 1980s. The programmes were designed to target the poorest; research and geographical information services were developed; and incentives were provided for civil servants to redeploy to local government (Casteñada, 1992).

Poverty must be reasoned separately – but with some interdependent cause and consequence relationships – among cash or calorific poverty, housing poverty and urban poverty. Cash or calorific poverty is about the amount of income which is necessary for subsistence. Housing poverty refers to standards, home-related health, rent-to-income ratios and price-to-income ratios in homeownership. Urban income can be ascertained from access to essential infrastructure services, health risks in squalid local environments and the value of neighbourhood (dis)amenity. Housing poverty depends on the distribution of prior incomes – that is, income from subsistence, from wages or informal sector entrepreneurship, and from capacities to save and engage in self-help activities. Of course, housing poverty, with its deleterious effects on health and the capability to work, can influence cash income and whether it falls above or below poverty lines. Urban income can be understood as the net amount of benefits and costs in urban conditions. Examples include the value of time in queuing for water, the time-distance costs of transport to work, and the implicit costs of time in self-help participation for environmental improvement. As in the case of housing poverty, the net amount of benefits and costs in urban contexts influence the capacity to achieve incomes above the poverty line. All of this provides the cause and reason why low-income living areas require multi-dimensional programmes to reduce several kinds of inter-acting poverties. One programmatic approach to this is the Grameen Bank, founded by Muhammed Younis (Younis and Jolis, 1998). The Grameen Bank provides micro-credit for enterprises and housing loans. It started as a mutual self-help saving and investment institution among famine-stricken people, and it has grown to a US$2.5 billion business-seeking access to international capital markets. Grameen has a relatively minor but important role in housing equity and welfare: in order to obtain a more comprehensive understanding of housing welfare, it is necessary to approach the subject in a more fundamental way.

HOUSING INEQUITY AND SUBSIDIES[1]

Questions of inequity and housing poverty are significant in housing in developing countries. They are relevant to sustainable development by virtue of the housing impact upon health, childrearing and various productive uses, including home-based industries. Infrastructural services and local environmental conditions are included in 'housing' because they make up a large component of its value. Evidence exists that low-income households consider self-help squatter housing in their range of preferences: Daniere and Takahashi (1999) have measured the preferences, showing that self-help is often the favoured choice relative to rental or formal sector homeownership. In fact, state-assisted sites and services housing are assimilated into the ordinary resales that occur in housing submarkets (Vijayalakshmi, 1998). Some subsidization occurs inadvertently – for example, in the failure to achieve full cost recovery in improved squatter settlements. Also, cross-subsidization can occur in voluntary neighbourhood improvement schemes. In the Orangi, Karachi, project, the lane committees often pay the costs for the very poorest households in their negotiations with the central coordinators in the project.

The housing literature on housing inequity and subsidies for developing countries is rather thin and fragmented compared with that for developing countries. In one perspective this is surprising because, as indicated in the collection of contributed chapters by Aldrich and Sandhu (1995), many developing countries have implemented various privileged and regressive schemes for formal sector workers and salaried public servants. The workers in the formal sector and salaried public servants have higher average incomes than informal sector residents. This has led to some reaction among international aid organizations such as the World Bank and the later American Development Bank which favour targeted subsidies for the poor. More is said about this in subsequent discussions. The reactions reflect the increasing relevance of subsidies in housing, especially as the aid agencies have placed greater significance upon housing finance in whole housing sector development. In the most general terms, housing equity is an aspect of the broad political economy of housing. Housing equity issues arise in housing delivery systems which can be understood as comprising production, consumption, finance to developers, price-access to consumers, resources for maintenance and conditions of occupancy and tenure rights. Much of this has impact upon affordability.

Affordability has three interacting factors. First is the income of the household and its capacity to save and / or engage in self-help. The relevant income is not just current income, but sustained medium-term income in the few years before and after the housing decisions are made by the household. Housing decisions are made in medium- rather than short- term contexts. Medium-term income is sustained better in city-regions where macro-economic frameworks and labour markets exhibit stability and growth. As discussed previously, those who are near the poverty thresholds are constrained to reallocate from housing to food in times of macroeconomic recession or adversity in labour markets. Second, urban property markets change the terms of price-access among squatter settlement, rental and formal sector homeownership. Third, housing policy development can influence overall housing supply, the availability of credit in housing finance systems, and any provision of subsidies. As elaborated on below, countries such as Chile have instituted reforms since the mid-1970s to expand supplies rapidly and have created subsidies in the social housing sectors of their housing systems. But many countries have much less housing supplies and thereby lesser housing opportunities. Developer finance is restricted, leaving the construction sector with small formal sector markets for the wealthier who can afford high downpayments for homeownership. Occupier finance is also underdeveloped and the poor are dependent on high-cost finance form money-lenders, their own savings and self-help. The most significant matter for welfare and sustainable development is the degree to which the absolute and relative incomes improve in the bottom 40 per cent of the distribution of household income, along with the (in)effectiveness of housing and land policies.

In many circumstances it can be expected that housing systems will exhibit both vertical and horizontal inequity. Vertical inequity occurs when higher income groups pay relatively less for their housing than lower income groups or when equal outlays lead to higher standards for the higher income groups. Horizontal inequity occurs when households on similar incomes have varying price-access and standards of housing. As suggested above, these inequities have been accentuated by regressive subsidies in some Latin American and subSaharan countries which favour housing for formal sector workers and salaried public servants. Some inequities can be structured within housing systems, especially in terms of occupancy rights, security of tenure, and access to social and infrastructural services. Unimproved squatter settlements are often disadvantaged in these aspects of inequity. For example, higher income households in formal sector housing are more likely to have clear property rights and to receive subsidized infrastructure.

Subsidies cannot be defined and operated in an economically or politic-ally neutral way. However, the normal general principle is to measure them by reference to market value, expressed in terms of rental value. Sometimes the value of the dwelling is referred to replacement value which can be above or below the market value according to the characteristics of local housing submarkets. Subsidies can be explicit or implicit. Examples of explicit subsidies are grants paid to residents for environmental improve-ment and loans paid at below-market rates of interest to developers or occupiers. A more transparent subsidy is a one-off capital grant, favoured by the World Bank, and implemented in Chile, in other Latin American countries and as part of post-apartheid restructuring in South Africa since 1994. Implicit or hidden subsidies include the difference between market rents and regulated rents or social housing rents which are set below market levels. Other implicit or hidden subsidies are tax remissions on mortgage interest rate payments and public sector improvements in the local environ-ment which add to the private asset values of housing. The environmental improvements are external social benefits which are capitalized into the value of the housing. And tax remissions are known as 'tax expenditures' because they are broadly equivalent in economic effect to increases in public expenditure. Some subsidies are demand-side, such as grants to households for housing improvement, and some are supply-side, including inducements to developers to increase housing supplies beyond the levels the free market would otherwise provide. The economic and social effects vary among different forms of subsidy, and distributionally they can be either regressive or progressive in themselves or as a set in an overall housing system. Sometimes subsidies are designed with their probable effects analysed technically and sometimes they are introduced without much care in design or technical analyses.

The discussion can now be turned to policy issues surrounding subsidies in the housing systems of developing countries. As noted above, various sorts of subsidies occur within national housing systems. But these have not been analysed and evaluated extensively to indicate their measured efficiency and distributive impact. However, some fragmentary information is available on various programmes which have been financed by the World Bank and other international aid agencies. In their evaluative review of the 1972–83 aided self-help projects, Mayo and Gross (1985) comment that the issue of subsidies had not been addressed rationally. They do not explore the principles or techniques which would be necessary to address the comparative efficiency and social effectiveness of housing subsidies. Various authors (Barton and Olsen, 1976; de Salvo, 1971; 1973; Murray, 1975; Pugh and Catt, 1984) have examined various applied policy contexts to establish cost-benefit ratios and social impact in demand- and supply-side subsidies in social housing programmes. Furthermore, Mayo and Gross (1985) observed that in the World Bank sites and services programmes, inducement subsidies up to some 90 per cent to total costs would be necessary to attract typical target groups.

During the late 1980s it was possible to discern the types of subsidy favoured by USAID, the World Bank and the Inter-American Development Bank. They have been influential in their loan support programmes to such countries as Sri Lanka, Chile, Uruguay, Costa Rica and Colombia. The experience in Sri Lanka and Chile is elaborated on for illustrative purposes. In Sri Lanka, USAID provided some US$60 million loans under its housing guarantee programme. During the 1970s and 1980s in Sri Lanka governments had initiated and progressively developed mass small loans programmes for new building and renovation. The programmes were aimed at low-, moderate- and middle-income groups, arranged in various categories, including below-market interest rates for lower income groups. USAID favoured the redesign of subsidy, using a one-off capital grant for transparency and efficiency, rather than the below-market interest rate form. The reasoning was that one-off grants were viewed in orthodox economics as less distortionary in markets than other forms, and that the costs in public sector budgets would be transparent, thereby promoting better assessment of housing among other budgetary priorities. Since 1973, Chile has made housing a strong political priority, pursuing progressive whole sector reform under both the militaristic regime of Pinochet and the Allwyn democratic regime elected to power in 1990. In the social housing components of the whole housing sector development, the form of subsidy used was the one-off capital grant – that is, a housing voucher supported by both the World Bank and the Inter-American Development Bank. These subsidies were carefully designed – for example, the design in the Inter-American Development Bank funds enables beneficiaries to commence housing improvement at an early stage – that is to say, the beneficiaries can add rooms and amenity to their government-built core sites and services housing.

It is useful to obtain a broader picture of how a housing system can be transformed towards greater roles in promoting housing welfare and alleviating housing poverty. This is necessary because unless housing supplies are increased among moderate- and middle-income groups, as well as among low-income groups, the more affluent groups will raid housing near the bottom submarkets. More than this, the broader housing system will indicate the conditions under which successful reform can take place. As in the case of Chile, this will normally include public and private sector integration, fundamental changes in housing loans and subsidy systems, and increasing the flows of saving and investment from the wider economy into the housing sector. Also, the broader scheme of things in designing and operating whole housing sector development has important aspects of governance in finance and institutional development. Some of the attributes of governance in finance occur in routine background ways, including loan appraisal, managing mortgages or subsidies, and allocating or reallocating financial instruments in primary and secondary mortgage markets. Governance also occurs in embedding reforms and operations into the policy, administrative and operational structures of housing.

A diagrammatic elaboration of the post-1973 reformed Chilean housing system is seen in Figure 10.1. On the left side, the production-consumption economy (ie, households and firms) produce goods and services in both the informal and formal sectors. Housing production is new building, housing improvement, and self-help provisions. The right side displays the income and allocation into the housing system. As can be seen from the flows of finance and resourcing, it is the central section which is highly significant, comprising government and housing financial intermediation through capital markets. This central section is where the role of institutional reform and enablement frameworks are displayed, but always linking the production-consumption economy to the housing system. In Chile's system, the linkages to the housing system have been highly effective, including housing allocations from mandated pension funds, macro-economic stability since the mid-1980s, and disciplined fiscal policy. Other important features can now be explained:

- Government land and infrastructure policy includes the upgrading of squatter settlement and attempts to limit further squatter settlement.
- The very poorest receive income support in schemes which are decentralized in sophisticated targeting, allocation and monitoring. The low-income housing programmes complement this.
- The general basis of broadspread housing finance is the Letters of Credit programme, with these issued by commercial banks to applicants. The Letters of Credit are purchased by pension funds and other institutions in the secondary market, thereby adding to the smoothing

of fluctuations in liquidity among financial institutions. Households save into indexed accounts (for deposits) and borrowing is limited to a 25 per cent (repayment) income limit. The Letters of Credit programme was introduced in 1976 and in 1988 it was supplemented with an Endorsable Mortgage Scheme operated through mutual societies. The balances in the Letters of Credit programme were US$2.1 billion in 1993, and by then the Endorsable Mortgage Scheme had provided some US$45 million to housing.

- Low-income schemes are several and varied. They are designed to restrict eligibility by income, to set limits on size-standards (but with provisions for incremental improvement), and to operate directly to households or through local authorities, NGOs and cooperatives. Although policy makers had originally planned to operate the pro-grammes through private finance, they are implemented by the State Bank owing to the diseconomies of scale for low volumes in the private sector. Subsidies come in various forms, including a one-off housing voucher grant and a subsidized interest rate. The World Bank provided US$80 million loans to the Chilean government to support the housing voucher scheme. The World Bank's micro-economic orthodoxy favours one-off capital subsidies because it is argued that it minimizes economic distortion and they avoid unplanned future liabilities in government budgets. One indicator of distributional change is that whereas only some 21 per cent of total housing subsidies were allocated to low-income groups in the 1970s, the proportion increased to 50 per cent in the 1980s. This is in a context where the whole sector reflects a development and welfare-society approach rather than simply a welfare-state approach.

In summary, the enabled Chilean housing system has the following essential characteristics. First, the macro-economic reforms based on open trade add growth and productivity to provide a framework. Second, housing sector response to increases in average incomes is positive in developing countries, with Mohan's estimates (1994) indicating some 8 per cent increases in housing expenditure from incremental increases in income. Third, the institutional and organizational reforms in housing finance have increased saving, investment and production in the housing sector, with some improved price-access among low- and moderate- income groups. Finally, all the foregoing adds to housing assets to society as a whole and to households with homeownership tenure. The growth of mandated pension funds have significance in this. The pension funds invest in housing to some 13 per cent of their total investment. Added housing sector supply also makes rental tenure more competitive in some regions. At present there is no systematic information on how the reformed housing system impacts upon social diversity with its social inclusion and exclusion features. But Chilean approaches have embedded an institutionally reformed framework for the long term of housing welfare and asset formation. Already since 1973 housing investment has doubled.

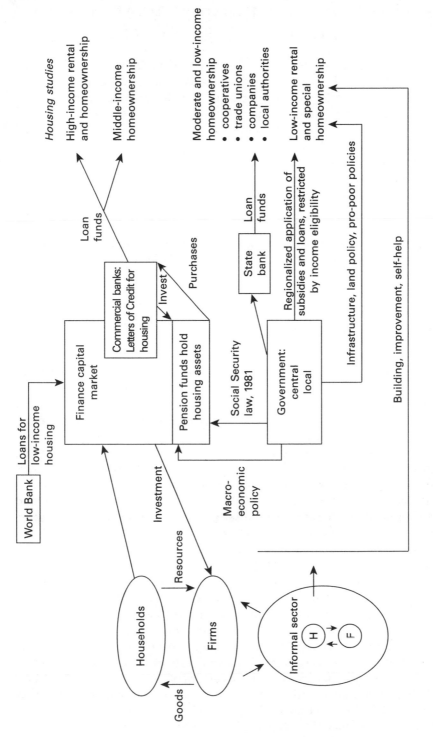

Figure 10.1 *Chilean Housing System: Finance and Resourcing*

Constructing New Theory in Agglomeration Economies and Urban Change

The idea of sustainable urban development can be fully appreciated only by understanding the rationale for the existence and development of urban areas. Their varying characteristics of development determine their individual patterns of environmental problems, their poverties and their relationships to wider regional, national and international economies. At once, it is clear that urbanization constitutes an enormous amount of capital investment in buildings and infrastructure. It is useful to recognize that the major early authors of the theory of capital (Fisher, 1906) defined capital in terms of usefulness and material qualities in producing flows of income. He included environmental capital such as fisheries, parks and waterways: this can be extended readily to the broad benefits of urban amenity and urban income, as discussed earlier. What tends to happen in urban areas is that firms colocate to exploit their backward and forward linkages to each other – that is to say, in agglomeration they purchase inputs at competitive prices and sell their outputs to other firms in the vertical production processes or to consumer markets. The early theorists of agglomeration emphasized various insights and perspectives, but no comprehensive theory. For example, Marshall (1919) explained that agglomeration is a response to increased trade, technological change and the organization of production. Within the consequent processes, learning and skilling takes place in ways which are both firm and industry specific. Myrdal (1957) also presented explanations related to processes. His theory of 'circular cumulative causation', indicates that something such as agglomeration can commence as a historical accident and then generate its own path dependence and cumulative advantage. Primary changes in production stimulate secondary changes which then reinforce the primary changes and raise their scales and efficiencies. Myrdal is interested in these processes as causing global and regional inequality, and he also applies them to poverty and racial discrimination. He thereby raises the issues of institutional causation as well as agglomeration in production.

Urban histories also add insights and perspectives. In the history of the Italian city-republics of the 11–13th centuries, their growth and nature rose from underlying increases in trade and a doubling of population in Italy. The trade was linked to the Middle East and northwestern Europe. Competing city-republics developed a class structure of merchants, professionals – for example, lawyers – artisans, smallholders and labourers. Economic change occurred in the immediate rural areas with a growing interdependence between agriculture and urbanization. More than this, the city-republics had to develop government, administration and law, all being necessary for urban development and relationships with other city-republics. The government also included the provision of infrastructure, property rights and citizenship. Clearly, the processes were at once economic, social, political and environmental. The urban history of medieval England was similar, influenced basically by demographic change and trade

(Miller and Hatcher, 1995). From the health and environmental perspectives, disease, early death and poverty were ever present characteristics of urban living conditions. Low-income housing was built by self-help methods, often durable for only a year or so before rebuilding. Water supplies were polluted and heaps of refuse were left lying in the streets.

All the foregoing provides some glimpses of causes, processes and outcomes in urban agglomeration, but not much in the way of rigorous theoretical explanation. However, in the 1990s, much led by the writing of Paul Krugmann (1991; 1995) the theory of agglomeration has been consolidated and given great significance as a central feature in development studies. As Krugmann states, agglomeration and the rationale for the existence of towns and cities has been 'stunningly neglected'. The essentials of Krugmann's theory – which I shall use below to develop a theory of urban change – can be stated as follows. Along with Myrdal, it is accepted that often initial agglomeration occurs as an historical accident. Examples include persons with skill commencing a small shoemaking or carpet workshop. Related firms colocate to take advantage of scale economies. Scale economies are associated with two related economic conditions. First, an existing plant can be operated at a higher, optimum rate of output. Second, and more significant in the longer term, a higher rate of output which is justified by increases in market size means that more efficient technologies can be introduced. This reduces the unit cost and provides external economies to related firms which purchase the outputs for their own inputs in their production. In terms of mainstream economic theory, the presence of economies of scale implies that 'the urban' has imperfect rather than perfect competition. The scale economies induce agglomeration and economic necessity in competitive contexts further induces technological innovation to reduce costs and/or to adapt or provide new products. Third, agglomeration is highly responsive to the reduction of relative transport costs which also increase sales in wider national and international markets. Finally, the cumulative processes and the underlying factors of growth in trade and population remain the elemental factors.

Krugmann's theory is presented in terms of both formal econometric models and persuasive speculative argument. The formal models are constructed as interactions between factor mobility, economies of scale and transport costs. Computer simulations reveal that the agglomeration and uneven urban concentrations will occur 'naturally'. As is the case in any development of formal theory, although the models establish basic reason and explanation, not all is accounted for within their bounded view of the world. Indications of what has been excluded are discussed by various authors. Henderson (1995) reasons that a wider urban systems approach is necessary, including the roles of local government and macro-spatial planning. Additionally, when firms choose their location, they often seek to match their requirements in a process of searching and reviewing labour market skills. For others (for example, Boddy, 1999; Cox, 1997; Storper, 1997) some further explanatory factors lie in the qualities of infrastructure, in the detailed empirical recording of interfirm exchanges and in recognizing that what is global or international is represented in the (urban) local. For developing countries, some of this needs qualification and adjustment. On the one hand, city-regions may exhibit dynamic, modern economic change, but this is more dispersed and uneven. Some of the less dynamic patterns of older agglomeration prevail in some centres. On the other hand, some change in competitive contexts can be rapid and locally detrimental. In earlier discussions it was indicated that the automobile industry in São Paulo, Brazil, experienced competitive disturbance. The study by Rodriguez-Pose and Tomaney (1999) shows that the cheaper land rent and labour costs in other Brazilian cities were more than sufficient to overcome the long-established agglomeration economies of the São Paulo metropolitan region. City-regions that do not adjust can be hit hard in the modern international economy.

Krugmann's formal models of agglomeration provide some large relevance towards developing a theory of urban change. But more is needed, especially in terms of drawing together the economic, the social, the political and the environmental. This is done by the 1993 Nobel prizewinner in economics, Douglass North, in his New Institutional Economics (NIE) (North, 1981; 1990). Institutions are norms, rules and ways of doing things. They are required because markets in themselves are insufficient and must be supplemented by designing and enforcing agreements. North's central propositions are that institutional reform often depends on quests for better economic production and productivity; that institutional conditions largely account for comparative differences in growth development; and that property rights for both markets and collective functioning matter. His methods in research have been based on a form of economic history which integrates economics, statistics, sociology and historical change. The evaluative content mixes the quantitative and the qualitative, with focus upon the reasoning and timing of economic change. It is not surprising that the influence of North's work has grown rapidly in the 1980s and 1990s. The work has relevance to property rights and state roles in sustainable development, to structural economic change, to spatial redistributions of economic activities and to the impacts of global-regional macro-economic crises. Furthermore, it provides a theoretical underpinning for a distinctive theory of the state, for reforms in governance, and for linking institutional reform to the patterns and speeds of agglomerated urban development.

North's theory of the state is written in these terms:

> It is for this reason that the whole development of the new institutional economics must not only be a theory of property rights and their evolution but a theory of the political process, a theory of the state, and of the way in which the institutional structure of the state and its individuals specify and enforce property rights. (North, 1986, p237)

For North, trade and external conditions may lead societies to set aside inhibitory institutions, replacing them with ones that achieve sustainability, growth and progressive developmental change. The underlying forces are demographic and trade transitions. But for updated relevance, the causes for environmentalism and the reduction of poverty can also speed up glacially slow institutional reform. In effect, North's ideas, along with those of Krugmann, offer the basics in a theory of urban change. They inspire new research agendas, including the linkages between general development, agglomerated urban development and redesigning institutions for improving the prospects for sustainability.

INTERNATIONAL POLICY AND POLITICAL ECONOMY

In the forerunner 1996 book, *Sustainability, the Environment and Urbanization*, it was shown that international organizations such as the UNCHS and the World Bank tend to operate within the principles of regime theory – that is to say, they use advocacy and influence to spread their theories and practices among governments and the NGOs. The World Bank has the power of loan finance, conditionality in lending, and a large technical and research service. By comparison, UNCHS has limited finance and relies more on technical advice and persuasion. Since 1996, some important events and changes have occurred in the management and policies of these organizations. UNCHS has reorganized its senior executive management and secured stronger internal financial controls. It organized the Habitat II conference in Istanbul in June 1996, placing its emphasis on 'shelter for all' and 'sustainable human settlements'. However, its overview of urban development was more wide-ranging than those themes suggest. The scope included roles of local governments, new principles of environmental planning and management, the reduction of poverty, and the reshaping of the political economy of 'enablement' and 'partnerships'. Compared with the Rio de Janeiro UNCED meeting in 1992, Habitat II was more reflective of the views of the developing countries, although Chapter 7 of Agenda 21 and the Habitat II Agenda were broadly similar (see the discussions in Chapter 8). Activities in UNCHS currently centre on the development of Habitat II + 5, a broad updating and review of the Habitat II Agenda for 2001. In 1998, UNCHS and the government of Finland organized a conference of experts and local government representatives in Helsinki. The main focus of the meeting was a document presented by Pugh and Tipple (1998). The document reviewed the progress and development of Local Agenda 21s, raising questions about the compatibility between principle and implementation. Accordingly, it explored institutional issues, capacity building, and the theory and practice of enablement (see Chapter 8 for details).

For its part, the World Bank has also been experiencing managerial reorganization and has commissioned some independent academic reviewing of its first 50 years by Kapur and his co-authors (1997). This has significance in environmental agendas. First, the reorganization has consolidated work in water and sanitation, but may reduce other elements in housing and brown agenda issues. This comes at a time when, as indicated above, reform for housing was set within an ambitious whole

sector development in 1993. It is in the green agenda issues that the Bank
has had the most critical attention since the mid-1980s. The history of this
has been written in extensive detail by Wade (1997) in the aforementioned
commissioned studies. Wade finds that in the 1990s, along with poverty,
the World Bank's programmatic work on the environment is among the
fastest growing in total allocations. The environmental budget has increased
by some 90 per cent since the mid-1980s. In part this was in response to
sustained criticism by international NGOs. They organized extensive
publicity and attacked the bank for its neglect of the impacts on indigenous
people in the tropical forests of Brazil and on resettlement in the Narmada
Dam project in India. The roading project in Brazil and the Narmada scheme
were virtually devoid of environmental assessment. When Barber Conable
became President of the World Bank in 1986 he was determined to reshape
the Bank's management and appraisal capability in green agenda environmentalism. All of that contrasts with the World Bank's brown agenda
environmentalism which has been progressively developmental since 1972,
as discussed in earlier chapters in this book.

Both the World Bank and UNCHS follow policies that favour the
political economy of 'enablement' in the 1990s. These policies have been
evolving, with some substantial modifications, since the 1980s. In the mid-
1980s the UNCHS view of 'enablement' was restricted to the social and
environmental functioning of local environments, but by the end of the
1980s it embraced total urban development (Pugh, 1996). Accordingly,
'enablement' was understood as creating frameworks that provided legal,
social, cultural and governance conditions whereby states, markets, the
voluntary sector and households could achieve improvements in urban,
housing and environmental qualities. This also approximates the World
Bank's position, although it gives more attention to economic issues and
its imperative to maintain good credit standing in the international finance
capital markets. In context, then, enablement is adaptable and, along with
governance, it provides steering and guidance to sustainable urban development. From the broadest perspective it has become a political economy,
differing from neoliberalism, socialism, dependency theory and other
ideological visions. It is possible to place some characterization on the
evolving political economy, drawing on the theories of North (1981; 1986;
1990) and those of the 1998 Nobel prizewinner in economics, Armatya Sen.

Sen's writing in development, welfare and poverty has been extensive
since the early 1970s and it is complementary to North's on the role of
institutions in development. The essentials of Sen's ideas are stated in his
recent work with Drèze on India's developmental experience (Drèze and
Sen, 1995). For Sen, the major purpose of development is that it expands
human capabilities, which are good in their own right and for enhancing
the chances of people pursuing values which are important to them. This
has roots in Aristotle's philosophy, with his argument that it is the central
duty of legislators to allocate and distribute the city's resources so that
individuals' capabilities are enhanced (Kraut, 1997). In practical elaboration,
this means that the model *polis* (city) would establish good governance,
and that collective goods such as the environment and education have

virtue in themselves. Conceptualizations of welfare that are based on capability differ from those that are restrictive to basic needs such as education, health, sanitation and shelter. Capability welfare is not for the material per se, but for freedom and pursuing lives of value. It does have much to say, of course, about poverty and inequality. Also, the capability approach is more inclusive of the positive and enhancing roles of some states, some households, some voluntary organizations and some characteristics of markets. The several roles in partnership can be mutually reinforcing, not just exhibiting conflict or with each confounding the good provided by the others.

The broad flavour of the Sen approach to political economy can be set out in a series of his statements. Poverty is socially wrong because it is a deprivation of capability. Within contingent conditions, economic growth and expansion of markets expand social opportunities. (Some of the contingent conditions are environmental.) Accordingly, the 'social' and the 'economic' are not divided in any simple way, except in some university lecture rooms. Basic education and health promote capability and choice and, along with other factors, including state roles, they may lead to patterns of growth which reduce poverty and improve sustainable development. Gender inequalities reduce freedom and inequality, and they should be a central concern in the theory and practice of development. State roles can be market-exclusionary or market-complementary, and each may be assessed in terms of their impacts upon social opportunity. Also, the state is not universally or inherently good: it can infringe on human rights, eliminate freedoms and act with excessive bureaucratic zeal. It is not simply a matter of arguing for more or less government, but more significantly for creating effective governance and institutional reform. The debates on economic liberalism in the 1980s and early 1990s were too narrowly drawn: the agenda needed widening to social policy and sustainable patterns of development. Research should proceed, then, on the capability and social development impacts of different patterns of growth. The urban is significant because some growth and expansion of capabilities is within path dependence from historically situated agglomeration economies. Finally, endemic and quieter deprivations – such as racial discrimination, the ill-health in some child labour and widowhood – are often much harder to bring to attention and public action than sensational events such as famine and natural disaster.

Necessarily in its context, the foregoing is a credo, a set of beliefs and principles that address political economy. Political economies, in their better forms, have literacy in economics, politics, philosophy and history. Writing a credo is not, of course, the only thing which Sen has done: his theoretical, technical and evaluative work review the limitations of political and economic policy (see Drèze and Sen, 1995). The credo has a purpose in social science, setting out some guideline principles. Sen's, as stated above, are not in terms of grand theory or ideological partisanship. Neoliberalism would fall foul of Sen's commitment to social opportunity; socialism would also be seen as inappropriate because it has a severe restraint on economic development; and dependency theory sheds light only on some aspects of exploitive inequalities in relations between the North and the South, but scarcely on anything to do with capability welfare and the precise policies which would create sustainable economic and social development. The Sen approach which gives focus to the practical conditions of economic and social reality would receive support from eminent philosophers of social science. For example, Winch (1958) argues that the task of social science is to develop concepts and principles related to the social, economic and political conditions of their time in a changing society. And Hayek (1998) warns against adopting populist moods of the times in propagating political economy. Instead, the approach should be based on scholarship in theory, statistical appraisal, and for addressing major issues such as social justice, economic efficiency and the course of public policy. For sustainable development, this means evaluation of performance among states, markets, the voluntary sector and households. This leads to some final comments on research agendas and sustainable development.

RESEARCH AGENDAS

Some of the major themes and discussions in the book can now be turned towards the importance of adding to and revising research agendas. The themes identify the city as a crucible, a place of dynamic agglomeration and interaction among the economic, the social, the political and the environmental. Studies of the rationale basis of urban areas and their development are studies of development. As Krugmann (1991) comments, they have been 'stunningly neglected' in development studies, leaving large gaps in the literature on developing countries. If included in more sub-stantive ways, sustainable urban development becomes more conspicuously a study of social, economic, political and demographic transformations. This places persistent poverties, inequalities and environmental degrad-ations into contexts of longer term change, but with some immediate social urgencies in health and other matters. Also, once attention is cast towards social and economic realities, the limitations of the grand theories of political economy become apparent. Dirty neighbourhoods and death from enteritis occur just as readily in capitalism, in socialism and in countries which sought autarky by way of economic protection from a failed import substitution as a means of promoting development. The social and economic realities indicate the contours of their own principles for political economy. Any market, state, voluntary group and/or household can add variously to welfare or cause diswelfare, either in neglect or unwittingly. Some of the main driving forces for development at the end of the 20th century have been international economic integration, the formation and spreading of human capital and the adaptation of institutions. Sustainable urban development requires these forces to be central rather than mere context requirements for research.

Another key theme which runs through several chapters in this book is the relationship between individualism and the social. This is most conspicuously shown in Carolyn Stephens' discussions of gross and persistent inequalities in wealth, power, health and broad educational influence. Set in contrasting examples, the moral tenor of the 'white sharks' can decapitalize a vast global region in Asia in 1997, but the refined ideas of Buddhist morality can inspire the social, economic and philosophical reasoning of Amartya Sen. The tensions and balances between individualism and the social also run through the main arteries of economics, sociology and law, all subjects which are basic for constructive debates on sustainable development. Individualism has permanent relevance at a more basic level. Society is not a system and neither are cities. They are open-ended entities in which individuals and groups can make differences, and that is why Carolyn Stephens raises questions about the commitment of the educated in the cause for health, equality and sustainability. This assumes greater importance in a period of rapid socio-economic change, where older economic and political frameworks are eroding, but newer ones require knowledge and legitimacy. This, of course, applies to the idea of sustainable development.

Some research agendas in urban sustainable development have set their own path dependence – that is to say, among limited available options such matters as theory, micro-studies, policy evaluations and so forth have arisen from the 1987 Brundtland Report and the UNCED meeting, Rio de Janeiro, 1992. The idea of sustainability has led to some partial reconstitutions of concepts, techniques and assembling new data bases in economics, political science, applied science, environmental health and sociology. Nonetheless, some glaring gaps are apparent, and some of these have been addressed in limited ways in this book. Central among these is relating concepts and interpretations in sustainable development to transformations. The relevant transitions are various, including the demographic, the economic, trade, urban agglomeration, institutional reform, poverties and inequalities. Why is this important? Simply put, what is observed in the here and now often requires a wider and deeper historical context for interpretation. Even useful micro-studies need some association to longer-term, underlying change. Comparative studies have been neglected. They do not produce basic theory, but they raise interrogatory questions about the conditions under which policies succeed or fail. It then becomes clearer what sorts of things can be done in specific situations. Some of this can guide institutional reform. In a context of rapid urban change and significant longer-term transformations, research agendas must be flexible and innovative. Some important aspects of this are the concurrent development of theory related both to abstracted models, such as Krugmann's on agglomeration, and to historical transformation, such as North's principles of institutional reform. For developmental relevance, the urban roles of expanding social opportunities and spreading human capital in health education and childrearing have central importance in sustainable development. For example, what is the price-locational access to education, training and essential personal and environmental health services? As argued in the introductory chapter, research in sustainable urban development has to become increasingly transdisciplinary, taking theory, methodology and evaluation from the mainstreams and heterodoxies of various social sciences. Finally, and most significantly, debates about the relationships between individualism and the social can be pursued beyond economics, sociology and law to ethics, leadership and education.

NOTES

1   This section on housing (in)equity and subsidies draws on my contribution to 'Housing Inequity' in the *Encyclopaedia of Housing* (1998) edited by Willem van Vliet (Sage Publications, Thousand Oaks, California, pp280–81). Thanks are expressed to Sage Publications for their use here.

REFERENCES

Aldrich, B and Sandhu, R (eds) (1995) *Housing the Urban Poor: Policy and Practice in Developing Countries*, Zed Books, London

Anand, S and Ravallion, M (1993) 'Human Development in Poor Countries: On the Role of Private Incomes and Public Services', *Journal of Economic Perspectives*, vol 7, no 1, pp133–50

Barton, D and Olson, E (1976) The Benefits and Costs of Public Housing in New York City, Institute for Research on Poverty, Madison, Wisconsin US

Blair, A, Ruble, J, Tulchin, S and Garland, A (1996) 'Introduction: Globalism and Local Realities: Five Paths to the Urban Future', in M Cohen et al, (eds) *Preparing for the Future: Global Pressures and Local Forces*, Woodrow Wilson Center Press and John Hopkins University Press, Baltimore, pp1–24

Boddy, M (1999) 'Geographical Economics and Urban Competitiveness', *Urban Studies*, vol 36, nos 5 and 6, pp811–42

Casteñada, T (1992) *Combating Poverty: Innovative Social Reforms in Chile during the 1980s*, ICS Press, San Francisco

Cox, K (ed) (1997) *Spaces of Globalization: Reasserting the Power of the Local*, Guildford Press, New York

Daniere and Takahashi (1999) 'Poverty and access: differences and communalities across slum communities in Bangkok', *Habitat International*, vol 23, no 2, pp271–88

de Salvo, J (1971) 'A methodology for evaluation housing programs', *Journal of Regional Science*, no 11, pp173–85

de Salvo, J (1973) *A Rationale for Government Intervention in Housing: Housing as a Merit Good*, Department of Housing and Urban Development, Washington, DC

Drèze, J and Gazdar, H (1997) 'Uttar Pradesh: the burden of inertia', in J Drèze and A Sen (eds) *Indian Development: Selected Regional Perspectives*, Clarendon, Oxford, pp33–128

Drèze, J and Sen, A (1995) *India's Economic Development and Social Opportunity*, Clarendon, Oxford

Drèze, J and Sen, A (1997) *Indian Development: Selected Regional Perspectives*, Clarendon, Oxford

Fisher, I (1906) *The Nature of Capital and Income*, Macmillan, London

Grindle, M (ed) (1997) *Getting Good Government: Capacity Building in the Public Sectors of Developing Countries*, Harvard Institute of International Development, Cambridge, Mass

Harris, N (ed) (1997) 'Cities in a global economy: structural change and policy reaction', *Urban Studies*, no 34, pp1693–703

Hayek, F (1998) *The Intellectuals and Socialism*, Institute of Economic Affairs, London

Haynes, J (1997) *Democracy and Civil Society in the Third World*, Polity Press, Cambridge

Henderson, J (1995) Comment on: 'Urban concentration: the role of increasing returns and transport costs, by Krugmann', in M Bruno and B Pleskovic (eds) *Proceedings of the World Bank Annual Conference on Development Economics 1994*, World Bank, Washington, DC, pp270–74

Jayarajah, C, Branson, W and Sen, B (1996) *Social Dimensions of Adjustment: World Bank Experience, 1980–93*, World Bank, Washington, DC

Kapur, D, Lewis, J and Webb, R (eds) (1997) *The World Bank: Its First Half Century*, Brookings Institution Press, Washington, DC

Kraut, R (1997) *Aristotle Politics: Books VII and VIII*, Clarendon, Oxford

Krugmann, P (1991) *Geography and Trade*, MIT Press, Cambridge, Mass

Krugmann, P (1995) 'Urban concentration: the role of increasing returns and transport costs', in M Bruno and B Pleskovic (eds) *Proceedings of the World Bank Annual Conference on Development Economics 1994*, World Bank, Washington, DC, pp241–63

Lindenburg, M (1993) *The Human Development Race: Improving the Quality of Life in Developing Countries*, International Center for Economic Growth, ICS Press, San Francisco

Lipton, M (1997) 'Poverty – are there holes in the consensus?', *World Development*, vol 25, no 7, pp1003–7

Marshall, A (1919) *Industry and Trade: A Study of Industrial Techniques and Business Organization; and of their Influence on the Condition of Various Classes and Nations*, Macmillan, London

Mayo, S and Gross, D (1985) 'Sites and services – and subsidies: the economics of low-cost housing in developing countries', discussion paper, Report No UDD–83, Water Supply and Urban Development Department, Operations Policy Staff, World Bank, Washington, DC

Miller, E and Hatcher, J (1995) *Medieval England: Towns, Commerce and Crafts*, Longman, London

Mohan, R (1994) *Understanding the Developing Metropolis: Lessons from the City Study of Bogotá and Cali, Colombia*, Oxford University Press, Oxford

Murray, M (1975) 'The distribution of tenant benefits in public housing', *Econometrica*, vol 43, no 11, pp771–87

Myrdal, G (1957) *Economic Theory and Under-developed Regions*, Duckworth, London

North, D (1981) *Structure and Change in Economic History*, Norton, New York

North, D (1986) 'The New Institutional Economics', *Journal of Institutional and Theoretical Economics*, vol 14, no 2, pp230–37

North, D (1990) *Institutions, Institutional Change and Economic Performance*, Cambridge University Press, Cambridge

Phang, S-Y 'Housing, housing wealth formation and the Singapore economy', *Housing Studies*, (forthcoming 2001)

Pugh, C (1995) 'International structural adjustment and its sectoral and spatial impacts', *Urban Studies*, vol 32, no 2, pp261–85

Pugh, C (ed) (1996) *Sustainability, the Environment, and Urbanization*, Earthscan, London.

Pugh, C (1997) 'The World Bank's millennial theory of the state: further attempts to reconcile the political and the economic', *Third World Planning Review*, vol 19, no 3, ppiii–xiv

Pugh, C and Catt, C (1984) 'Cost-benefit and financial analyses of public housing in South Australia', *Urban Policy and Research*, vol 2, no 2, pp27–33

Pugh, C and Tipple, G (1998) *Local Implementation of the Habitat Agenda with Particular Attention to Local Agendas 21*, UNCHS Theme Paper, Nairobi

Rakodi, C (1999) *Tackling Urban Poverty: Principles and Practice in Project and Programme Design*, Paper to seminar: 'From Welfare to Market Economy: the State, Aid and Policy Shifts in Urban Development and Shelter Programmes', Oxford Brookes University, 6 July 1999

Ramachandran, V (1997) 'On Kerala's development achievements', in J Drèze and A Sen (eds), *Indian Development: Selected Regional Perspectives*, Clarendon, Oxford, pp205–356

Ravallion, M (1990) 'Income effects on undernutrition', *Economic Development and Cultural Change*, no 38, pp489–515

Ravallion, M, Datt, G and Van de Walle, D (1991) 'Quantifying Absolute Poverty in the Developing World', *Review of Income and Wealth*, vol 37, no 4, pp345–61

Rodriguez-Pose, A and Tomaney, J (1999) 'Industrial Crisis in the Centre of the Periphery: Stabilisation, Economic Restructuring and the Policy Responses in the São Paulo Metropolitan Region', *Urban Studies*, vol 36, no 3, pp479–98

Sahn, D (ed) (1994) *Adjusting to Policy Failure in African Economies*, Cornell University Press, Ithaca

Sandhu, K and Wheatley, P (eds) (1989) *Management of Success: The Moulding of Modern Singapore*, Institute of Southeast Asian Studies, Singapore

Storper, M (1997) *The Regional World: Territorial Development in a Global Economy*, Guildford Press, New York

Vijayalakshmi, M (1998) 'Implications of settlement status and housing moves in sites and services in Chennai', PhD thesis, Faculty of Architecture and Planning, Anna Univesity, Chennai

Wade, R (1997) 'Greening the Bank: the struggle over the environment, 1970–93', in D Kapur et al (eds) *The World Bank: Its First Half Century*, Brookings Institution Press, Washington, DC

Whittington, D, Pearce, D and Morgan, D (eds) (1997) *Economic Values and the Environment in the Developing World*, Elgar, Cheltenham

Winch, P (1958) *The Idea of a Social Science (and its Relation to Philosophy)*, Routledge & Kegan Paul, London

World Commission on Environment and Development (1987) *Our Common Future* [The Brundtland Report], Oxford University Press, Oxford

Younis, M and Jolis, A (1998) *Banker to the Poor*, Arum Press, London

INDEX